Musings
of a
Middleton Boy

GOWER

Burry
Holms

Llanmadoc

Landimore

Cheriton

Weobley
Castle

Llanrhidian

Llanmadoc
hill

Llangennith

Burry
Green

Hardings
Down

Cefn Bryn

Rhossili hill

Sluxton

Reynoldston

Kings
Hall

Llandewi

Home
Tower

Rhossili

Middleton

Pitton
Cross

Scurlage

Penrice

Worms
Head

Pitton

Margam
Corner

Brittel

Oxwich

Pilton

Paviland
Cave

Overton

Port
Eynon

Castle

Slade

Oxwich
Green

BRISTOL

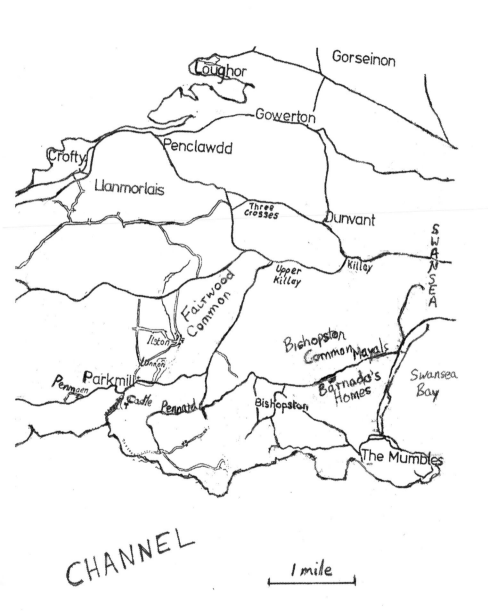

Gorseinon

Loughor

Gowerton

Crofty

Penclawdd

Llanmorlais

Three Crosses

Dunvant

Killay

Upper Killay

SWANSEA

Fairwood Common

Ilston

Bishopston Common

Mayals

Swansea Bay

Vannon

Parkmill

Pennaen

Castle

Pennard

Bishopston

Barnado's Homes

The Mumbles

CHANNEL

1 mile

Musings
of a
Middleton Boy

✦

Growing Up on the Gower Coast

Cyril Jones

iUniverse, Inc.
New York Lincoln Shanghai

Musings of a **Middleton Boy**
Growing Up on the Gower Coast

Copyright © 2007 by Cyril Jones

iUniverse books may be ordered through booksellers or by contacting:

iUniverse
2021 Pine Lake Road, Suite 100
Lincoln, NE 68512
www.iuniverse.com
1-800-Authors (1-800-288-4677)

Because of the dynamic nature of the Internet, any Web addresses or links contained in this book may have changed since publication and may no longer be valid.

ISBN: 978-0-595-46658-0 (pbk)
ISBN: 978-0-595-70515-3 (cloth)
ISBN: 978-0-595-90953-7 (ebk)

Printed in the United States of America

This book
is dedicated to the Rhossili boys and girls
of my generation
and to
our hardworking parents—

The Greatest Generation

In graves where drips the winter rain,
Lie those who loved me most of men: …

Ernest Rhys

Contents

Acknowledgements

Although I had been considering the possibility of writing about my upbringing in Rhossili for several years, I finally got started in the autumn of 2003, after I returned to Canada, from New Zealand.

I am pleased to acknowledge the encouragement of many of my cousins, especially: Richard Rosser, for continually prompting me to get on with the job; Pat Stafford, for encouraging me to keep in touch with my Middleton roots; and Clive Jones, for posting news cuttings to me in New Zealand and Canada.

Many of those who lived in southwest Gower when I grew up there, have confirmed (in some cases, corrected) my recollections. They really are too numerous to mention. I am especially pleased with their genuine interest and approval.

Lastly, I must express my appreciation to my wife, Lena, for her patience with "the one-finger typist" over the four years it took me to search my memory files and convert them into print; and for her intense critiquing and editing, in the final phase of the work.

Preface

THE writings contained in this book are a collection of stories and reflections about life in the parish of Rhossili, during and after the Second World War, as seen through the eyes of a boy who grew up there.

The stories are based, somewhat precariously, on my personal recollections and experiences. Furthermore, the anecdotes and interpretations of events essentially reflect my own perceptions of various situations and incidents. In the case of my earliest memories, such as tumbling out of an upstairs window at the age of two, I cannot be certain how much is due to my own recollection and how much is due to my parents recounting the incident, in later years—yet there is a memory and an enduring fear of outward-sloping windowsills.

Other than crosschecking the timing and details of events with some of those who lived in the parish of Rhossili during the 1940s and 1950s, I have done little to validate the stories. They are simply meant to provide interesting reading for those who would join me in a journey to the Rhossili of more than half a century ago. If the people who lived there in those days see fit to endorse the honesty and general accuracy of these stories, that will be sufficient reward.

I have mentioned many of the names of present and former inhabitants of Rhossili in the stories. The reader will know they are represented in a respectful way. There is no intention to offend. In the few instances which might embarrass the individuals concerned, I have omitted the names, even though my own recollections may be quite clear.

The Author

1

Prologue

✦

(Anatomy of a Parish)

You secret vales, you solitary fields,
You shores forsaken, you sounding rocks!

Henry Constable

IN the parish of Rhossili during the 1940s, about eighty percent of the men were either farmers or farm-workers. After all, farming was the chief reason for the existence of the community. For more than a decade preceding the war, some of the larger farmers were known to recruit much-needed workers at the annual Brecon Agricultural Fair. With the increased demands for agricultural production in the war years, farm labour was soon augmented by the Women's Land Army, displaced persons (DPs) from Europe and German POWs. Another constant source of farm help was Barnardo's Homes. The young recruits were invariably accommodated at the farmhouse where they worked.

Other members of the community were involved in providing some of the basic services needed by the bustling village. These included schoolteachers (Ada Thomas; Lily Button), shop-keepers (Alf Richards; Will Williams), bus-drivers (Jim Brockie; Harold Jones; Jack Bevan), coastguards (Dorling; Payne; Parker), a cobbler (Harry Gammon), a road-man (Alf Shepherd), a vicar (The Reverend Scudamore) and chapel lay-preachers (Jack Bevan; Mansel Bevan). A few, including Jack and Mansel Bevan, Marsden Jones and Mansel Thomas commuted to their businesses or professions in the Swansea area.

There was one hotelier (Guido Heller), while some operated large guesthouses in Rhossili Lane (the Williamses; the Croziers). One farm-worker (Alec Thomas) offered a part-time butchering service (mainly for killing, drawing and quartering pigs and sheep), while a couple of others (Sid James; Vaughan Price) offered "short back and sides" haircuts in the evenings or at weekends. (The women gave each other home perms.)

Even so, Rhossili depended very much on neighbouring parishes, especially Reynoldston, Porteynon and Llangennith, for such services as public-houses, police, blacksmith, undertaker, baker, carpenter, haulage contractor, threshing contractor, farm hardware and supplies, and tractor fuel and repairs.

During the war years, the men of the parish shouldered such additional duties as the Home Guard, Auxiliary Coastguard, Royal Observer Corps and Auxiliary Fire Service. The women, as well as being traditional housewives at a time when that, alone, required up to twelve hours of hard work every day, often needed to take on part-time farm-work "to make ends meet".

Rhossili was a hive of agricultural activity, bustling with hardworking men, their self-sacrificing wives and underprivileged children. Horses still competed with tractors for the farmers' favour, and many of the farm-workers lived in "tied" accommodation, with no guarantee of permanent employment or shelter.

In contrast to the village of Llangennith, where even the small farmers owned their own land, at least eighty percent of the farmlands in Rhossili, along with the associated buildings, were still owned by the Penrice Estate, headed by Lady Blytheswood. (Great Pitton farm was the major exception.) This was a throwback to the feudal system. Tenant farmers were subject to a strict code of practice that was generally honoured by both parties. Rent was paid by the tenants; building repairs and maintenance were the responsibility of the estate. Professional game-keepers, such as Woodward, Gibson and Jones were employed to ensure that poaching was minimised.

It was the right of tenancy (as opposed to the actual ownership of property), which was jealously guarded and passed down from generation to generation, in the traditional farming families. Even the large, modern bungalows and houses that were built in the 1920s, along the newly-paved road between Pitton and Rhossili End, were subject to ninety-nine year leaseholds from the Penrice Estate.

But the seeds of change had already been sown in the preceding quarter of a century—paved roads, the wireless, motorised transportation, electric power, the telephone and the farm tractor. Then came the war; first drastically increasing the demand for farm produce, then accelerating technological development so rapidly that, within a couple of decades, small farmers and farm-workers would become akin to "endangered species".

Even the Penrice Estate was subject to the whims of fate and political change. It was a combination of these two that would bring about its downfall.

2

Gower Roots

People will not look forward to posterity, who never look backward to their ancestors.

Edmund Burke

I HAVE never been overly excited at the idea of tracing my family tree, based entirely on my paternal family name. For one thing, modern science tells us that our mothers' genes are generally dominant; for another, only mothers are absolutely certain who their offspring are; thirdly, to focus on the paternal family name smacks of chauvinism. On the other hand, I must admit that tracing my maternal family tree would be rather challenging. For the moment, I prefer to muse on the idea that I should have been named Cyril Powell-Rosser-Richards-Jones—and that's only going back as far as my grandparents!

It seems that the first of my paternal ancestors to reside in Rhossili—my great-great-grandfather, Francis Jones—migrated all the way from Oxwich, about 160 years ago. He had already married a Rhossili-born girl, Margaret Bevan, who had borne him ten children by the time they moved from Oxwich Green to Hoarstone. Their youngest son, William—one of my eight great-grandparents—spent a number of years at sea. He sailed around Cape Horn and experienced the seamy side of such ports as San Francisco before returning to Rhossili to settle down. He was, at times, a ship's master in the days when Wales had a huge involvement with maritime traffic.

Following the death of his first wife, Anne, in 1887, William married the widow of one Samuel Bevan. He thereby assumed the tenancy of Middleton Hall farm, which eventually included more than seventy acres of land—scattered from Hoarstone to Lewis Castle, and from The Chapel to The Vile. Most of the land was good for such staple crops as corn, potatoes, cabbages, swedes, beetroots and carrots. A few rough fields were suitable mainly for grazing or hay.

Middleton Hall farmhouse was centrally located in the village, at the cross-roads formed by the junctions of the Vile Lane and School Lane with the main road running between Pitton and Rhossili End. For some reason, the figure-eight shaped area at the crossroads was always known as Middleton Bank, or simply 'the bank'. (Perhaps the name derived from the sloping bank of the stream, before the main road was paved.)

In the late 1880s, a group of God-fearing men of the village decided to build a new Methodist Chapel because the one near Great Pitton farm was no longer considered adequate. William Jones was one of those altruistic souls. As a result of discussions about the best location for the new chapel, he donated a piece of land from one of "his" fields, known as Bestatown. (Of course, this would have required the approval of the Penrice Estate.)

The location selected for the chapel was on level ground, close to the quarries in Mewslade valley, where most of the stone must have been obtained. It was equally accessible by both Pitton and Middleton people. (Unfortunately, they could not be aware of the imminent invention of the motorcar. Hence, the chapel was located at a rather blind corner, where it would always be risky to stop a vehicle. A larger plot of land could have provided safer, off-road parking.)

Almost forty years later, in 1926, William's son, Francis (Frank) Jones, must have agreed to donate a small parcel of land from the rough field known as Broad Hay, so that the village hall could be built. Francis, the offspring of William's first wife, married Anne Rosser of Oxwich, just prior to the turn of the century, and they made their home at Hoarstone. They began raising a family which would eventually number eight sons and five daughters. Following the death of William, in 1909, Francis moved his fledgling family to Middleton Hall.

My father, Joffre Jones, was the tenth child in the family of thirteen: he was born at Middleton Hall in 1915. He was twenty-four years old and still living at the family farm when he married nineteen-year-old Joyce Powell, the youngest of six children, in 1939. She had worked at an hotel in Loughor before coming to work as a general help at Bay farm at Rhossili End.

My mother was born and raised in Gorseinon, but her mother, Sarah Jane Powell (nee Richards), was born and bred in the Horton/Porteynon area. Sarah was a first cousin to "aunty Mag" (the wife of "Little Johnny" Beynon), who lived at High Priest; "aunty Vi" (the wife of Alf Shepherd), who lived at West Pilton; and "aunty Min" and "uncle Lem", who both lived at Fernhill Top. Thus, my mother had ties with some of the families in Rhossili.

Although I spent the first twenty-one years of my life in Rhossili, I was actually born at my maternal grandparents' house at 13 Brynhyfryd Road, Gorseinon, because my mother wanted to be taken care of by her own family during child-birth, as was quite common in those days. My maternal grandfather, Fred Powell, was a collier and lay preacher, who hailed from the Forest of Dean.

When I was a few weeks old, I was borne to Middleton Hall, where I lived for the next two years. There, I enjoyed daily attention, not just from my parents, but also from Granny Jones; aunties Gladys and Margaret (Peggy); and uncles Arthur (Robin), Phil and Leonard. After all, I was the first baby to appear there for eighteen years. From all accounts, I never complained about anything, except being put to bed.

Granny Jones had become the matriarch at Middleton Hall when my grandfather, Francis, died in 1931, at the age of fifty-seven. She suffered from diabetes and thyroid problems, so she was obliged to have daily insulin injections and use saccharin to sweeten her tea. She wore wire-rimmed spectacles on her full, round face: she must have been very short-sighted because her eyes appeared huge through the lenses.

Granny would sometimes send me to collect watercress—a healthy delicacy she was especially fond of—from the well near the "rocket house" (which housed the wagon loaded with land-to-sea rescue equipment), at the base of Rhossili Down. On other occasions, she would ask me to fetch a bunch of flowers. Sometimes it would be primroses, which grew wild in many locations. In late spring, cowslips abounded on the hedges in Sid Thomas's field, next to the Post Office; at other times, there were blue-bells or foxgloves.

Having raised so many children of her own, Granny did not have much energy in her sixties, but she was quite tolerant towards me. She sometimes told me stories about her own schooldays at Oxwich, in the late 1880s: "The teacher asked us what caused thunder and lightning. I put my hand up. I said it was God showing His anger at the sinfulness of people. The teacher said it was the right answer." Perhaps it was. Granny was seventy when she died, in 1947.

I would like to learn more about all my grandparents, as well as the names and backgrounds of each of my great-grandparents and great-great-grandparents. However, it would take a lot of effort to discover all their names; even then, I could hardly claim to know them very well. I represent only a small part of each of them, and they would each represent only a small part of me.

Suffice it to say that approximately three-quarters of my ancestors for at least the past two centuries were residents of southwest Gower.

3

'The Cottage'

I can see the little homestead on the hill,
I can hear the quiet murmur of the rill;

W.S.G. Williams

MY parents always believed they were fortunate to obtain the tenancy of Middleton Hall Cottage when it became vacant in 1942. My father caught the bus to the Home Farm, in order to plead his case to Mr. Pritchard and Mr. Anthony, the agents for the Penrice Estate. I had just turned two. From shortly after my birth, we had lived in overcrowded conditions in my father's family home at Middleton Hall.

'The cottage' was about a hundred years old. Its full name implied that it had, at some point, been a "tied" cottage—intended to house a farm-worker's family as long as he was employed at Middleton Hall farm. A long time ago, that tie had evidently been broken, as it had been occupied by the family of a shoemaker, William Morgan, since before the turn of the century.

Sometimes described in old records as "the last house in Middleton", 'the cottage' nestled on the south-eastern slope of Rhossili Down, commanding an unbroken view over fields and farms, from Cefn Bryn ("the backbone of Gower") all the way around to Worms Head. To the southeast was an expansive view of the Bristol Channel. In fair weather, the outline of Lundy Island, and even the North Devon coast, could be clearly seen.

The roof was thatched and the whitewashed walls were built of large stones—most likely hewn from the quarries at Rhossili cliffs. The "pine end", where the chimney was located, was more than a yard thick. A cobblestone pathway, bounded by a yard-high stone wall, extended from the gate at the southwest corner, around to the only external doorway, located in the centre of the south-easterly face. There was an enclosed garden and a small field—in total, more than one-third of an acre of land.

There was a lean-to shed at the leeward end, which must have once served as the workshop of the shoemaker, William Morgan. We used it as a coal-shed. It also served as a kennel for our black spaniel. Apparently I made the poor dog's life quite miserable at times, by pelting it with handfuls of coal-dust while it was tied up, or with green tomatoes when it followed me into our small garden. That I could enjoy being such an annoyance, perhaps signalled a negative trait in my character.

Shortly after we moved into 'the cottage', I tumbled out of an upstairs window. The windowsills were almost two feet deep because of the thick walls, and sloped outwards, so that when a window was open, it was quite easy for a two-year-old to make a mistake. I have vague recollections of the incident, of which bedroom window it was, and of falling helplessly. In later years, my mother would recount: "My heart was in my mouth as I rushed down the stairs. I found you on your hands and knees on the cobblestones. There was a bump on your forehead and you slept for hours, after". In those days, it wasn't so easy to get prompt medical attention.

About five years later, following the death of Lady Blythswood's daughter, my parents had the opportunity to purchase 'the cottage' outright. The Penrice Estate had to be dismantled because of the pressure of "death duties" (which were very severe under legislation introduced by Clement Attlee's post-war Labour Party government). It is therefore somewhat surprising that my father would remain a lifelong Conservative Party supporter (mainly because of his admiration for Winston Churchill, I think), even though it was the taxes imposed on the rich by a Labour government which gave him the opportunity to become "king of his own castle". Life is full of ironies.

Although sitting tenants were given the first option to purchase their rented properties, a local farmer (who was my father's employer at the time) offered to purchase 'the cottage' and rent it to him. But my parents wisely insisted on saving to buy it themselves. My father was earning less than four pounds a week, and they needed to save about four hundred pounds to buy our humble home. My parents were able to purchase 'the cottage' rather cheaply because it was classified as "condemned" due to the state of the thatched roof and the woodwork around the doors and windows. Even so, it was a tough struggle for them. From time to time, they would count out their savings from a tea-tin which was kept hidden in the cupboard under the stairs. "Scrape and save" was their byword.

'The cottage' was draughty and chilly for much of the year. There was no bathroom. The whole family took a bath once a week, usually on Saturday evenings. Water had to be heated in a bucket balanced precariously over the open coal-fire. As each member of the family bathed, an additional bucket of water was being heated up for the next one. First my little sister, then me, then our mother, finally our father; then the flimsy, metal bathtub, which had a handle at both ends, would be carried out and emptied into the small field beside the garden.

There was no indoor toilet. We used a stout zinc and timber outhouse located in a sheltered spot, below the garden. The need to take laxatives was an unpleasant fact of life, as most adults seemed to need monthly treatment for constipation. This must have had a lot to do with the predominantly starchy diet, particularly white bread, cakes made with white flour, and biscuits. We children were sometimes given a cup of Andrews Liver Salts, mixed strongly enough to taste quite bitter. If Andrews didn't work, a tablespoonful of Syrup-of-Figs was tried; otherwise, a cup of detestable Senna tea would be administered.

To add to the general discomfort of our chilly outhouse, which was located about ten yards from 'the cottage', newspaper served as toilet paper. My sister and I had to report to our mother if there was any sign of worms, so that we could be dosed with a suitable remedy. At the other extremity (so to speak) a fine metal toothcomb was used to check for nits and lice, especially after I had started school. My blond, curly hair was usually tangled, and my mother would struggle to force the toothcomb through it, while I yelped in protest.

Chest colds were a common ailment. We battled them with slices of lemon soaked in hot water, bowls of hot bread-and-milk, flannel vests and vapour rubs (or goose-grease, when it was available). Occasionally, cough mixture and cod-liver oil was purchased from one of the chemist's shops in Swansea; but visits to Drs. Morton and Harris's surgery in Reynoldston to obtain prescriptions for medicine were rare. Sometimes, the doctor could be waylaid while making house-calls to other patients in the village; otherwise a telephone call from one of the farmhouses would see him arrive in a day or two. The doctors were quick to quarantine children who came down with infectious diseases such as measles, chicken-pox or whooping cough.

Until I was about ten years old, my little sister and I shared a bedroom (indeed, a bed) which helped greatly in keeping us warm on damp, chilly nights. Even so, rubber hot-water bottles were necessary in the winter months. Under the thatched roof, we read our books with the aid of a couple of candles placed on the whitewashed stone ledge, which formed part of the massive chimney wall behind our bed. Sometimes we lay staring up at the golden-brown, herringbone-patterned straw matting (which supported the thick layer of thatch), trying to spot spiders or exploring the mysterious shadows thrown by the candlelight.

A bucket had to be placed in my parents' bedroom to catch the drips at the southeast corner of the roof whenever it rained hard. There were times when I would accompany my father out past Kinmoor Lane to help collect bunches of rushes, which he bound into small sheaves to patch the leaking corner of the roof. When the cold wind or rain drove in hard from the east, the bottom of the front door had to be sealed with an old blanket or sack to keep out the draughts and rainwater. The window frames, too, were prone to leak on occasion.

The coal-fire was constantly in use, so my father needed to borrow a set of chimney brushes at least once a year. When he delayed too long, we risked a roaring chimney fire, which could be frightening when it occurred. We were so dependent on the coal-fire that, even in warm weather, it had to be coaxed into life most days, if only to provide a cup of hot tea; but it was also essential for cooking, laundry, ironing and personal ablutions. The bellows, the poker and the coal-scuttle were essential implements in the home. When the bellows wore out, we folded the daily newspaper into a fan and used it to good effect. Sometimes we used our lungs to encourage the reluctant sparks.

The mantelpiece bore witness to the fireplace's position as the focal point of the working man's living room. It ensured an air of importance and gave visitors something to focus on. It received a fresh coat of paint more frequently than did the doors or window frames. Perched in the centre of the mantelpiece was the clock. This was the official family time-piece—though my parents kept a tinny alarm-clock near their bed to ensure an early start to each grinding day. A couple of small glass vases, painted plates or pottery ornaments completed the display. It was also where the front door key was usually kept.

We had no electricity; therefore, our lighting was mainly by oil-lamp (downstairs) and candles (upstairs). Wicks were trimmed, threaded through the brass mechanism, lit and turned up after the glass globe was put in place. The two-gallon paraffin can was usually replenished every couple of weeks, when the Holwells van came around. Holwells also sold miscellaneous household hardware such as clothes-pegs, scrubbing-boards, hair-clips, curlers, door-mats, hot-water bottles, graters, brushes and scissors.

Needless to say, every last hour of daylight was utilised before the lamps would be lit. This was not so much for the sake of economy, but because, in the end, the light from an oil-lamp would be little better than twilight, unless you were sitting near it. Therefore, our parents often strained their eyes to read, knit, darn or sew.

If I stood in front of the window before the oil-lamp was lit, my mother would comment: "You make a better door than a window, Cyril."

I loved books and I was a night-owl by nature. I liked to read late by candlelight, in bed. In the mornings, though, I was very much a daydreamer—and so absentminded that my mother would endeavour to wash me as I stood in an enamel bowl. A kettle or saucepan of water had to be heated on the fire, first. This ritual continued until I was about ten years old, when my mother realised that, although I still wore short pants, I was rapidly approaching puberty.

The radio was unreliable, being dependent on a dry battery and an accumulator (wet-cell), one or other of which always seemed to need recharging or replacing. When it worked, there was only one station to listen to—the good old BBC. My parents enjoyed the Saturday night plays, the Sunday church-services, and of course, the daily six o'clock news. As a ten-year-old, I was fascinated by suspenseful serials such as *Dick Barton: Special Agent* and *Journey into Space*. On the lighter side, there were comedians Arthur Askey and Billy Cotton, and long-running situational comedies like *Life with the Lyons*. In the 1950s, the incomparable *Goon Show* and *Hancock's Half Hour* were hugely popular. Of course, all rural folk enjoyed *The Archers*. Some would discuss the latest crisis, involving Dan, Doris, old Walter Gabriel and a mysterious stranger, named John Tregorran, as they went about their chores.

After another "scrape and save" marathon, my parents were able to afford to have 'the cottage' modernised in 1953. The architect was one Howell Mendes, who was very well known in Gower. While it was being renovated, we returned to live at Middleton Hall for about four months, with uncle Len, his wife Doreen and their three small children—Pamela, Colin and Susan.

After more than four months, we returned to a very different home from the one we had left. It was taller, had a slate roof, a front porch, metal-framed windows, a back-kitchen, a bathroom, a third bedroom, electric light and a limitless supply of piped water, which heralded a completely new era. It was one of the last houses in the parish to get electricity. Now my mother could cook with an electric range—instead of having to depend on the temperamental coal-fire (even in summer). Now, we didn't have to go to the bottom of the garden in foul weather to use the lavatory. Now, my mother could use an electric washing machine and gradually dispense with her scrubbing board; but old habits die hard—it didn't happen overnight.

It seemed like another huge step of modernisation when my parents were able to buy one of the popular new Rayburn stoves, which was much cleaner and more efficient than an open fire. It cost about eighty pounds, so it was a major expenditure. They had to buy it on hire-purchase (or "the never-never", as it was commonly known). It boasted several hotplates, so that potatoes, cabbages, and salted ham could all be boiled at the same time. The stove was set up in what had been our parlour, so our living area moved away from the old fireplace. Henceforth, the fireplace was used mainly on special occasions, such as Christmastime.

Furthermore, indoor plumbing freed us from the tit-for-tat annoyance of stones being thrown at the zinc-sheeted outhouse when it was occupied. I had been the worst offender. Throwing stones at just about anything (whether it moved or not) had become a bad habit. On one occasion, when I was ten, I made my father so angry that he chased me across the hill towards Windy Walls. But running and dodging between gorse bushes was another talent I had developed. He couldn't catch me, and he never bothered to chase me again.

Life seemed to be a little more relaxed after the renovations. My sister and I now had our own bedrooms. My parents had a little more time for light-hearted banter. Amongst many humorous interludes, my sister and I would sometimes march around behind my mother, each holding on to one end of the strings of her apron, while chanting: "We're tied to mother's apron-strings." Our poor mother would laugh so hard, she could hardly catch her breath.

Although my parents made further improvements to our home over the years, it was in 1953 that it was transformed into a relatively modern house. 'The cottage'—as well as much of the traditional way of life it represented—had vanished.

[Endnote: My parents continued to live at 'the cottage' until their final days (in Dec. 1994 and Dec. 1995, respectively). It was sold to the present owner in 1996.]

4

The War Years

It was the best of times, it was the worst of times ...

Charles Dickens

SINCE I was born in April 1940, the many effects of the war on the parish of Rhossili have provided useful reference points for the scant recollections of my first five years or so. These effects resulted from compulsory enlistment, the rationing of food and clothing, the British soldiers encamped at Middleton, the Royal Air Force radar installations, the American GIs encamped at Scurlage, the child evacuees from English cities, the displaced persons from European countries, the "land-girls" (Women's Land Army) and the German prisoners of war. In addition, there were the Home Guard, the Royal Observer Corps, Fire Crew, and Auxiliary Coastguards—part-time duties which were shouldered by local men who had been exempted from military call-up.

In the early years of the war, a couple of large corrugated-zinc Nissen huts were installed in Broad Hay (a rough field belonging to Middleton Hall farm, located between Middleton Lodge and the village hall) to accommodate soldiers of the Royal Sussex Regiment. As we lived at Middleton Hall until mid-1942, I saw these soldiers frequently.

My mother often repeated the story of how she rescued me from a ring of laughing soldiers who I was entertaining with some eloquent speech-making, while clad only in a short vest. I was less than two years old, so I don't remember the incident, though I do remember the soldiers and the Nissen huts. By late 1942, this regiment had embarked to participate in the battle for Tunisia. Several months prior to that, one of them, Ernie Rayner, had eloped with aunty Gladys, to his home near Manchester. I never saw her again.

We moved to 'the cottage' in mid-1942. One year later, the Royal Air Force began the construction of a new roadway up the hill, opposite the gate leading to Talgarths Well. This was partly to facilitate the construction of a radar installation (consisting of several tall lattice-steel masts, interlaced by a network of insulated wires) which was erected in front of the waterworks compound on the hill, overlooking 'the cottage'.

The new roadway also provided better access to the waterworks, and an alternative, drier route to the RAF camp overlooking Hillend. I worked as a volunteer on the construction of that roadway. I had a child's wheelbarrow, a coal shovel from home, and a bricklayer's hammer for a pickaxe. I could not have been more than three years old, but the memories of the tiered excavations would never be forgotten. On occasion, I would invite my RAF acquaintances to our house for a cup of tea and a couple of my mother's delicious Welsh-cakes.

My father was first involved in the Home Guard; then he switched to Auxiliary Coastguard lookout duties. I learnt not to expect much of his time or attention: it was normal for him to be at work ten or more hours a day. In the summer months, it could be thirty-six hours at a stretch, as harvesting could mean working until dusk; then, if it was his night on watch, he would have to be at Thurba Head from midnight to 6:00 AM, returning to the farm after breakfast.

I have little recollection of the Home Guard, except that they were led by our respected Postmaster, Will Williams, a veteran of the Gower Yeomanry, which was disbanded after the First World War. They sometimes trained in Will Morris's rickyard. My mother often recounted that, on the night a German invasion of the Gower beaches was considered to be very possible, the Home Guard was deployed along the brow of Rhossili Down, gallantly facing the wide expanse of Rhossili Bay. Having first raided the Post Office and relieved it of most of its supply of biscuits, they spent quite an enjoyable night, until the alert was lifted, early next morning. Meanwhile some of their wives, left at home with their children, were quaking in their beds. My mother sometimes recalled: "I was sure I could hear the blooming church-bell ringing". (This was the prearranged signal to indicate that the Germans had invaded.)

We kept our government-issued gasmasks in their individual cardboard boxes carefully stored in the cupboard under the stairs. My parents' masks were plain black, but mine was orange-coloured and had a flat, almost diamond-shaped "nose", which I presumed was meant to make the mask a fun thing to wear. My parents dutifully familiarised me with my gasmask at an early age; but as the war wore on, and the threat of invasion diminished, it became an occasional plaything on rainy days.

A number of child evacuees from English cities were billeted in the village to escape the 'blitz'. Most of them must have stayed in the village for at least a couple of years. I hadn't started school, but in my frequent trips to the farmhouse at Middleton Hall, I came to make friends with one or two of them. One in particular, was a special friend. His name was John Harris, and he and his mother stayed on at Rose Cottage for a couple of years after the war. Then, there were the Weston children, who lived at Windy Walls. With Marion and her younger brothers, I diligently studied various kinds of flies, spiders, caterpillars and butterflies.

The "land-girls" (Women's Land Army), another special wartime group, have been frequently written about: and at least one film, *The Land Girls,* has been made about them. They were distinguishable by their smart fawn breeches and olive-green sweaters. There were eight or nine of them scattered throughout our parish. Two of them, Venus and Doreen, were billeted at 'the cottage' for about four months in 1945. Four of the land-girls eventually married local men; one, Doreen Guppy, married uncle Len in late 1945. They lived at Middleton Hall farm, which they eventually purchased from the Penrice Estate. They raised four children: cousins Pamela, Colin, Susan and Stephen. The other "land-girl" brides were Gwen Beynon, Avril Tucker and Rona Richards.

The brick-a-brack of war increased as the war progressed and soldiers were allowed home on leave. At least five of my uncles served in the forces, but uncle Ollie and aunty Peggy's husband, Wilfred, lived at Middleton Hall. Sometimes they left surplus equipment behind when they returned from leave. There were steel helmets, dress hats, webbing, gaiters, khaki jackets and trousers, regimental badges, a German bayonet—even clips of .303 rifle bullets or spent ammunition cases. One or two of the older boys sometimes brought .303 bullets to the school and demonstrated how to extract the gunpowder and transfer it to a pop-bottle, perhaps to make a crude firework.

All kinds of things were salvaged for the war effort, including discarded pots, pans, books and metal fittings. Newspapers and cardboard were major salvage items: they were collected and stored in Jack Richards's shed near the bus-stop at 'the bank'. Small metal badges were issued to those who provided good service for the salvage effort. Some of the older children managed to win them, and so earned my envy and respect. They sometimes used discarded prams to make their collections. The commendable salvage effort continued for a while after the war; it was the forerunner of today's "re-use, repair, recycle" philosophy.

One indelible memory of wartime living was the rationing. There were Ration Books for food and Clothing Coupons for off-the-rack clothing. Of course, many items could not readily be controlled; for example, knitted clothes and home-pro-duced food such as eggs, poultry and vegetables. There was also the inevitable "black market"—a term I heard often, but only vaguely comprehended. Even so, the controls were effective. There was little point in going shopping without your Ration Book: even when you did take it, the shops were sometimes out of stock.

In addition to Ration Books and Clothing Coupons, a bus-ride into Swansea required Identity Cards for adults, if only to pass through Scurlage, where the Americans were encamped for about a year prior to D-Day.

Buses avoided crossing the Fairwood aerodrome during the war years, instead taking the route through Bishopston, so we didn't have much chance to see the spitfires or hurricanes. We knew that, especially during the blitz, the planes based at Fairwood were used to defend Cardiff; while those at St. Athans were scram-bled to defend Swansea. This was to avoid the runway lighting becoming a marker for the German bombers.

As the red double-decker Rhossili bus rushed across Bishopston Common, towards the top of The Mayals, several huge ships would invariably be seen anchored in Swansea Bay or moving slowly in or out of port. Anti-aircraft guns and barrage-balloons were much in evidence as the bus travelled along the Mum-bles Road past Singleton Park, then past the St. Helens rugby ground, and turned left at the Brangwyn Hall.

As I accompanied my mother on rare shopping expeditions around Swansea towards the end of the war, I was able to view the "bomb sites", including some houses and St. Mary's Anglican Church opposite The Market. It hadn't gone unnoticed that the grinning effigy of the Devil at The Market, had seemed to protect it from the bombs, while the church had suffered very badly. The ruined church stood patiently awaiting repair for several years after the war was over.

Soon after the Americans moved out, in the spring of 1944, the DPs (dis-placed persons) were next to occupy the camp at Scurlage. From what I recall, they were mostly men in their thirties and forties, who had fled their homelands in eastern European countries such as Poland, Hungary, Czechoslovakia and The Ukraine. Local farmers could afford to hire one or more of them because they were paid only about one shilling a day.

Near the end of the war, people spoke, with more apprehension than humour, of the V1 rocket planes. These unmanned flying bombs were first launched by the Germans shortly after the June, 1944, landings. They were commonly referred to as "buzz-bombs" or "doodlebugs". The V2 version, a potentially more serious threat, was more like a space rocket. They were used primarily to attack

London in retaliation for the massive bomber raids being mounted against German cities, such as Dresden.

After about eighteen months, the DPs were moved elsewhere so that German POWs could be imprisoned at Scurlage (probably because the camp had good security features). The POWs were allowed to work on Gower farms in much the same way as the DPs had, though farmers tended to treat them with suspicion, at first. Nevertheless, many of them proved to be strong and willing workers. Like the DPs, they were hired at a daily rate and many of them became regular workers at a number of farms. Two of them worked for about two years at the family farm at Middleton Hall. Another one, Joseph Niwa, settled permanently in Rhossili. He married my cousin, Frances, and lived at Hoarstone.

Finally, the war was over. Japan had capitulated. I helped to collect scrap wood, tires, gorse—any rubbish that would burn—to be transported by tractor and trailer or horse and cart to the crest of the hill above Windy Walls. Good use was made of the roadway I had helped to build just two years earlier. I enjoyed a couple of trips on uncle Len's tractor and trailer to the pine-tree plantation between Sluxton and Kings Hall to load up dead branches and trunks of fallen trees for the VJ Day bonfire. I had started school just the previous month.

The bonfire was lit by one of the prominent parishioners—probably Jack Richards, JP, or Gower RDC councillor Will Williams. As we celebrated, we could see other bonfires at several locations in southwest Gower. It was the second bonfire that year. The first had been a few months earlier to celebrate VE Day.

About this time, many of us villagers attended a ceremony in the village hall to honour some of the Rhossili servicemen who were being demobbed. One by one, they were called forward to receive documents (which I believe included a civilian Ration Book and Clothing Coupons). They were also presented with a small stipend. Each one was loudly applauded. In addition, they were entitled to a blue-serge demob suit. For some time afterwards, the ex-servicemen were readily identifiable by their best suits. Local men who returned from serving with the armed forces included Raymond Shepherd, Harry Morris, Oliver Jones, Harold Hinton and Wilfred Pugh.

No doubt there was a positive community spirit in the village (indeed, in the whole country) during the war years. Of course, there were always some who were inclined to be freeloaders, in one way or another. However, people were generally hardworking, unselfish and considerate to others. We had a glimpse of how the world might be a better place.

But all too soon, the spirit of those days would begin to fade.

[Endnote: Volunteers in local wartime auxiliary services included (lists may not be complete):

<u>Royal Observer Corps</u>: Lloyd Williams; Glyn Williams; Will Button; Phil Richards; George Grove; Sid James; Ingram Chalk; Jack Bevan (Rhossili); Johnny Beynon (Meadowside); Albert Griffiths.

<u>Home Guard</u>: Will Williams; Bevan Tucker; Gwyn Beynon; Norman Tucker; William Harry; Morgan Jones; Joffre Jones; Bert Fisher; Leonard Jones.

<u>Auxiliary Coastguard</u>: Stan Beynon; Bill Beynon; Joffre Jones; Phil Jones; Will Jones; Bowen Richards.

<u>Auxiliary Fire Service</u>: Jack Bevan; Mansel Bevan; Alf Bevan; Ron Densley; Glyn Richards.]

5

The Yanks

WELL before the end of the war, a new phenomenon occurred in my life—soldiers with strange, sandy-coloured jackets and rounded helmets. People called them Americans, or sometimes, "Yanks". I was aware only that they were from some distant land and that they were on our side in the war.

It must have been some months before June, 1944, that I recall the American soldiers rolling through the village to train with their DUKW amphibious vehicles (known as "ducks") at Rhossili Bay, though they favoured the easier accessibility of Oxwich and Porteynon Bays, for the most part. Although no one knew at the time, we later realised they were preparing for the D-Day invasion of occupied Europe.

They were encamped at Scurlage, roughly in the area which would be developed as the sports grounds and the Grass-dryer Co-op by 1950. They seemed to control any kind of traffic around Scurlage, making it necessary for locals to carry ID cards even when taking the bus to town.

Some of the local farmers apparently found them rather overbearing—even questioning the movement of cows along the road from the pasture to the milking shed. When on maneuvres, their convoys sometimes blocked traffic completely, on the narrow Horton, Porteynon and Oxwich roads.

With their strong emphasis on security, the Americans did not socialise easily with the local population in Gower, as the Canadians and other Commonwealth personnel did. Besides, they didn't play football or cricket and the locals didn't play baseball, so there was little in common.

The older boys taught us to chase behind the jeeps and ducks as they chugged along the road past The Ship farm and the Post Office. "Give us a gum, chum!" we had learnt to shout. It was a strange language to us, but low and behold, the Americans would often respond to this strange phrase by tossing small packets of "candy" (sweets) or chewing-gum, which were quite unlike anything we had seen in the village shops. We were used to hard-boils, jubes and peppermints.

Sometimes a couple of vehicles would stop at 'the bank' for a while. On one occasion, a "duck" was parked outside Jessamine farm. A youthful officer, who would always be a lieutenant in my mind, engaged me in small talk. I remember nothing of the details of the conversation, but he eventually reached inside his jacket and took out a thin brown flute, which he gave to me.

After D-Day, the newspapers were full of large black headlines, and maps showing dramatic arrows sweeping across the countries of Europe. At four years of age, though, I only had some vague impressions that our side was winning some kind of contest—after all, the war had been going on since before I was born. In Rhossili, life was quite wonderful for a pre-schooler bursting with energy and curiosity, who understood little of the hardships that our parents endured, let alone the life-and-death struggle that was going on in Europe and elsewhere in the world.

One legacy of the American "occupation" of Scurlage occurred when my father was involved in ploughing over the campsite about three years after the end of the war. (He was still operating a Fordson tractor for the War Agricultural Committee.) He sometimes brought home tin cans containing biscuits, processed meat and other food, which had been turned up by the ploughshares.

Although I subsequently heard many derisive stories about the wartime exploits of the unpopular Yanks, my own childhood experience had made me aware of their good intentions. What happened to that flute? Almost a decade later, my mother told me that, because I was too young to take much interest in it, she had loaned it to one of my older cousins; but by then, she could only guess who that might have been.

In any event, I never saw it—or my American friend—again.

[Endnote1: Over the years, I have sometimes wondered about my American friend. Did he bring that flute all the way from his hometown in America, only to give it away to a four-year-old, curly-headed Welsh boy who had the gall to carry on a man-to-man conversation with him? Did he survive the aftermath of D-Day? Or did he pay the ultimate price for coming all those thousands of miles to help ensure a good future for kids like me? I will never know.]

[Endnote2: As far as I have been able to ascertain, the Americans encamped at Scurlage were part of the US 28th Division which was stationed at several locations in England and Wales, including Haverfordwest and Tenby, prior to D-Day. They did not take part in the D-Day landings, but probably landed in Normandy a few weeks after the initial invasion.]

6

Hardworking Parents

Man goeth forth to his work, and to his labour: until the evening.

Anglican Prayer Book

MY parents, Joffre Jones and Joyce Powell, were married in October 1939. I was born at the end of the following April. My modest gifts of observation and arithmetic have led me to conclude that I was probably conceived in Sluxton Woods about the end of June, 1939; thus the marriage did not get off to an ideal start. They began married life at the already-overcrowded Middleton Hall. It was the beginning of many years of hard work to improve life for themselves and their children. No one who knew them would disagree that they were good examples of people who lived by old-fashioned work ethics.

As an agricultural worker, Joff was excused from wartime conscription. Because of that, he felt he had a duty to work as long and hard as he could, especially throughout the war years. In those days, in any case, it was expected that a farmworker would work a five-and-a-half or six-day week, plus any overtime needed to get the harvest in. There was seldom any overtime pay, though there might be an occasional reward of "a few bob" extra, at the end of the week—or a chicken at Christmastime.

In addition to the long hours on the farm, Joff served in the Home Guard at the beginning of the war; then he transferred to night-watch duties at the Thurba Head lookout, which was a temporary zinc and timber hut about the size of a garden shed. He sometimes worked round the clock—coming off his night-watch in time for breakfast, before going back to work all day on the farm. The march from 'the cottage' to Thurba was quite challenging—all the way down to the bottom of the rugged Mewslade valley, then up the steep grassy slopes to the top of the Head—taking the best part of half an hour, each way. Of course, this involved travel by foot, sometimes at night, regardless of weather conditions.

From well before the end of the war, until early 1948, Joff was employed by the War Agricultural Committee. This organisation managed a pool of farm equipment, including several Fordson tractors, located in a fenced compound at Knelston. His job took him all over Gower, as this equipment was rented out to farmers who did not have their own. He travelled as far as Pontarddulais and beyond. He became known as one of the hardest working men in Gower.

From 1948, he worked for several local farmers, including Jack Richards, George Thomas and Alf Bevan. In the late 1950s, he worked for the Glamorgan County Council as a roadman for several years, before switching to construction work in the mid-1960s.

For many years, Joff dug graves at several churches from Rhossili to Reynoldston as a source of additional income for his family. The heavy clay and limestone rock ensured that this was physically exhausting work, which he often did after finishing his regular day's work (or on Saturdays), regardless of weather conditions. There was one particularly rocky grave-site at Llandewi churchyard in the mid-1950s. In Joff's words: "'Twas solid limestone. I was damn lucky Reggie Beynon came over from Lake farm and gave me a hand. I'll give 'n a couple o' quid, now, when I get paid."

It was sometimes painful for my sister and me to see how hard our father worked. We would often be looking out for him to come into view by the school, having surmounted the steep slope of Sheep Green hill, his handsome blond head bobbing, marching tiredly but vigorously towards his evening meal. Indeed, I imitated his ways of walking when surmounting the steep slopes in our parish. Normally, he would lean slightly forward from the waist, his arms swinging freely, toes pointing forward; but at the end of a long day, perhaps carrying a couple of shopping-bags or a sack of vegetables on his back, he would "stave" up the hill (as he would put it), toes turned outward, swaying from side to side.

We knew he would have little time or energy left for us, but we understood. We would wait around him expectantly, until our mother had our tea on the table, listening to his every word, as he spoke whatever was on his mind—perhaps something that had happened at work, or some local news he'd heard. Sometimes it was just about the chores he needed to do after supper (whether it was dark or not), such as chopping firewood, walking to the Post Office for the bread and the *Evening Post*, carrying a bucket of scraps to Middleton to feed our pig, or fetching a pint of milk from Jessamine farm.

I saw my father break down and cry only once—that was when he'd been out of work for a couple of weeks. To him, as with most of the proud working men, going on "the dole" was all but unthinkable: it was regarded as a kind of joke, spoken of with disdain. Certainly, there would have been a stigma attached to it.

Quite possibly, my mother, Joyce, worked even harder than my father. Joff would light the fire each morning, so that breakfast could be cooked. Joyce's day began with preparing his breakfast and his lunchtime sandwiches, and ended with such chores as ironing, knitting, sewing and darning, before she went to bed. This, in itself, was not unusual for the housewives of those days; however, until 1953, we lived in a thatched cottage without electricity, so even the clothes iron had to be heated over the fire. Spitting was the best way to check whether the iron was hot enough; then it had to be used with caution, usually with a tea-towel wrapped around the scorched wooden handle.

Clothes were washed by hand, using a washtub and a scrubbing board, again with buckets of water heated up over the fire. Every drop of water had to be carried from the communal water-tap which (fortunately) was located only about thirty yards from our house. The clothes had to be rinsed and wrung out by hand. Then Joyce would pray that there wouldn't be any unexpected rain or that the wind wouldn't blow the clothes off the line. On a bad day, both of these undesirable events might occur while she was out working on one of her part-time jobs.

Preparing the main meal of the day, alone, could involve a considerable amount of work. It required a housewife to be able to clean fish, poultry or rabbits—which would usually include scaling, feathering or skinning, respectively. Then the vegetables had to be prepared. Of course, no meal was complete without the appropriate sauce for the meat, and homemade pie and custard for dessert. Especially when the children were young, a housewife would expect little help with the washing-up, drying and storing of all the utensils and crockery.

In addition to all the housework, Joyce (like many other women) pitched in wherever she could, doing some of the farm-work that the men balked at, such as weeding fledgling field crops, like beetroots or carrots. The men didn't mind hoeing, monotonous though it was, but hours of weeding on their knees was too much, even for them.

Around the end of the war, Joyce found extra work delivering mail to all of Rhossili End, beyond the Post Office, including the allegedly haunted Old Rectory at Parsonage, where the Reverend W. Scudamore had lived until the New Rectory was built near the church, in 1925. Occasionally, she would take me along with her. It was an interesting, though long, tramp to the Old Rectory, as we walked from The Green, down the lane towards the "rocket house", past the well with its abundant watercress, then along the cart-track which hugged the dry-stone wall at the base of Rhossili Down. In some places, the track was deeply rutted and tended to flood when it rained, so that we had to scramble along the bank on the hill side of the track. The round trip must have been more than a mile, just to deliver letters to one house!

One of the jobs my mother took on in order to "make ends meet" was caretaker/cleaner of the village school (conveniently located less than a hundred yards from our house) when Florrie Williams retired in 1947. This also gave my father extra work, as the two large coal-burning stoves needed to be supplied with buckets of coal, as well as kindling wood. He would use any odds and ends of wood he could find to chop up for the fires. He made regular trips to Fall Bay to fetch driftwood for this purpose: sometimes, I would go along and carry whatever I could manage.

Joyce was able to add a little more to her income a few months later, when the delivery of school dinners began. She first served the food; then she washed up all the crockery, cutlery and containers. Every couple of weeks or so, she scrubbed and disinfected the wooden floors (which required moving all the desks). Daily, she cleaned out the stoves; then charged them with newspaper, kindling wood and coal. The cloakrooms and toilets were additional chores.

About 1950, Joyce also took on the caretaker duties for the village hall. That included setting up and clearing the chairs and tables, in accordance with the requirements of each function held there. Sometimes, after public dances, film-shows or private parties, all four of us would be there to sweep and tidy up afterwards. Often, after dances, the ever-popular farmer/musician Ron Parry would linger on to offer an encouraging word or two.

After the war, as the demand for bed-and-breakfast services began to increase in the village, my mother helped out at the large guesthouses along Rhossili Lane. Several of them had been built earlier in the century with that function in mind. The Broad Park guesthouse, which was operated by the Crozier family for a few years around 1950, was the prime example. My mother worked there several hours a day, several days a week as a cleaner, maid or assistant cook. Later, she worked for the Williamses at Dainsbury, before they moved to Oxwich.

There was very little social life for my parents. Joyce loved sharing a pot of tea with friends and neighbours, children's birthday parties, rare afternoon trips to take us kids to Mewslade bay for a paddle and a picnic, or chatting with other wives on the bus to town. Joff depended on chance encounters with various village characters while going about his work, fetching things from the shops or performing his other chores.

After the war, there were weekly film-shows in the village hall and annual trips to a Christmas pantomime, a circus or a fun-fair resort such as Barry or Porthcawl. These provided a little more variety in entertainment. There were also the Saturday shopping trips to town. My mother might fit in a visit to her family in Gorseinon. My father was more likely to watch the Swans play at the Vetch Field. But these diversions were not frequent.

Sundays were mostly days of less work, rather than complete rest. After tea, we could look out for Ron Parry, who operated an ice-cream van which also doubled as a mobile chip-shop (no fish, though). This was a weekly treat for my parents, who, like many other working-class people, could afford few recreational diversions. By 1950, there was a choice of Lyons ice-cream from The Green or Walls ice-cream from the Worms Head Hotel. My father liked to unwrap a cylindrical Lyons ice-cream (meant to make an ice-cream cone) and drop it into a large glass of Spooner's lemonade to make a foamy "iced drink".

Apart from an unreliable wireless, newspapers were Joff's main source of intellectual activity. In the week, it was the *Daily Express* and the *Evening Post*; on Sundays, the *People* and the *Sunday Express*. Like most of the women in the village, Joyce would look forward to the next weekly instalment of some historical romance, such as *Forever Amber*. She also loved her *Woman's Own* magazine. Crosswords, jigsaw puzzles and various newspaper competitions gave her some sense of entertainment.

In the late 1940s and the 1950s, mail-order shopping became very popular with most of the housewives. The latest *Littlewoods* catalogue was eagerly awaited and soon became well-thumbed. There were only two issues each year: one for the autumn/winter seasons, and one for spring/summer. For the most part, this mode of shopping proved effective and reliable for rural families. By contrast, mail orders through national newspaper advertisements often provided unanticipated problems.

In the 1940s, the supply of home hardware and cleaning products usually depended on the Holwells van, which came round about once every two or three weeks. Home and Colonial was another mobile shop, mainly for groceries that weren't rationed. It could be a real nuisance if either of the vans came by when there was no one at home: then, we would have to wait another couple of weeks for something we needed, or else put it on the shopping list for the next bus-trip to town.

The only other vendors who made house-calls were the "Little Jew" and the "Big Jew". They would each call around every two or three months. They dealt exclusively in textiles, including basic items of clothing, towels, dishcloths, etc. They carried their goods, tied up in a blanket or sheet, on their shoulders. When one of them was invited into a house, he would set down his bundle and open it up on the parlour floor, so that the housewife could shop. In fine weather, this might be done outside. After the shopping exercise was completed, the bundle would be tied up again and the vendor would be on his way to the next cottage or farmhouse—with a lighter bundle, but a heavier pocket.

Will Williams at the Post Office knew that our family budget was more than a bit tight, at times. In the case of particularly hardworking, honest people, he would make it clear that they could run up a bill "on tick" and that they could pay whenever they had the money. He knew that they would use that privilege as little as possible and pay what they owed as soon as they were able—certainly before spending money on anything other than absolute necessities. This helped to provide my parents with the financial flexibility to achieve as much as they did.

I could only benefit from their example.

[Endnote: Only the independence of their children and the advances in technology would eventually relieve my parents from the drudgery of their lifelong hard work. Only then, could they look forward to retirement and a meagre pension. In the end, they were able to live out their post-retirement years in peace and quiet, in the cottage that was their home for half a century, enjoying the comforts of television and modern appliances which are so taken for granted nowadays. They even enjoyed an occasional vacation in their senior years. How times had changed! It is fitting that their monument at Rhossili churchyard bears an acknowledgement of their industry: "The day is o'er; the toil is done."]

7

Hoarstone

Share my harvest and my home.

Thomas Hood

I WAS indeed fortunate to have so many of my father's brothers to tag along with, especially since he worked such long days and always had additional chores to do. There were uncles Robin, Ollie, Len, Phil and Will. Only Jack and Clifford had moved away from Gower: Jack worked in a steelworks, near Llansamlet, and Clifford worked as a bricklayer in Hereford.

Robin, Ollie and Len were all living with their mother at Middleton Hall, so I saw a lot of them, yet my favourite was Will. He treated me as though I were his own son, while his only child, Frances, loved me as an older sister might.

Born in 1900, Will was the eldest of the eight boys in the Jones family. When he married Ceinwen Thomas, a nurse from Aberdare, he struck out on his own, leaving the overcrowded family farm at Middleton Hall. About 1930, Will became the sitting tenant at Hoarstone, which had already been the home of four previous generations of his family. It was a slate-roofed cottage with a couple of outbuildings, a large vegetable garden, a pigsty and a small rough field.

As a boy, I didn't realise that Hoarstone had such a long history in our family. My great-great-grandfather, Francis Jones, became the first Jones to live in Rhossili for about half a century when he moved there from Oxwich Green, in the winter of 1846. However, his wife, Margaret, was a Rhossili girl who had been born and raised at Hoarstone. Their youngest son, William, led an adventurous life as a seaman, before returning to live at Hoarstone until he married a widow, Elizabeth Bevan, who was the sitting tenant at Middleton Hall farm. Then William's son (my grandfather), Francis, lived at Hoarstone for about a decade, after he married my grandmother, Anne Rosser, in the late 1890s.

Uncle Will was one of the old-timers who always wore a cloth cap, flannel shirt, waistcoat, corded britches, and leather gaiters which fitted snugly over his work-boots. Gaiters were only partly effective in keeping water out of boots, but they helped protect the shins when working around horses and farm equipment. They took extra time to lace up, so they lost their appeal with the increased use of tractors and the advent of the popular Wellington boots (which kept out water, much more effectively). But on Sundays, Will changed into a suit and trilby hat to attend St. Mary's church where he, like his younger brother, Phil, served as a warden for many years.

There were several amusing incidents involving Will and me. One such story tells how I was helping him to plant potatoes in his garden when he "ran out", just before he got to the end of a row. I called out, "'s alright, I've got some 'taters, uncle Will." It was only then that he realised that I had been busily picking up the seed-potatoes that he had been planting. Yes, we kids could be daft; there was no doubt about it.

On another occasion, I have a faint memory of being attacked by an aggressive cockerel as I approached Hoarstone from the direction of Professor Stephen Lee's bungalow at Talgarths Well. The cockerel scared me with its flapping wings, then pecked and scratched me on the arms and legs. Aunty Ceinwen and cousin Frances heard me yelling. They rescued me, slightly scratched and bleeding. They took me into the house and made sure there was no serious damage. About an hour later, I went home, having almost forgotten the incident.

Uncle Will, who worked at Donald Button's farm for most of his working life, did not arrive home until well after I had left. Aunty Ceinwen and Frances had been complaining about the cockerel for some time, because they were afraid of it, but Will had seemed in no hurry to do anything about it. Well, the story goes that, as soon as he arrived home from his day's work, they told him how the cockerel had attacked me. He listened and said nothing; but before he sat down to his tea, he went out and killed the cockerel.

In 1944, my older cousins from Hereford, Frank and David, spent several months at Hoarstone, because their father, Clifford, was in the army and their mother, Clara, was hospitalised. They found that aunty Ceinwen was a strict disciplinarian. Each day, when they returned across the fields from the school, she required them to fetch enough buckets of fresh water from Talgarths Well to provide for the following day's household needs. Only then, would they receive their tea.

About three years later, I lived at Hoarstone for about six weeks when my mother abruptly decided to return to her parents' home in Gorseinon. However,

Frances made sure I wasn't burdened with too many chores. Therefore, I settled in quickly and enjoyed my sojourn.

Cousin Frances, who was a decade older than I, was well-versed in all the chores needed to keep the home going, whether it was fetching water, washing clothes, feeding the pigs, milking the cow, scrubbing floors or helping plough the garden and field. For several years, during and after the war she delivered the post on foot, around the whole of Pitton and Middleton. Even so, she always found time to treat me as a special guest.

In 1948, Frances married a German prisoner of war, Joseph Niwa, who was employed by Reg Howells at Fernhill. Joe soon became "one of the locals". Like his father-in-law, he worked at Donald Button's farm until he retired. Frances and Joe soon had two little daughters, Julie and Marie, so Hoarstone became a busy household, comprising three generations under one roof.

In the mid-1950s, Frances and Joe invested in a television set. Will and Ceinwen, who were both suffering from deteriorating eyesight, did not show much interest in it, always preferring their beloved wireless. Even so, these early black-and-white TV sets did much to reduce the sense of isolation of many rural residents and elderly people. I was a regular visitor, eager to enjoy some wonderful long-running western series—*Cheyenne*, *Rawhide* and *Maverick*—which followed one after the other. It had to be a very wild night to make me miss "western night" at Hoarstone.

By the mid-1950s, turkey had become a realistic option for a farm-worker's Christmas dinner. At Hoarstone, there seemed to be cold turkey sandwiches for a late supper for weeks after Christmas was over. Frances was a wonderful cook, who specialised in homemade pies such as gooseberry, rhubarb, apple and blueberry. She also learnt from her mother, Ceinwen, the art of making homemade wines, especially from elderberries. The folk at Hoarstone always enjoyed a magnificent yuletide feast.

It was truly my "second home".

8

A Trip to Town

Travelling is the ruin of all happiness.

Fanny Burney

IT is a Saturday morning in 1945. My mother, Joyce, wakes me for breakfast at about half-past eight. She wants us to catch the ten o'clock bus to town. My father has left for work already. A kind neighbour has offered to look after my placid one-year-old sister. I have mixed feelings: I can usually avoid going to town, except when my mother wants to buy me some new clothes. But there are some Clothing Coupons to be used up, and my short trousers are all well worn from the daily rough and tumble around the farms.

"You'll be starting school in September and you'll need something decent to wear," my mother reminds me, as she takes the kettle off the fire, pours hot water into an enamel bowl sitting on the floor, then adds some cold water from a bucket. Our thatched farm-worker's cottage has no bathroom, or even a water tap. Standing me naked in the bowl of lukewarm water, she washes me with a flannel and soap, then helps me dry myself and sits me on a kitchen chair.

I am busy indulging in my favourite early-morning pastime—daydreaming. Mam holds a clean shirt in front of me; I obligingly lift up a foot. "Not your leg, your arm, boy," she tells me. After the shirt is on, she proffers a pair of short trousers; I extend an arm. "Stand up, Cyril," she commands, "Now lift up your leg." Then, while I enjoy my breakfast of Quaker porridge oats, cooled with milk and sweetened with a dessert-spoonful of Tate & Lyle's "golden syrup", she turns her attention to my little sister. Eventually, Mam and I are hurrying past the school, watching to see if the bus is coming down Pitton Cross hill. We know it will take several minutes to go out to Rhossili End and return to Middleton.

31

A few other people are already waiting at 'the bank' when we get there, some with children. Among them are Ella Howells and her two-year-old daughter, Margaret. Ella is going to visit her family for a few days. Reg and Ella Howells have been farming at Fernhill for only the past three years. My mother, who has been living in Rhossili for about six years already, always enjoys a chat with Ella. They are both from the industrial valleys, so they have similar "Welshy" backgrounds—quite different from the Gower culture.

Suddenly, the red United Welsh double-decker bus, flies round the corner and screeches to a halt, well past the bus-stop: it never seems to want to stop in Middleton—sometimes it doesn't, if people don't make themselves clearly visible to the driver. We get on the lower deck of the bus and see that three or four people from Rhossili End are already there; a few others are on the upper deck. As we ride along, we look to see who else will get on, that we know.

Only one man, Phil Richards, gets on in Pitton. As the bus struggles up Pitton Cross Hill, dropping all the way down into bottom gear before it reaches the top, the friendly conductor comes shuffling along. "One-and-a-half return to Swansea, please," says my mother. "Oh, is 'e five? That will be ten-pence-ha'penny for both of you, then ... thank you," replies the conductor, "Lovely day, isn't it?"

By now we are gathering speed on the downward slope across Pitton Cross common. We see Will Tucker's young wife, Averil (who had come to the village as a "land-girl") running from the farmhouse door, down the farm roadway, waving frantically. Her mother-in-law, old Mrs. Tucker, is running behind her. Fortunately, the bus-driver sees them and stops. We wait patiently until they arrive, breathless and grateful. Averil, an eternally cheerful, dark-haired, big-boned young woman, flashes a bright smile at everyone, asking how they are.

There is a renewed chorus of "good morning ... lovely day, isn't it ... how are you?" after every stop. Once we get past Pyle Well, though, the greetings become fewer and more muted. Rhossili people have a strong community feeling. By the time we have been around Horton and Porteynon then back to Scurlage, the bus is filling up. It still has to divert through Reynoldston; then continue through Penmaen and Parkmill, before crossing Bishopston Common. Soon, I have to give up my seat for a grownup and sit awkwardly on my mother's lap, while staring out of the window.

Halfway across Bishopston Common, the bus stops to pick up a couple of people, waiting in front of a magnificent building, set in its own grounds. "That's Barnardo's Homes," my mother tells me. She goes on to explain that youngsters without parents live there, until they are old enough to find work. I can't quite comprehend the idea of being without parents (or at least uncles and aunties) to live with. The bus gathers speed, while I continue to ponder the idea of children without families of their own.

It is still wartime, even though the Allies are clearly winning in Europe. Although identity cards are no longer considered as important as they were in the early years of the war, people still carry them "just in case, isn't it?" As we approach the top of The Mayals, we can see several huge merchant ships anchored in Swansea Bay. There are also still a few high-flying barrage balloons (with their funny, fat "ears") floating majestically in the air, holding taut the wires which threaten enemy dive-bombers.

Travelling along the Mumbles Road, I try to spot the anti-aircraft guns. I see some, but there is no one manning them, these days: they will never be needed again. We catch up with a "Mumbles train", which is really a double-decker tramcar, as it shakes and sways along its tracks. It stops opposite Singleton Park to pick up a few passengers, so we quickly leave it behind; then, turning up past the Guildhall, we approach the United Welsh bus-garage.

It feels so strange to be in town; quite unnatural, really. I must walk (not run) with short, stiff steps, watching out for obstacles—mostly human ones, in the form of crowds of Saturday shoppers—while holding on to my mother's hand to make sure I won't get lost. I must stop and turn mechanically, first one way, then the other, at all street crossings, while the noise and fumes from buses, vans and lorries threaten to overwhelm me. There seem to be concrete steps and curbs to trip over, everywhere.

All the time there is a dazzling array of strange faces—old, young, very young, very old, mysterious, menacing, pretty, happy, weary and unshaven. For a country boy, who is used to seeing less than a dozen (always familiar) faces around at any one time; a boy who mostly uses his ears to detect approaching vehicles or horses; a boy who is used to dashing off in any direction according to whim, town feels more like a prison camp. I am already feeling weak and pallid in this foreign environment.

"First," says my mother, "we must find somewhere to have a cup o' tea." We have already passed several small cafes; but it's Saturday, so they all looked crowded. We go into the next one we come to. It is stuffy and crowded inside; we have to share a small round table in the corner with a middle-aged couple. They politely acknowledge our presence; then, keeping their eyes averted so as not to intrude on our privacy, continue conversing quietly but earnestly in Welsh.

Several men are smoking as they drink their warm beverages. Soon we are enjoying a cup of hot tea with two teaspoonfuls of sugar, and a pastry. I don't really like pastries and I wonder why grownups do. I finally decide to try one of the Welsh-cakes, because they look familiar. Ugh, it tastes rubbery, nothing like the ones my mother makes at home. "Do you want an ice-cream, Cyril?" asks my mother. I shake my head. I've only ever had ice-cream about three or four times in my life: it is a strange delicacy to me, and awkward to handle. My mother says we should share one "while we have the chance, isn't it?", so we do.

Now my mother charges off in earnest on the shopping expedition with me in tow. We first head for Oxford Street, then High Street, stopping at Woolworths, British Home Stores, Marks and Spencer, then Woolworths again. I hear my mother say, "Try this on, Cyril" so many times that I begin to protest. My legs are feeling tired, which they rarely do in Rhossili. "Just one more shop," promises my mother, "Then we'll go to The Market to buy some food." Soon, with my mother already carrying a large brown carrier-bag, as well as her own bulging shopping-bag, we head to The Market.

We buy apples, oranges, pears, some green grapes, a leg of Welsh lamb (for Sunday roast), a fresh cauliflower, half a pound of laver-bread, a quarter-pound of cockles and a few other delicacies not available in our village shops. By now, I can only think of going home. My mother ponders whether there's time for another cup of tea and a pastry, in the Market Café; or whether we should head for Belles, opposite the bus-garage and have a "feed of fish-and-chips". Fish-and-chips seem like the lesser evil. I express my enthusiasm rather weakly. That's it, then; we have nearly an hour to wait for the twenty-to-five bus. No more shopping, we'll have a meal instead.

At Belles, the atmosphere is bright and airy, compared to the other cafés. There is plenty of room at that time in the afternoon. "What do you want, Cyril?" asks my mother, "We can share if you like. Fish-and-chips, pie-and-chips, egg-and-chips, sausage-and-chip ..." "Fish-and-chips please, Mam," I reply. There is a generous portion of deep fried chips; the fish is delicious fresh cod, fried in thick batter; and there are two rounds of rubbery white bread, smeared with margarine—all for eight-pence-ha'penny. Sugar, salt and vinegar are on every table. A cup of tea and a small bottle of Corona pop are extra.

The tasy fish and salty chips barely calm a growing queasiness in my stomach. Then we stroll over to the bus-garage and take our place in the queue behind the tubular iron railings for the Rhossili and Porteynon bus. The garage reeks with the smell of diesel fumes, spilt fuel and cigarette smoke—sometimes relieved by the pleasant odours of coffee and freshly-baked pastries drifting from the Garage Café. My mother encourages me to visit the toilet—after I first watch over the shopping-bags, while she goes—so off I go. The stale odours of the bus-garage toilets do little to help my increasing nausea.

Suddenly, our bus sweeps into view and roars through the garage to where we are waiting. We get on, choosing a seat just in front of the side-seats, and wait impatiently for the driver and conductor to take their ten minute break. A cup of tea is essential before a two-and-a-half hour return trip. My mother searches her purse for our tickets. I am already longing to get to Middleton.

The crew strolls back to the bus; then we slowly manoeuvre out of the garage and through the narrow, busy streets of the town, skilfully avoiding the pedestrians who are more frequent obstacles than the vehicles. The bus jerks and shudders. Finally, we turn the corner at the Albert Hall cinema; a few more minutes and we are powering our way up past the Odeon in Sketty. We turn down towards the Mumbles road. We seem to crawl up The Mayals, then fly across Bishopston Common.

By now, my face has turned quite white. "Not feeling well, is 'e?" asks a well-meaning man in a trench-coat, leaning over from the side-seat behind us. My mother explains that I'm not used to travelling on the bus. He says we should move down to the front because there will be less fumes. We move to a spare seat near the front, but the vibration from the engine is much stronger there. I hang on for another ten minutes or so; then I tell my mother I'm going to be sick. We have just climbed Penmaen hill; we're about halfway home.

My mother takes me to the back and informs the conductor. He asks whether I'd like to stand on the open step at the back, where I can get some fresh air. The man in the trench-coat says he'll stand out there with me to make sure I don't let go of the handrail. Soon, the bus is bowling along the curvy road between The Towers and Home Farm. It doesn't feel safe, standing out there. I'm glad the man has got hold of me by the collar of my jacket. The cool, rushing air feels like a tonic. I won't be sick, after all; not on this trip.

Luckily, this bus is going to Rhossili first, before Horton and Porteynon. Arriving at last at Middleton, I step shakily off the bus, glad to feel 'the bank' under my feet again. The sky is dull grey and it's trying to rain. My father is there, waiting. He takes two of the heavy bags from my mother and asks what she's brought for him to eat—he's only had a jam sandwich for tea, he tells us, but he's lit the fire, so it's all ready for my mother to make "something with a few chips" for his supper.

We march steadily uphill towards 'the cottage'. For once, I'm glad to get home well before dark. My father won't need to be searching for me tonight.

[Endnote: Laver-bread is a traditional sea-weed dish, peculiar to The Gower Peninsula. The weed is dark green and clings over the surface of relatively smooth rocks. It is collected as the tide ebbs; then subjected to thorough washing in fresh water, to remove sand and grit. It is boiled and strained, then chopped up to form a pulpy mass. Pepper and a little oatmeal may be added. A dollop of laver-bread is a mouth-watering component of a fried breakfast (especially with lean bacon).]

9

Farm-work

The ploughman homeward plods his weary way ...

Thomas Gray

GENERALLY, both farmers and farm-workers worked very hard. However, the farmers had the privilege of choosing what they did and when they did it, so they could accommodate their personal commitments. They also enjoyed a much better standard of living (unless they were subsistence farmers), as well as higher social status. The farm-workers were subjected to a day-in, day-out obligation to provide eight to ten hours (or more) of hard work for at least five days a week without overtime pay.

But what was so difficult about a farm-worker's life? First consider the tools of the trade—such artefacts as scythes, hooks, hoes, shovels, spades, forks, rakes, sheep-shears, pitchforks, bill-hooks, sharpening stones, sledgehammers, buckets, seed-boxes, dibbers, sacks and sisal ropes. These tools were wielded or manhandled when feeding and watering stock, milking by hand, mucking out sheds, spreading dung, planting vegetables, sowing grain or fertiliser, weeding rows of crops, harvesting, threshing, hedging, fencing and shearing sheep. Farm-work in the 1940s was undeniably physically-intensive work. Even work performed with the aid of horses was hard, especially ploughing.

Next consider the long hours. Harvesting and threshing meant extremely long workdays when the weather was dry. Generally, there was no overtime pay, though farm-workers would be encouraged to help themselves to vegetables for their own use. Double daylight-saving time during the war years ensured a very long day's work. Even with normal daylight-saving time, it didn't get dark until about ten o'clock, in July. For some, the annual dipping and shearing of sheep were additional chores (though there were few farmers who kept sizeable flocks, due to the strong focus on vegetables). Often, two or three farmers would put their small flocks together for dipping.

Harvesting corn, in the days before the invention of combine-harvesters or balers, required handling the crop several times. First, a corn crop was cut with a reaper-and-binder. Then the sheaves were "stooked" in sets of six or eight, so that the breeze could dry and ripen them. After several dry days, the sheaves were loaded onto a cart or trailer. Secured tightly in place with sisal ropes, they were transported to the rickyard where they were unloaded and carefully formed into a square (usually oblong) or round mow. But the manual labour wasn't over: the annual threshing operation would require more hard work.

Harvesting hay required almost as much work as the corn (except for the threshing operation). Within a few days after cutting, the hay had to be turned to allow it to dry out thoroughly. This might be done with a wooden hay-rake, or a horse-drawn rake. The operation sometimes had to be repeated when there was showery weather. Finally, the hay was pitchforked onto carts or trailers for the journey to the rickyard. As with sheaves of corn, the load had to be tied down tightly to ensure that it didn't slip during the journey, as the cart swayed and bumped along the Vile Lane.

Usually, the shortest distance to the paved road was preferred to the shortest overall route. My father, Joffre, was adept at securing the loads with a couple of one-inch sisal ropes, which were tied securely underneath the rear of the trailer, and thrown over the load to the front. He would use bowline knots to set up a system where the ropes could be "reefed" as tight as possible, so there would be no risk of slippage on the bumpy ride to the rickyard. We kids often rode on top of the load.

The normal working day was underway by 7:00 AM, lasting until at least 5:00 PM. Breakfast was eaten when it could be fitted in. Noon was time for dinner. Traditionally, this was the main meal of the day, since most workers could return home, or at least to the farmhouse kitchen. It was often a heavy meal of meat, potatoes and gravy, with any other garden or field vegetables available. For dessert, there might be a homemade tart, some fruitcake or Welsh-cakes and a mug of hot tea. When it wasn't practical to get home for dinner, the men took sandwiches to work; then, dinner had to wait 'til teatime.

In wet weather (which often caught them working in the open fields) or when cutting cabbages, the men tied potato-sacks around their lower legs and draped them across their shoulders (secured with binder-twine, a piece of stiff wire or a nail) to help keep themselves as dry as possible. For head-cover, they would push one bottom corner of a sack inwards to fit into the other corner, thus creating a hood, with the rest of the sack draped behind their shoulders.

But damp, chilly weather occurred all too frequently. At other times they took hard knocks (resulting in bruises or cuts) from livestock, implements or machinery, though such injuries were invariably ignored, except for whatever crude first-aid was at hand.

One could observe the differences in behaviour between men a decade apart in their ages. By the age of fifteen they had already begun their working life, in earnest. By twenty-five, they were in the prime of their energy, strength and vitality; they were carefree, risk-taking and probably about to get married. By thirty-five, their best years were past, except for putting in a hard day's work. At forty-five, work consumed the lion's share of their energy; they needed to pace themselves in order to have enough left for household chores, gardening and perhaps a little fishing. At fifty-five, they were old men, never moving faster than a steady walking pace. In many cases they did not live to see sixty-five.

Admittedly, these comparisons are generalisations, based on a snapshot in time. Of course, there were exceptions. Some lived longer, perhaps because of their persistence in keeping active well into their sixties and seventies. Others were wise enough to "take care of themselves" by living a healthy lifestyle and avoiding unnecessary exposure to the elements.

But almost all the men smoked; some of the older ones smoked pipes, while most of the younger ones smoked Woodbine, Players or rolled their own. Though smoking was often called a "dirty habit" because of the nicotine stains on fingers and teeth, people were not aware of the more deadly effects. Smoking was the main self-indulgence for most farm-workers, though some preferred to carry "a quarter of hard-boils" in a small white paper bag.

As a boy, I observed that the men had mostly abandoned participation in even impromptu sporting activities by the time they were in their mid-thirties. By the age of fifty or so, they had resigned themselves to old age. Though they rarely complained, they suffered from arthritis, gout, sciatica, torn muscles, bruised bones and a host of other untreated ailments. There was no doubt that traditional farm-work was both back-breaking and health-destroying.

The advent of the first tractors (though often stubborn to respond to the starting-handle), simplified many farm operations, but they did not greatly reduce the hardship of many farm-workers' jobs. On many farms there was competition to be "the tractor driver". Farmers (or their sons) would naturally have first claim. The others did the bulk of the manual work.

At Middleton Hall farm, the first tractor was a standard Ferguson (usually called a "Fergie"). It ran on a fuel called TVO, which was similar to paraffin. There was no battery; the spark-plugs were energised by a magneto. Tractors had to be started by "swinging" the starting handle. Sometimes, trying to get them going was a challenge, especially on cold mornings. It was necessary to manipulate the choke and avoid flooding the carburettor, while swinging the starting handle.

Uncle Len, a fit twenty-five-year-old, would make half a dozen rapid turns on the handle. Getting no results, he would examine the glass fuel-gauge, adjust the throttle to about one-quarter open, give a few more swings, tell me to push the choke halfway in, try a few more swings, check to see if he could smell the carburettor flooding, tell me to hold the choke halfway out, then swing the handle a few more times. "Hast thee got the choke halfway in, by?" Len would ask. "Aye, halfway," I'd answer.

What a performance. Most of the time, the tractor would sputter into life. Then, Len would drop the starting handle and rush round to take control of the choke and the throttle, so that the engine wouldn't die—but sometimes it did.

It was important to know when to allow the starting handle to disengage. My father cautioned me when I was as young as eight, that I should never swing the handle with my thumb on the opposite side from my fingers (as in a handshake); rather, I should keep my thumb alongside the forefinger. Some of the men used their cloth caps as pads when swinging the starting handle. "An' keep thee head well clear," Joff told me. One of the older farmers at 'the bank', Will Morris, had received a nasty clout under the chin when a starting handle had "kicked back".

Farm-workers who had families lacked the transportation or the money (even if they'd had the time and energy) to seek relaxation from the daily routine of hard labour. Fortunately, perhaps, there was no pub in the village. The concept of a family vacation was all but unknown to them, though children were sometimes sent off to stay with relatives for a week or two. The main objective of the farm-workers' lives was to stay out of debt while they fed, clothed and sheltered their families.

There was little relief from the treadmill. It was a hand to mouth existence, where the wives did their best to inject some fun and pleasure with birthday and Christmas celebrations or traditional culinary treats. Otherwise, relief came on Bank Holiday weekends (which meant an extra day's rest) or the annual Gower Show.

Opportunities were taken, in between busy spells, to enjoy a Saturday afternoon's shopping in Swansea. In the winter, whole families would book tickets for an evening at the annual pantomime at The Grand theatre. The talented comedian, Harry Secombe, was always a special attraction. *Mother Goose, Cinderella* and *Jack and the Beanstalk* were the favourite pantomimes. On rare occasions, a circus would set up on the recreation area on the Mumbles Road, near the St. Helens ground. It was always important to get there an hour before the show to view the animals in their cages. Along with the annual Sunday-school trips, these were about the only family outings for most farm-workers' families.

In the mid-1940s, football matches were often arranged for a Sunday morning, perhaps at the field opposite Meadowside (when it was fallow), one of George Thomas's fields in Rhossili Vile or on the firm sands of Rhossili Bay. Almost all the men played in their work-clothes and hobnailed boots. The young men in their mid-twenties, like uncle Len, had plenty of energy for this. But my father, then in his early thirties, sometimes found it tiring to make the long walk to the field, play a rough and tumble match, then trudge home afterwards. The young single men, full of life and energy, also enjoyed dances in the village hall, as well as fishing and shooting.

One thing that always amazed me was that the local men never swam in the sea, though one or two of them claimed to be able to. Most had gathered laverbread and periwinkles, hunted crabs and lobsters in deep pools, fished with rod and dragnet, and served in the "rocket crew", yet they never did more than roll up their trouser legs to paddle in the sea—and that was on rare occasions.

Religion was not a major part of their lives. The only day of the year that the Church or the Chapel could guarantee a full attendance was at the annual Thanksgiving service. Then, the venerable buildings were truly resplendent—spring-cleaned (in October), decked with the finest samples of field and garden produce, and with whole families in attendance.

The annual Harvest Supper was held at the village hall, at about the same time of year: it was invariably sold-out. By comparison, Christmas and Easter church attendances were quite modest. Without organised religion (and lacking other social outlets), the pressures of their austere lives led to frustration within households, which sometimes resulted in family quarrels.

Without a doubt, farm-workers and their wives were amazingly resilient in an era when there were few social benefits—when it would have been considered a disgrace to be "on the dole". Rarely affording the time to visit a doctor, they would work through many common ailments. No matter how hard they laboured, the family income was always below what would be described as "the poverty line" for later generations.

Being a farmer was one thing, being a farm-worker with a dependent family was quite another. Only the larger farmers, particularly the generation that grew up with the tractor and the motor car, could genuinely regret the passing of those days. Most of the small farmers and especially the farm-workers—those who spent long, relentless days slaving in the fields, just to scratch a living for their families—would certainly not wish their children to repeat their experiences.

After his uncle, Johnny Beynon, sold Fernhill farm, George Beynon went to work at Great Pitton farm for more than forty years. Although he was not a robust man, George loved farming and all the country traditions. He had a quiet air of serenity about him and he had the stamina to go fishing after a long day in the fields—usually from the base of the cliffs below Thurba Head. But even this man would not have wanted his children to spend their lives as farm-workers. Another farm-worker, Vaughan Price also worked more than forty years at Great Pitton farm.

Despite all the hardships, many of the farm-workers loved their work and they certainly loved Rhossili. After all, they had invested just as much of their time and sweat in the land as any farmer. To be physically fit, strong as an ox, breathing the fresh, salty air on a brilliant, still morning in spring, working up an appetite for a traditional country breakfast, was the kind of feeling that money couldn't buy.

[Endnote1: The farmers of the late 1940s included:
Rhossili End: George Thomas (Rhossili Farm); George Richards (Bay Farm); Sid Thomas (Glebe Farm); Bowen Richards (The Green/Ash-tree Farm).
Middleton: Wilfred Beynon (The Ship); Stan Beynon (Riverside); Alf Bevan (Old Farmhouse); Len Jones (Middleton Hall); Jack Richards (Jessamine); Will Morris (Middleton Lodge); Ingram Chalk (Hampstead/Ivy Dene); Jack Gibbs (Mewslade View).
Fernhill/Sluxton: Tom Williams (Fernhill Top); Reg. Howells (Fernhill); Doug Shepherd (Sluxton); Alf Bevan (Old Farmhouse/Kings Hall).
Pitton: Bevan Tucker (Higher Pitton Farm/Corner House); Donald Button (Lower Pitton); Gwyn Beynon/Christopher Beynon (Great Pitton).
Pitton Cross/Pilton Green/Pylewell: Ingram Button (Pitton Cross); Will Tucker (Pitton Cross); William John Harry (West Pilton); Norman Richards (Kimley Moor); Bert Fisher (Pilton Green); Morgan Jones (East Pilton); Fred & Arthur Morris (Pilton Green); Gwyn Williams (Pylewell); Roland Morgan (Paviland).]

[Endnote2: The farm-workers of the late 1940s included (list may not be complete):
George Beynon; Bill Beynon; Enoch Beynon; Reggie Beynon; Ernie Beynon; Harry Morris; Will Button; Ron Densley; Eric Gibbs; Len Gore; George Grove; Sid James; Oliver Jones; Joffre Jones; Phil Jones; Will Jones; Arthur (Robin) Jones; Leighton Kent; Douglas Kent; Alf Moulding; Percy Golding; Jim Morse; Joe Niwa; Jim Price; Vaughan Price; Cuthbert Pugh; Wilfred Pugh; Albert Pullen; Ivor Pullen; Phil Richards; Harold Hinton; Raymond Shepherd; Alec Thomas; Stan Walters; Alec Pym; Vic; Ralph.]

10

The DPs and POWs

Alien they seemed to be:
No mortal eye could see
The intimate welding of their later history ...

Thomas Hardy

THE Displaced Persons (DPs) were wartime refugees—many of them were from the Ukraine, but some were from Czechoslovakia, Poland, Hungary and other parts of Eastern Europe. They were encamped at Scurlage soon after the Americans moved out for the D-Day invasion. From those I saw, they were mostly able-bodied men in their thirties and forties. Each weekday, they were transported in old army lorries to local farms, where they were employed as cheap labour. Generally, they were placid men, glad to be away from their war-torn countries, though one or two of them caused problems among the various ethnic groups. I recall hearing that one of the drivers, Cliff Eaton from Llangennith, had fights break out in the back of his lorry.

Most of the larger farms hired DPs. Two of these men, a Czech and a Pole, who were a little older than most of the DPs, were hired by my uncles at Middleton Hall. I became friends with them. They really were salt of the earth people—they just seemed thankful to be safe and working in the fresh air in a free country—yet they were treated as aliens, to be governed by strict rules. They were delivered to their respective work locations each morning, and collected and returned to their camp at night, where they were confined. I don't think they were allowed out much at the weekends, due to wartime security concerns.

I watched them work around the farm, helping them when I could. I rode with our DPs on the trailer behind the little Fergie tractor, driven by uncle Len, as it clunked and clanked across 'the bank' on its steel wheels, then down the Vile

Lane, heading for one or other of our fields scattered around the Vile. One of our fields was at Meard; another at Lewis Castle, overlooking Fall Bay; others were at Sandylands; yet others were among the land-shares in the lower Vile.

The tractor's back wheels were large steel discs about four feet in diameter, with steel appendages (which we called spugs), bolted around the circumference. These were not well suited to the paved road; the road surface suffered and the spugs tended to be jolted loose. In the laneways and fields, though, they gave excellent traction. The front wheels were smaller, steel-rimmed discs. If we happened to meet another tractor in the Vile Lane, a convenient gateway would serve as a passing point. Farmers would often take the opportunity to exchange a few words of news or opinion, or discuss when and where to borrow (or return) a piece of farm equipment.

The DPs were usually left to eat their own lunch, comprised of about four rounds of white bread with cheese, jam or marmite for a filling. There was perhaps an apple or slice of cake for dessert. Mostly, the farmers would provide only a mug of hot tea for them. They were not invited to eat their dinner in the farmhouse kitchen; they could pick their spot outside or in the barns, according to the weather.

Even at my tender age, I sometimes felt uncomfortable with the way these men were treated. I understood that they were essentially homeless, had very few possessions and lived in a camp. They were poorly paid (perhaps a shilling a day) and they were expected to follow instructions without question. Some local farmers addressed them as "vassal" rather than use their real names. Some thought that "Vasal" must be a popular Ukrainian name. In the case of our two DPs, we did use their names (or at least the English equivalents). They worked at Middleton Hall for a year or more and they were genuinely sad when their time with us came to an end.

When they knew they had to leave Gower, probably being moved to a less secure campsite to make way for German POWs, they seemed particularly sorry to say goodbye to me—an inquisitive kid with curly, blond hair. One of them marked the outlines of my feet on a piece of brown paper, then spent much of his spare time for more than two months, painstakingly making a pair of slippers from some sort of thin rope, which was wound around and around. He proudly gave me his goodbye present. It made a lasting impression on me, even though I was only five years old, because I had never owned a pair of slippers.

Soon after, the camp at Scurlage was filled with German prisoners-of-war. Most of these POWs worked hard on the farms they were assigned to. My older cousin, Frances, married a POW, Joe Niwa, who had been assigned to work on

Reg Howells's farm at Fernhill. He had served with the German infantry on the Russian front, before being moved to the Western front, in the aftermath of the D-Day invasion. The POWs were at Scurlage for several years. They were used to help open the roads during the blizzards of 1947, so that tractors-and-trailers could eventually get through to deliver bread and other essentials to isolated villages, like Rhossili and Porteynon.

At Middleton Hall, two of the POWs found steady employment for perhaps a couple of years. One of them was named Hans. By this time, though, I was spending my weekdays at school, so I didn't get to know them as well as I had the DPs. One year, they were invited by uncle Len and aunty Doreen to spend Christmas Day at Middleton Hall.

On one occasion in the school holidays, we got started rather late in the morning, cutting cabbage at Sandylands. Rather than interrupt the work to return to Middleton Hall for lunch, uncle Len sent me back to the farmhouse with a message for aunty Doreen. At six years of age, I struggled to understand exactly what he said, because I hadn't learnt the name of this particular field.

I found my way back through the Vile alright, but when I arrived at Middleton Hall, all I could say was "Uncle Len wants tea and sandwiches and sandals". Fortunately, aunty Doreen was able to figure out what the real message was.

At an early age, though, I had discovered empathy for people of very different backgrounds from my own. I had learnt to judge them on their merits.

11

Boots Maketh a Man

One should always have one's boots on, and be ready to leave ...

Montaigne

EVEN before starting school, I had come to realise the importance of a good pair of boots. I rarely saw a local man who was not wearing them for at least five days of the week. On Sundays, some of the men would dress up for church or chapel, or to take a walk "out the end" with their families. Of course, it was also expected that a working man would wear his "good shoes" to go to Swansea; to the doctor; or to attend a social function.

I was always impressed by the story of how a new pair of boots had saved the life of my grandfather, Francis Jones. During a rescue operation at Paviland cliffs, he had slipped and fallen in the blackness. He had always maintained that the only thing that had prevented him from plunging to his death was his new boots, one of which became jammed in a rock crevice, as he overbalanced. Of course, it might have been the new boots that caused him to slip in the first place.

Our boots were always made and repaired by our village cobbler, Harry Gammon, who lived in a cottage at Sheep Green. Mr. Gammon (as I was obliged to address him) was a tall, big-boned man of about sixty years. He had a shock of reddish-grey hair atop his narrow, sombre face and a heavy moustache which reminded me of pictures of Germany's Kaiser. He was quite lean and fit-looking. His wire-rimmed spectacles added to his studious appearance. He was a man of few words. He and his wife generally kept to themselves and they weren't seen around the village very much. I heard they had two grown sons who were working away in England, somewhere—"offalong" as my father would say.

Mr. Gammon did his work in a stone-built extension to his cottage, which doubled as a coal-shed. I'm sure that the outbuilding had had a quite different purpose before it was occupied by a cobbler. Joffre told me that, in the early part of the century, the village shoemaker had been one William Morgan, who had occupied 'the cottage' where my parents were now the tenants. It was a trade that could be readily plied from almost any house or cottage.

Joff took me to be measured up for my first pair of real boots when I was about four or five years old. I had to stand on a piece of brown paper, while Mr. Gammon drew carefully around my feet. Then, I felt disappointed when I realised it would be at least two weeks before the boots would be ready. Mr. Gammon and Joff discussed the finer points of good boots, while I wondered why it needed to be such a long process. It was important to allow for at least a year of growth, they agreed.

It was almost three weeks before it was time to go back for the fitting. Final adjustments were agreed on; then I had to wait for a few more days. When we returned, a week later, I was fitted with a fine pair of black boots which laced up to just above my ankles—just like the working men I spent every day with. Now, I was one of them—a real farm boy. Those boots would be worn from dawn to dusk, without protest.

The boots had steel tips under the toes and heels; the soles were dotted with rows of steel studs. At first this made them feel like a pair of ice-skates on the paved roads. But soon, I had gained so much confidence that I mastered the art of crouching on my haunches while holding on to a cow's tail and being towed down Sheep Green hill. Of course, the cow had to be coerced into a trot, first. At that time, farmers were not so sensitive about their milk yields; so they didn't get overly upset at such childish pranks. "Dang thee, by!" was about all they would say.

Getting boots repaired was a different experience. I would watch Mr. Gammon intently, as he placed the worn boot on a child-sized last. Next he would pry away what was left of a worn-out tip; then cut away any worn leather with his incredibly sharp, hooked knife. He would then select a sheet of new leather of appropriate thickness, and cut a piece from it. This he would measure against the removed part of the sole, and cut it closer to size.

Holding the new piece of leather in position with his left hand, he would pick up a handful of short nails from a tin or jar and pop them into his mouth. With long-practiced accuracy, he would spit them one at a time into his left hand, without lifting it from the sole of the boot, while he wielded the hammer with his right hand. Following this, he would take his knife once more, and carefully trim the edge of the new leather to match the outline of the existing sole. Finally, he would nail on a new metal tip and studs. The process was essentially the same, whether it was a toe or the heel that needed attention.

Mr. Gammon kept a greenhouse which extended along the front of his cottage. He paid careful attention to his tomatoes and flowering plants. I had not failed to notice that in the upper reaches of the greenhouse, he grew black grapes. I was one of those who sometimes sampled Mr. Gammon's grapes when he left his greenhouse windows open. The fact that the grapes usually tasted rather sour did little to deter our appetites for such an exotic treat. "Beggars can't be choosers," as my mother would say.

By about 1950, boots were no longer considered necessary or even economical for children. Shoes could be readily bought in town. Henceforth, the only time I would wear boots would be to play football or rugby; but those boots were not made to measure and my feet would suffer accordingly. I sometimes crammed my feet into football boots that were too tight—a mistake I would suffer for, in future years. The nails tended to come through the soles as the leather studs wore down. It's a wonder some of us football fanatics didn't get tetanus.

Thanks to technological progress, even the farm-workers could buy their boots ready-made from retailers, in Swansea. The days of the village cobbler were over.

[Endnote: In old records, cobblers were usually referred to as shoemakers. The term "cordwainer" is sometimes found in older census records. This refers to a more general expertise in working with fine-grained leather, often stripped from horse-hide—a skill historically associated with the town of Cordoba, in Spain.]

12

Rhossili School

*It should be noted that children at play are not playing about; their games should be
seen as their most serious-minded activity.*

Montaigne

RHOSSILI School served only its own parish, in contrast to the one at Knelston,
which served children from Llandewi, Scurlage, Horton, Porteynon and Reynoldston. Schooling normally commenced in the September following a child's
fifth birthday. There were few exceptions to that rule, though some were made
for those born in the autumn months.

I attended Rhossili School from 1945 to 1951, spending about three years in
Miss Button's infants' class and a similar period in Miss Thomas's senior class.
The two classes were separated by a removable wood and glass partition. There
must have been at least a score of lively children in each classroom, but the partition was effective as a noise barrier.

My contemporaries (i.e. those within about a year or so of my age) included:
Howard Chalk, Ron Beynon, Alice Thomas, John Bevan, Hildegarde Thomas,
Sylvia Williams, Alan Button, Mary Davies, John Moulding, Beryl Shepherd,
Peter Crozier, Mary Price, Pamela Richards and Norman Parker. Unfortunately,
there were no class photographs taken in that era.

When I started school at the end of the summer of 1945, everything seemed
strange and uncomfortable at first. I think my mother was apprehensive because
I'd become so used to running wild on the farm and the hill. But under the
watchful eye of our wonderful infants' teacher, Lily Button, I settled down quite
quickly.

I soon came to enjoy all aspects of school life, except for the free, yet (paradox-
ically) compulsory, one-third pint of milk at the morning break. Many of the

other children seemed to enjoy the milk, while others did not object. For me, it was an unpleasant daily experience, particularly when the milk was pasteurised. When I didn't drink it all, Miss Button would be displeased; when I poured some down one of the china washbasins in the cloakroom, one of the other children would "tell teacher".

On the first Monday of each month, Miss Button would pin a fresh sheet of paper to the front of her desk, titled: "Wild Flowers Found Growing in the Neighbourhood." Anyone who brought a freshly-picked wild flower to school had the privilege of adding its name to the list. Sometimes, flowers were pressed and dried by those students who were enthusiasts.

If we persisted in behaving badly in the classroom, Miss Button would make us stand on the seats of our desks with our hands placed on our heads until she decided we'd been punished enough. It was on one such occasion that I uttered the immortal words: "Please, Miss Button, can I sit down? My arms are aching and my legs are tired …" Barely suppressing a smile, Miss Button replied, "I think you mean '*may* I sit down', Cyril."

About a year after starting school, I was able to take along an inflated bladder from a freshly killed pig. My father told me that was what they played football with, when he was a boy. It had to be allowed to dry out before being inflated with a bicycle pump. The neck was tied off as tightly as possible with binder-twine. Although it was far from perfectly round, it was the nearest we could get to a real football in those days. Its distinct odour faded slowly, but after a week or two of being kicked around the schoolyard, it was worn out.

After that, there was little to amuse rambunctious young boys, so we charged wildly around the infants' playground, in various formations. On one occasion, Howard Chalk tripped over the step by the school gate; Ron Beynon was so close behind that he fell over Howard; I landed on top of them.

Both teachers were adept at setting daily challenges for four or five groups of kids working at different levels, while somehow providing individual direction, encouragement and feedback to all of them. In the infants' class, groups of two or three were assigned small gardens in which to sow flower or vegetable seeds. Class-time was allotted for gardening, during the spring and summer months.

In Miss Thomas's senior class, the busy schedule included a weekly Arts and Crafts session, in which her scholars were introduced to rug-making, weaving, knitting and crocheting. The library service consisted of flat, wooden crates filled with reading or illustrated books, which were exchanged every month or so.

Eventually, rubber and sponge balls were provided at school, though we were very short of recreational equipment. We mostly relied on traditional forms of amusement. At playtime, the older children indulged in such timeless favourites as rounders and shinty, using sticks lopped from tree branches. Football was an ongoing favourite with the boys, as well as with some of the girls. It was not uncommon for us boys to join in the girls' perennial favourite—hopscotch.

At other times, we drove imaginary tractors or flew war-planes around the playground. At such times, the girls would indulge in imaginary games of a social or cliquish nature, to which they applied such fancy names as *Balmoral*. Sometimes, "L-O-N-D-O-N" or "You're it!" were in vogue. In the late 1940s, steel hoops became popular again. The hoops were made of about a quarter inch, circular cross-section steel; they were about thirty inches in diameter. They could be rolled and guided along with a short hooked piece of metal, shaped like a gatehasp. Then it was yo-yos for a while.

There were times in my senior years when our class was allowed to spend our playtimes on the hillside, adjacent to the school. At such times, tribal instincts could take over. We would form dens or simple dwellings from the clumps of tall ferns. We would build defensive palisades around our village. As the reigning "chief" I exercised my right to select a "wife" (or even two) to share my fernhouse. I even painstakingly allocated "wives" to those who were slow to choose. A chief had important responsibilities.

When the ferns were past their best, we boys would turn to other adventures. Peter Crozier and I were particularly imaginative. The pathway leading directly up the hill towards Windy Walls was perfect for the re-enactment of a Cowboy-and-Indian story we had read. We imagined that the path led up the face of a narrow butte, where we intrepid cow-hands could defend ourselves against a war-party of savage Indians. We might have to end up eating horsemeat, but at least we had the benefit of a natural spring—and gorse bushes which would conceal our defensive positions.

I was privileged to live very close to the school. Other children had quite a long way to walk, especially Hidegarde and Gareth Thomas, who lived at Alveley; Marlene and Gloria Shepherd, who lived at Sluxton; and the Dorlings, Paynes and Parkers who lived at the Coastguard Houses. They needed to bring their lunches with them (at least before the advent of school dinners), whereas I was able to go home to 'the cottage' at dinner-time.

Such was the spirit of cooperation and goodwill which continued into the post-war years, that the children from Upper and Lower Pitton could count on a ride to school in the box-shaped mail-van, especially in inclement weather. Of course, there were frequent stops along the way, so it was no joyride for the six or seven kids crammed into the van. One day, the handbrake was left disengaged when it stopped to deliver mail at Jessamine farm, so the van rolled backwards across the road, bumping into Will Morris's farm buildings. Some of the kids near the front were able to jump clear, through the sliding side-door, but it was a bit of a fright for those in the back of the van. Unfortunately, that was the end of the free rides to school.

In September 1948, just as I moved into Miss Thomas's senior class, my mother, Joyce, was appointed as school caretaker, following the resignation of Mrs. Florrie Williams. Two months later, she also became the server of the first school dinners, which were prepared at Parkmill School and delivered in shiny metal containers. Soon, almost all the children were taking advantage of this innovation. My mother, clad in the white uniforms issued to kitchen staff, was responsible for serving the food and washing up afterwards.

Initially, the meals were white-bread sandwiches; a piece of bland pudding with custard and a cup of very weak cocoa, which my mother was obliged to prepare with prescribed quantities of milk and hot water. Eventually, we had hot dinners (often, tasteless rissoles made from chopped-up meat of some sort); otherwise, it was sliced beef, pork or corned beef. Invariably, there were mashed potatoes and one or two other vegetables, such as swede or cabbage.

The tasteless gravy was delivered in a large cylindrical container, which had an insulating air-space. There was a similar container for the custard, which we poured over whatever was provided for dessert—often squares of a khaki-coloured, spongy cake dotted with raisins. Sometimes, we had rice pudding, though it never tasted like my mother's. We paid about four-pence a day for these meals.

While school dinners inevitably became monotonous, at least we weren't forced to consume them, as was the case with the compulsory bottles of pasteurised milk. However, Miss Thomas kept a bottle of cod-liver oil and a tin of Virol (a molasses-like product) in a cupboard near her desk, which she doled out, almost daily in the winter, to those children she considered to be too thin or pallid-looking.

In support of my mother's care-taking responsibilities, my father looked after the other end of things, so to speak. He routinely buried the contents of the buckets from the school toilets in the corner of George Richards's field, almost opposite the school. Each summer, a crop of tomato plants would emerge from this fertile spot, bearing testimony to one of the most popular components of sandwiches, during the summer months.

In 1949, we welcomed an unusual visitor to our school. She was Miss Womala, a schoolteacher from Uganda. She told us she was one of the Buganda people.

Since I had only seen Africans in photographs or in illustrated children's books, the experience became quite indelible in my memory. She was very dark, but she showed us that the palms of her hands and the soles of her feet were almost as white as ours. As she gave us a short talk about her country, a dozen queries raced through my mind. When we were invited to ask questions, up shot my hand. After Miss Womala had answered, Miss Thomas asked if there were any other questions: up shot my hand again. I asked three questions before anyone else got a chance.

About 1950, there was a district handwriting competition, sponsored by the Brooke Bond tea company. From the time we started school, we had all been painstakingly taught how to use steel-nibbed pens, inkwells and blotting-paper. I expected I would have a very good chance of winning the competition; but when the results came through, Hildegarde Thomas, who was more than a year my junior, had won first prize. As it turned out, I wasn't even second in our school (let alone the district).

In the late spring months, Miss Thomas's class had the opportunity to participate in at least one ramble, each year. These were usually arranged for a Friday afternoon. On one occasion, we tramped through Berry Lane, then across the fields to Brinsel; another one (which I missed, due to unfortunate circumstances) was to King Arthur's stone on Cefn Bryn; yet another took us down through the Vile, examining the flora of the fields and hedges, as we went.

St. David's Day was the major cultural event of the school year. Both real and crepe paper daffodils and leeks abounded. Every child was involved in something—recitation, song or pageant. Twelve children represented each of the counties of Wales, while another represented Monmouthshire, which always pleaded to be included in Wales. This latter role was usually assigned to Peter Crozier, who had been born and raised in England. The national anthem was sung with fervour, in both Welsh and English. At other times of the year, Welsh patriotism and passions were stirred with such dramatic rhymes as Gogerddan and Bedd Gelert.

Miss Thomas loved music, which was a particular talent of her family. With the help of her tuning fork and the small school organ, she taught us the scales until she was sure they were ingrained in us for life. One by one, she would make us sing solo. I had no ability to hold a tune for more than a few seconds, so my unwilling efforts were usually dismissed as "bass" (or perhaps it was "base"), accompanied by a distasteful look. However, I did enjoy other aspects of cultural activity, such as reciting poetry or playing a role in a play. On at least one occasion, singing, poetry and speech competitions were also held at the village hall.

The annual 11+ examination was a serious matter to Miss Thomas. She decided whether a student was ready to attempt it on their first or second year of eligibility. Candidates were carefully drilled and prepared for the big day, which was a holiday for all other students. Alice Thomas and I were the only ones to sit the exam in 1951. One of our invigilators was Mr. Reg Crozier, Peter's father, who was also appointed as one of the village census-takers, that year.

Although these exams were supervised by independent volunteers from the community, Miss Thomas would leave a supply of sweets (such as sugar-coated almonds) to be doled out at the morning and afternoon breaks, in the hope that the sugar would give our brains a boost at the critical time. The following day, she would make the candidates rewrite all the exam papers, emulating as closely as they could, what they had written the previous day, so that she could gauge their individual performances. I still recall her barely-veiled disappointment when she realised I had misunderstood a passage from *Silas Marner*, which had served as our reading-comprehension test. I had completely blanked out on what a loom was, even though I had actually used one to produce a scarf, at school.

Nevertheless, because she was sure that we had both passed the County exam, Miss Thomas rewarded Alice and me by taking us to enjoy a performance of *The Pirates of Penzance* by the pupils of Penclawdd Secondary Modern School. We caught the half-past four bus to Killay; then we waited patiently for a bus to Penclawdd. Miss Thomas had done her homework on the bus-schedules.

By the time we arrived at the school auditorium, it was almost dusk. Some of the "pirates" were skirmishing and yelling in the playground as they waited for the performance. They were racing and swinging around the steel poles which supported an overhang alongside the auditorium. I wondered whether it was all meant to provide entertainment while we were queuing to get inside.

Having never seen a musical play, except for the Christmas pantomimes, Alice and I were quite impressed. Miss Thomas, though, had a much more discerning ear when it came to music; but she seemed reasonably happy with the performance. Then we had to reverse our earlier journey. There were long waits for both buses, so it was about eleven o'clock by the time we reached Middleton.

In July 1951, we children in Miss Thomas's senior class joined our counterparts from Knelston School on an educational trip to Bristol Zoo. Beyond that, there were no interschool activities at all—no cultural, athletic or sports competitions. As a result, most of us experienced some difficulty adjusting to the secondary school environment, even though we never gave it much thought.

Even during my father's generation, the same two teachers at Rhossili School had provided an excellent grounding in the basics of education. Virtually all my contemporaries at Rhossili School were either coerced or cajoled into achieving their maximum potential.

[Endnote1: Many of the students of my day went on to achieve good results in secondary and/or tertiary education. John Densley and I, who both spent the major portion of our professional careers in Canada, are the sons of farm-workers who sometimes worked together, both on the farm and on building work.

We offer an interesting contrast in our academic achievements. John attained the distinction of a Ph.D. in electrical engineering and has been following a highly specialised career, ever since. I, on the other hand, have graduated in engineering, business and linguistics, in three different countries. We seem to be ideal models for the famous witticism:
  • A specialist is someone who learns more and more about less and less, until, in the end, he knows everything about nothing.
  • A generalist is someone who learns less and less about more and more, until in the end, he knows nothing about everything.]

[Endnote2: In 1969, the village school closed after 87 years. The building was soon converted into an Outdoor Pursuits Centre. More than a decade earlier, both of the local teachers had retired. They had served the school since before 1920. Prior to 1882, the building was a workhouse, while schooling (probably poorly attended and executed) was done in long-disappeared sheds or barns, elsewhere in the parish.]

[Endnote3: Rhossili School pupils at September, 1950 (may be incomplete):
Ada Thomas's Senior Class
Howard Chalk; Ron Beynon; Alice Thomas; Cyril Jones; Peter Crozier; Sylvia Williams; John Bevan; Alan Button; Mary Davies; Beryl Shepherd; Hildegarde Thomas; Mary Price; John Moulding; Norman Parker; Pamela Richards; Susan Fayres; Clive Jones; Keith Hopkins; Margaret Howells; Brian Beynon; Cynthia Williams; Pat Pugh.
Lily Button's Infants Class
John Densley; Russell Jones; Gareth Thomas; Thelma Jones; Christine Hinton; Pat Davies; Gareth Thomas; Sandra Parker; Gloria Shepherd; Leo Harding; Roger Button; Rowland Button; Wilfred Price; Janet Payne; Mary Bevan; Mary Jones; Mary Moulding; John Morris; Elaine Grove; Alan Pugh; Pamela Jones; Caroline Fayres.]

13

A Boy's Christmas in Middleton

One Christmas was so much like another, in those years ...

Dylan Thomas

CHRISTMAS was always a special time, of course. Our mothers made themselves incredibly busy with extra work—feathering poultry, mixing Christmas cakes and puddings, cleaning, decorating, shopping for once-a-year treats, and searching Swansea's Oxford Street and High Street for Christmas presents they could hardly afford. The all-important presents were secretively accumulated in the bottoms of wardrobes, in cupboards under the stairs or even at a neighbour's house, waiting patiently for Father Christmas to deliver them.

Some farmers killed and dressed quite a lot of poultry, which they sold locally or through Swansea Market. Farm-workers fattened up their own poultry or ordered a bird locally, if they were not given one as a Christmas bonus from their employer. The birds were killed in the time-honoured way, with a sharp knife slipped into the open beak, down the inside of the throat; then they were held up by their feet to allow the blood to drain out. The flapping wings soon became limp. Men and women would sit in barns or sheds, on milking stools or old kitchen chairs, feathering frantically while the birds were still warm. Uncle Robin, his cap pushed to the back of his head, would feather a goose like a man possessed.

Children were subjected to age-old myths and tricks. When there were some snow flurries prior to Christmas, we were told: "It's the Old Lady in the sky, feathering geese." Robin would ask me, "Dost thee know how t' put a chicken t' sleep, by?" Then he would pick up a wildly-fluttering bird, tuck its head under its wing, swing it from side to side in his hands for about fifteen seconds and set it down on the ground. I was always fascinated to see that the chicken would just

57

stand there, its head still tucked under its wing. Uncle Len would tell me a yarn about poultry hiding under the low footbridges to escape the attention of ravenous foxes.

In the whitewashed farmhouses and cottages, Christmas decorations were often homemade chains made with coloured paper-strips and glue. These were usually complemented by store-bought elaborately-patterned paper balls, bells and chains which opened up like concertinas, so they could all be used again, the following year (if you were careful not to tear them). Christmas trees were rare in the homes of farm-workers' families, but sprigs of holly (with or without berries) were plentiful. Often, a sprig of mistletoe was brought home from town with other last-minute paraphernalia, such as crackers and tinsel.

Christmas was never a deeply religious occasion for most of the rural families, even though the carols were hugely popular and goodwill and best wishes exuded from all and sundry. Most parents were loath to walk to church with so much else to attend to: better to enjoy a Christmas service on the radio, perhaps.

About two weeks before Christmas, the Methodist Chapel would organise a group for door to door carol-singing, in support of charities and missions. Except for the summer months, Ron Beynon and I were constant companions. Though neither of us had any musical talents whatsoever, from the age of about eight until we were around twelve, we would somehow find the nerve to sing carols in the dark, outside the doors of local folk who we thought might be kind enough to give us tuppence or thruppence without embarrassing us too much. We'd sing "Good King Wenceslas" or "The First Noel"; then we'd chant the well-worn rhyme which begins: "Christmas is coming; the geese are getting fat ..."

We were almost always given something, even if it was only a piece of cake or a couple of sweets. It was one thing to sing outside in the dark, but some people, like Sid James, would ask us in and make us sing another carol—to their great amusement—before deciding to give us a small reward. It was hard-earned money, alright.

Most Christmases, Ron and I would also join in with the Chapel carollers. Sometimes we would run ahead for a couple of hundred yards, sing our own carols at a couple of houses, then run back in the darkness to rejoin the official party. We particularly wanted to be with them when they reached Professor Lee's bungalow at Talgarths Well. Professor and Mrs. Lee always offered everyone a warm drink and a piece of pie—a treat not to be missed by a couple of energetic young scoundrels.

We were sometimes brave enough to sing irreverent words to some of the carols (knowing, of course, that we would be safely drowned out by the crowd):

"We three kings of orient are,
One on a bike and one in a car,
One on a scooter,
Blowing his hooter,
Following yonder star ..."

Telephones and cars were affordable only to the larger farmers and business-people, so rural working-class people did not do a great deal of visiting at Christmas time. Being poor, as well as very busy, they usually concentrated on their own family's celebrations. However, there was a regular Christmas Eve visitor to our house who always seemed to arrive about an hour after my bedtime: I could sometimes hear blurred voices. The next day, I would notice that the Christmas cake would be served with a slice missing. After several years, I discovered that the mystery visitor was not Father Christmas—it was uncle Oliver.

I never saw Father Christmas, no matter how early I woke next morning; but he was real, because I wanted him to be. Peering through the gloom, I would eventually make out a bulging brown lady's stocking lying across the foot of the bed. Somewhere nearby would be a lumpy white pillowcase. For us kids, this was the greatest moment of the whole year, when anticipation reached a level beyond reality.

The one day a year when we would experience a feeling of unlimited prosperity, had begun—at 4:30 AM. I would shout, "Father Christmas has been!", as I rushed into my parents' bedroom. My poor parents, exhausted from the preparations and having had about three hours' sleep, would feign surprise and excitement at my discoveries. They would encourage me to go and look through the stocking first, before getting into the pillowcase. In vain, they would crave a little more rest, before the hectic day began.

The stocking contained an apple, an orange, sweets and novelties (perhaps a couple of magnets, disguised as black and white Scotch terriers); and any small toys, such as whistles, lead soldiers, a packet of crayons, or small tin frogs that clicked, then hopped when you pressed them on the floor. The pillowcase contained the larger presents, including books of all sorts, items of clothing, a pencil box, pens, or board games like Draughts, Ludo and Snakes-and-Ladders. A perennial favourite was the ever-fascinating kaleidoscope.

There was usually a special present, such as a mouth-organ, a basic meccano-set, a crane, a clockwork car, a multi-bladed penknife; or a six-gun and holster with rolls of "caps" for ammunition. The most valuable (if not the most exciting) Christmas gifts were the books. My mother always ensured I had plenty of them to read, from a very early age. There were adventure books, comic annuals, football annuals, books of traditional prose and poetry. She would never tire of reading or explaining them to me, if I needed help.

Then there were the really big surprises. When I was eight, it was a whole cowboy outfit, complete with a hat, waistcoat and fringed buckskin trousers for breaking in even the wildest horses. Perhaps the best present I ever received was a football kit, when I was nine. There was a green jersey (just like South Gower), white shorts, green and white socks and—real football boots! There was also a plastic football with real panels. I couldn't wait to dress up, boots and all, to run down to Middleton and find somebody to play football with. The fawn-coloured boots were ankle high, made of hard, unyielding leather, perhaps a little tight for me—or they soon would be. Each one had six leather studs fastened to the soles with three nails, the sharp points of which would inevitably work their way through to the inside, as the studs wore down.

I was ten when I received a new maroon-and-white bike. My mother spent several sessions helping me to learn to ride in the school playground, before I could venture onto the road. Even then, she would run along behind me holding the seat. On one occasion, when I realised she had let go, I lost confidence and veered into the shallow stream opposite the school. Although I enjoyed the bike, I hardly ever took it to the village because I liked to wander around the farmyards and through the fields, so the bike would quickly become a nuisance; but it was often useful to pedal to Scurlage when South Gower was playing at home.

When I had finished enjoying the excitement of opening all my presents, I would become impatient to see what my little sister had received. She was about four years younger than I, and she was not so excitable or inquisitive; thus I would think of ways to wake her and point out that Father Christmas had been. I gave the impression that it would be most unappreciative of us not to examine our presents as quickly and enthusiastically as possible. Her presents of course, were quite different from mine and they were of little interest to me; but there would always be something that I would find interesting enough to help her play with.

It was the food, as well as the presents and decorations that made Christmas so special for us kids. The centre-piece of our Christmas dinner would usually be a tasty free-range chicken; but occasionally it was a duck or even a goose. (Excess goose grease was often saved to be rubbed on our chests, if we caught a winter cold.) Other treats included the inevitable Christmas pudding, served with custard. The Christmas puddings were dark and fruit-filled, but did not usually contain liquor. One or two silver thruppeny-bits were mixed into them to add some excitement. To a farm-worker's family, a bottle of wine would have been a rarity—indeed, an expensive luxury—though a few made their own from elderberries and other home-grown produce.

The rest of the day, we enjoyed sampling a whole range of delicious and exotic fruits, some of which were rarely available during the rest of the year: there were russet apples, tangerines, grapes, pomegranates, dried figs, a box or two of sticky dates and a fine selection of nuts in their shells. If a nut-cracker could not be found, a hammer would be used (with caution). The old favourites, apples, oranges and pears were in abundance. Then there were chestnuts, which we would roast in the hot ashes below the grate. How magical was the day! The bright metallic colours of some of the decorations and novelties would become forever associated with Christmas.

Our wireless (when it was working) provided Christmas music, but more often than not, most of the noise emanated from me and my sister. After Christmas dinner was done, I would arm myself with a couple of my presents and run down to Middleton to share the excitement with my close pal, Ron Beynon. Sometimes, if the weather was bleak or rainy, Ron and I would play with our new toys at the The Ship farmhouse, until teatime. At 'the cottage', our tea would include jelly and blancmange, mince-pies, Christmas-cake, tarts and other treats. There was more than enough.

On Boxing Day, I would invariably be down at 'the bank' by mid-morning, searching for a few more pals, such as John Bevan or Howard Chalk, with whom to share the spoils of Father Christmas's unfailing generosity. Sometimes we joined others of my father's family at Middleton Hall. On those occasions, I might get a small taste from a flagon of brown ale or cider. I learnt to enjoy the bitter taste of the ale—which I would frequently revisit in later years. Often though, farm-workers' families kept to themselves and enjoyed some well-earned relaxation on those two days.

There was hardly ever a white Christmas. But even when the snow came later on in the winter, it was pure magic. It was like a second Christmas—nature's own celebration. There were long, clear icicles hanging from the corrugated zinc roofs of cowsheds; there were snowballs with which to terrorise or be terrorised; but mostly, it was the crunch of the fresh snow underfoot and the way it changed the face of the countryside—covering and re-shaping fields, trees, hedges and buildings.

No Christmas decorations could possibly match that.

14

Country Fare

He hath filled the hungry with good things ...

The Bible: Luke 1:53

THROUGHOUT the 1940s, both during and after the war, food-rationing was in force. You could bring a great deal of cheer to a visiting neighbour or relative if you could offer them two or three fresh eggs; or a few sticks of rhubarb, some kidney beans, peas or tomatoes from your garden. Of course, neighbourly borrowing was commonplace—a cup of sugar, milk or flour; half a loaf of bread; a dollop of lard; a few potatoes; a cabbage or an onion.

For most of the year (especially for those few who did not have electricity), everything in the home centred round the open fire. It provided the only source of heating for the house; including hot-water bottles at bedtime. The coal-fire also provided the heat for roasting; baking; boiling vegetables or meat; hot water for laundry or personal ablutions; boiling the kettle for frequent cups of tea; frying breakfast; and toasting uneven slices of white bread, suspended on the ends of dinner-forks.

A round iron bake-stone, placed across the top of the grate, was used to make Welsh-cakes or pancakes. When the oven was hot enough, a fruitcake, a rice pudding or a tray of jam tarts could be baked. Sometimes, large green cooking apples were baked in their skins and served with custard; then there were homemade pies made with apples, gooseberries, rhubarb, blackberries or wind-berries (from the hill). For variety, cooking apples could be stewed in a saucepan with some water and a couple of tablespoons of sugar.

Welsh-cakes were a regular treat for dessert; so were homemade cakes and pies, rice puddings with cinnamon and raisins, bread puddings and stewed apple and custard—though they were all sadly lacking, in a nutritional sense. Every home had a cake-tin, which was rarely empty. After dinner, my mother might ask: "Would you like a piece of plain cake with currants in, Cyril?"

Needless to say, running out of coal presented a serious situation. There was barely enough wood available for kindling. It was sometimes necessary to "beg, borrow or steal" until the coalman came again—then, there would be another bill to pay. The anthracite coal was of excellent quality; but while waiting for the coalman, people would sometimes use their bare hands (and a little water) to mould the coal-dust accumulated on the floor of the coal-shed into nuggets which would burn in the grate—though this was often not very successful.

Our diet was plain but ostensibly wholesome. The Sunday roast at 'the cottage' was a freshly-killed rabbit, as often as not. Those who owned shotguns and enjoyed hunting rabbits on Sunday mornings would often sell them for about a shilling (less, if there were a lot of shotgun pellets in them). Vegetables such as cabbage, swedes and potatoes were mostly free to farm-workers, or could be bought locally at a very reasonable price. Other vegetables in season, such as home-grown peas, kidney beans, broad beans, carrots and cauliflower, offered ample variety. Unfortunately, the traditional method of cooking was to boil vegetables in water and then strain them before serving; which effectively ensured that most of the vitamins and minerals were wasted.

The special flavour of "new potatoes" was a seasonal treat, enjoyed by all. They would be rinsed, then boiled whole, in their paper-thin jackets and eaten with fresh garden salad, vegetables or cold meat. Always, they were smeared with butter, because almost everything "tasted lovely with a bit o' butter". All summer long, garden salad was served for tea at least a couple of times a week. Lettuce, tomatoes, cucumbers, radish and shallots were favourites for making salad. Shallots were a special favourite of many adults, who would trim off the roots and repeatedly dip the end in salt, as they munched contentedly.

When a farm-worker, or perhaps a kind neighbour, killed a pig, there would be plenty of salted ham and bacon. Sometimes you could buy a ham, flitch or shoulder. It would provide the family with breakfast meat for a few months. No one complained about constantly having to dodge around a home-cured flitch, wrapped in muslin cloth, dangling from the beams in the kitchen. A couple of sticky flypapers hung nearby helped to protect it.

For breakfast, fried eggs were enjoyed with mushrooms, laver-bread, tomatoes or bacon. A couple of slices of fried bread were always added for good measure "to keep the cold out, isn't it?" Quite often, though, there was only scrambled (or poached) egg on toast; or a boiled egg with some bread fingers to dip in the yolk.

Baked beans or spaghetti on toast were good standbys for any meal—as were pil-chards and sardines.

But everything, it seemed, was served on white bread, even though whole wheat bread was available. Hovis bread was popular with a few health-conscious people. While meals were invariably accompanied by a cup of tea, I developed a preference for Camp Coffee, which came in a similar bottle to HP sauce (another favourite indulgence of mine). The coffee was a dark brown, viscous liquid, which (the label claimed) contained an ingredient called "chicory essence".

As well as fresh garden salads, mackerel, flat-fish (lemon sole, Dover sole or plaice), sea-bass or a few crabs, were summertime treats. The sea provided a variety of fish and crustaceans, as well as periwinkles and the ever-popular laver-bread for those who had the time and enthusiasm to make the effort. Penclawdd cockles were always a nice change. Several locals such as Fred Marks, Alec Thomas, Johnny Beynon (Meadowside) or "aunty Mag" (High Priest), would catch and sometimes sell various kinds of seafood, though lobsters were usually reserved for family members. In the winter, kippers, hake or haddock could be bought in Swansea Market, as a change from beef, mutton or pork.

About late April, each year, my father would make a couple of trips to collect freshly-laid seagulls' eggs from the cliffs around the Devil's Chair or Thurba Head; not surprisingly these had a strong, fishy taste. Only a stomach already used to eating free-range chicken and duck eggs could hope to accommodate them. Nevertheless, when they were boiled and eaten with a pinch of salt and some butter, they were an enjoyable treat.

Farm-workers rarely enjoyed poultry, other than at Christmas. If they kept a few chickens or ducks, they were mainly meant for providing a supply of fresh eggs. Those free-range chickens and eggs really did taste good. Larger farmers had a greater variety of poultry, sometimes including such exotic species as Chinese geese, Guinea-fowl or bantams. At Christmas, if they didn't have their own poultry to kill, farm-workers usually placed an order with one of the farmers for a young cockerel, either alive or freshly-killed and feathered.

There is no doubt that the families of the farm-workers, as well as those of some of the small farmers, led a Spartan existence, yet their diet was remarkably varied. However, it included such rich delights as fresh butter and cream, cheese, full cream milk, eggs, salted ham and fat bacon. A favourite dish of some of my uncles was a hunk of boiled, fat pork covered with white parsley sauce, served with potatoes mashed up in butter and milk and some peas or kidney beans. When roasted, even the skin of pork ("crackling") was enjoyed as a tasty treat.

When food supplies ran short, main meals were reduced to boiled eggs; or treacle, jam or marmite sandwiches. In season, cheese with lettuce, tomatoes or cucumber sandwiches was popular. But always, they were made with white bread. Deep-fried chips or fried, scalloped potatoes alternated with the more traditional mashed potatoes to accompany fried eggs, sausages, meat pies, or fresh fish.

In Middleton, everyone fetched their milk from Jack Richards's Jessamine farm, unless they had a cow of their own. Rhossili and Pitton had their own milk-farmers. Everyone could buy bread, cigarettes, sweets, chocolate bars and general groceries from the Post Office (Will Williams) or the Lower Shop (Alf Richards).

Of course, you would take a large shopping-bag with you, if you were buying bread or groceries. Even so, customers would generally avoid carrying what they'd bought in the Lower Shop into the Post Office and vice-versa. Most people would make two separate trips, but sometimes my mother or father would give me a bag of groceries to look after, while they went to the "other shop" for something they couldn't get in the first shop.

We had to fetch the weekday papers from the Post Office and the Sunday papers from The Green. In the 1950s, The Green, which was run by Bowen and Rona Richards, had the widest variety of sweets, chocolates and snacks. It also had a wide range of bottles of pop, ice-creams (cones or wafers) and lollipops. Youngsters, adults or families could relax on the benches inside the shop and enjoy their favourite treats. Bowen and Rona were always welcoming, polite and ready to chat with their customers.

White bread and refined sugar (often in the form of Tate and Lyle's "golden syrup" or a variety of Robinson's jams) became a regular part of most working families' diets in Britain. Along with biscuits, sweets and pop, bad dietary habits were formed. No doubt these took a toll on the health of many of our parents. Many of us kids had molar teeth extractions before we were ten years old; while the school dentist did a steady business with fillings.

In spite of my parents' best efforts, in my early teenage years I was a scrawny kid with weak joints, missing teeth and soft nails, who never felt particularly robust. I was a little under average height and weight, but there was plenty of fire in my belly. I was wiry enough and could chase a football from dawn 'til dusk. I often walked with a slight limp, due to arthritis resulting from an ankle injury at birth; or from a bruised kneecap, caused by frequent collisions with the road.

For several years after I started grammar school, I suffered from chronic neuralgia. Cold weather would start my gums aching; but sitting in front of an open fireplace would make them ache even more. My mother would give me warm bread-and-milk and a crushed aspirin; but there was not much else she could do.

Abscesses developed around my molar teeth, which resulted in at least two more extractions by the time I became a teenager.

It seemed such a performance for my parents to take me to see the doctor (in Reynoldston) or the dentist (in Swansea), that we didn't bother, unless it was something quite serious. In any case, I was terrified of the dentist, whether it was for a filling or to be gassed for an extraction. I just thought that pain must be a normal part of life, so I complained as little as possible.

[Endnote: The traditional farmhouse diet included much rich produce which would be considered risky nowadays. Due to indulgence in sweet or starchy foods and the irregular brushing of their teeth, many children needed premature extractions. Many middle-aged adults were overweight and suffered from the effects of an excessively salty or fatty diet, often resulting in heart-attacks and strokes in their fifties and sixties.]

15

Pig-meat

Even butchers weep!

John Gay

ALEC Thomas was a diminutive, energetic, feisty man. He had apprenticed in his family's butchering business before migrating to southwest Gower. For a while he was employed, mainly for his butchering expertise, by the Tucker family at Pitton Cross; but he became a farm-worker during the war. He and his wife, Olive, lived at Faircroft (his father-in-law Joseph Richards's house) in Rhossili Lane. Alec was a great asset to the village because most of the local farmers and farm-workers fattened their own pigs, during and after the war. In the 1940s, he killed about sixty pigs a year, as well as a number of lambs.

Uncle Len kept a breeding sow at Middleton Hall farm, while uncle Will continuously kept a pig or two at Hoarstone. My father also fattened a pig on several occasions, but not regularly. Even for several years after the war, families who killed a pig were required to give up a whole year of bacon ration-coupons; for some reason, they were not required to forfeit their lard coupons, even though a pig yielded pounds of excellent lard that would last for months.

Farm-worker Ron Densley and his wife, Gwyneth, would regularly buy a weaned piglet, usually a boar, from a local farmer, which they would fatten up for about ten months in a pigsty they built in the field adjacent to their modern agricultural worker's house, named Morawel. Pigs were fattened up to as much as twenty score (i.e. four hundred pounds) and killed in November; then another one might be fattened for just five months and killed no later than March. The pig-killing season was timed to avoid flies and mild weather, since the pig had to be hung for a few days. After that, salting would take two or three weeks.

Pigs were fed scraps of just about anything, because they would eat almost anything. The bulk of these scraps were carbohydrates, from bread crusts to surplus grain to shrivelled seed-potatoes. This, combined with a lack of exercise as they grew bigger, meant that pigs were inclined to be composed of more fat than muscle. Much of the meat, especially on the flanks, was almost entirely fat.

After making an appointment for Alec's services, customers would need to arrange for a block-and-tackle and a form—a wooden bench about two feet high and at least two feet wide, which served as a killing platform—to be available. Also a couple of paraffin lanterns and several gallons of very hot water were necessary. The appointed time was usually about 7:00 PM, which was after dark; or on Saturday mornings, depending on Alec's availability.

Then, of course, the pig had to be persuaded to approach the form. This, in itself, could be a bit of a game. A pig could be as stubborn as a donkey. A strong twist on the tail was often needed to persuade the pig to move forward. Pigs never liked being coerced. Protesting loudly, the pig would be flipped onto the form: it required a lot of physical strength to hold it in place. Alec preferred to have three men to assist him—one to control each back leg and one to hold the front legs.

From about five years of age, Howard Chalk, Ron Beynon and I tried to watch a pig-killing whenever we had the opportunity. Pigs would "scritch" for just about any reason. As soon as they were forcibly rolled onto the form, they would scream as though they were being murdered (which, of course, they were about to be).

It took us boys several attempts before we could resist the urge to run as soon as the pig began to scritch. The men would sometimes taunt us with "Where's thee gwain t', by? Casn't thee howld an t'n, by?" Finally, at about the ripe age of seven or so, we stood our ground and saw the whole process through.

When the pig's throat was slit, through the layer of fat, the blood was collected in a clean enamel bucket, because it could be made into "black pudding". As it cooled, the blood had to be stirred constantly (traditionally with a piece of branch from a blackthorn bush, about fifteen inches long) to ensure a uniform mixture of fat globules and blood cells. "Black pudding" was essentially dried blood, but it could be made tasty with the addition of salt, pepper and onions. It was popular as part of a fried breakfast, or sliced to make a tasty sandwich.

Gradually, the pig's struggles and noise would subside as its strength ebbed away. Then, buckets of scalding hot water were slopped over sections of its body, so the coarse hair and outermost layer of skin could be removed with a scraper. Then the heavy pig had to be turned over on the form to complete the process.

After all the coarse hair was removed, Alec would make incisions to isolate the Achilles tendons on the hind legs. Next, a steel bar would be inserted to spread the legs. An elaborate system of pulleys known as a block-and-tackle was needed to raise a 400 pound pig. The main block was attached by several wraps of one-inch sisal rope to a stout beam in the barn or shed. The carcase was elevated, until the head cleared the form.

It was only after this exercise had been completed, that the belly was slit open from the top, downwards through the rib cage, allowing the steaming innards to fall into a metal bathtub. Special organs such as the kidneys, the liver, the lights (i.e. lungs) and the apron (the lining between the stomach and the lungs), were carefully removed. In the 1940s, the bladder was usually saved for boys to convert into a football.

After allowing the pig to hang for about three or four days in cool conditions, Alec would return and begin separating the portions of the carcass. The head was first removed and chopped in half; the brain was saved to be seasoned and converted into "brawn". The torso was split into two halves as the backbone was removed, from the curly tail to the shoulders. The pig's carcase was then divided into hams, flitches (sides) and shoulders. Once these six main sections had been separated, salting could commence.

Over the next three weeks, pounds of salt and saltpetre were rubbed and forced into the meat. The flesh around the bony joints was cut away, so that the saltpetre could be forced deep into the space around the bone. After about three weeks, the well-salted meat was ready to be wrapped in muslin sacks and hung up to dry, protected from house-flies and warm weather—the two worst enemies. The meat was then usually suspended from kitchen or back-kitchen ceiling joists. Usually, sticky fly-papers were hung near them, as an extra precaution.

In those days there were no refrigerators, so the best cuts of meat—lean loin-steaks and chine (sections of the meaty backbone) were used up in a week or so. People gave packages away to relatives and friends, knowing that they could expect similar favours to be returned in the future. The choice portions included beautiful steaks and chine. Very little was wasted; even the tongue, tail and trotters could be boiled or included in a stew. In addition to his reasonable ten-shilling fee, Alec would invariably be rewarded with a package of fresh pig-meat in recognition of his highly-professional standards.

Wives were adept at collecting lard from various parts of the innards, before they were disposed of. A popular treat from a freshly-killed pig was faggots, which included the liver, the lights (i.e. lungs) and other odds-and-ends, which were minced, seasoned and wrapped up in pieces of the apron, before being baked.

By the age of eight or nine, I usually attended any pig-killings in our family (I think, mainly to test my nerve). Alec began to joke that he would teach me the butchering trade and I would be his future son-in-law. Since Alec's daughter, Alice, who was about half a year older than I, was an exceptionally pretty girl, with black hair and dark eyes, I didn't feel too alarmed at the prospect.

[Endnote: In retrospect, pig-meat formed a dubious part of our diet. Fresh cuts of meat, such as steak, kidneys and chine were generally lean and deliciously tasty; however, the fat and salt content of the preserved meat was a threat to our health. But in those days, bacon could never be too salty or too fat. Indeed, salt and fat were considered to be beneficial. Faggots, brawn and black-pudding are an acquired taste, still favoured by some.]

16

Blossom and Bess

… for want of a nail, the shoe was lost;
for want of a shoe, the horse was lost …

Benjamin Franklin

MY earliest and fondest memories of farm animals are of the two big carthorses at Middleton Hall farm, which spent much of their non-working time grazing peacefully in the meadow, as the weather allowed. Otherwise, they shared a cosy stonewalled stable. Their leisure time increased as farmers became more used to their new-fangled tractors, which, although sometimes difficult to start, required much less physical effort and skill to operate, especially when ploughing.

Horses took a lot of handling, even when simply pulling a cart. They needed to be controlled at all times. They had some useful forward gears, but a very poor reverse gear. It was difficult to back them out of a tight corner by shouting "Whoa, back!" Often it didn't work unless you grabbed them by the bridle and forced them backwards. Even turning a horse and cart in through a gateway had to be done skilfully. Left to itself, the horse would never make allowance for the tight turning-circle of the cart.

Blossom was a little more reddish brown than old Bess, but they both had a white blaze on the forehead. She was the younger of the two; therefore she survived for several years after the older mare had gone, though I have only vague recollections of the demise of either one. All animals, including horses, dogs, cats, cows, poultry, pigs or sheep had one of two important functions—either they were working partners or they were a source of food. When the time came to put them down (or if they simply died of old age), feelings of regret were brief. Larger animals were usually removed by Tomkins's lorry. Whenever we saw that lorry in the area, we suspected that some local farmer had lost a cow or a horse.

I have a clear memory of falling off one of the carthorses, probably old Bess, as she was being led around the corner of Middleton Hall farmhouse from the main road. We must have been returning from work at one of the fields near the Chapel. I was no more than three years old at the time. From then on, I was always nervous when left alone on the back of either of the gentle mares; somehow, I always seemed to lean the wrong way when the horse changed direction. It was just as terrifying when the horse dropped its head to chew at a tuft of grass.

It was near the end of the war when I spent a day with uncle Arthur (better known as Robin), while he and Blossom were ploughing the steep field just across the lane from Hoarstone. It was a warm and sunny early spring day. He ploughed the field lengthwise—up and down its steep slope. It was a long hard day's work for both man and beast, with Robin alternately "gee-ing" or "whoa-ing" at the horse to get its cooperation.

It amused me to watch Robin, sweat wetting the wavy brown hair under his cloth cap, grumble or curse under his breath whenever the ploughshare struck a large stone. It was a job that really needed two horses, but it was a sign of the times that old Bess had not been replaced when she had died about a year earlier.

Robin would tug on the "lines" to steer the horse left or right, while heaving on the handles of the plough to guide it around offending obstacles. The "lines" were about one inch thick, sisal ropes, attached to either side of the bit in the horse's mouth: they passed through rings on the sides of the collar. Robin would adjust the iron wheel at the front of the plough to reduce the depth of the furrow when working uphill. He could set the angle at which the horse was pulling, by adjusting where the batkin was hitched to the head of the plough.

At lunchtime we stopped for a can of tea and a sandwich, supplied by aunty Ceinwen and my teenage cousin, Frances, who lived at Hoarstone. In between, we drank from a tin can of clear, delicious water from Talgarths Well, using the lid for a cup. The mare made do with a couple of buckets of rainwater from the rain-barrel, until we got her back to Middleton.

The uphill furrows were indeed hard work. On the downhill turns, though, Robin's mood was quite different, especially since it was a beautiful day. He would intermittently break into what has probably been the natural song of the ploughman since time immemorial. I quickly learnt the words and the cadences; they seemed so natural. I tried them for myself. "Tie-rie-rie ... tie-rie ... rie-rie ...," I sang.

It was about 4:00 PM when Robin must have felt some pangs of hunger. He knew that his mother and his sister, Peggy, would have saved a home-cooked dinner for him. He didn't want his young brother, Len—who would have had his dinner at dinnertime, because he was working in Middleton—getting home before him and scoffing his share, too. After one more furrow up the slope, both he and Blossom had had enough.

Robin unhitched the mare from the plough, coiled up the chains and the lines, leaving the former with the plough and the latter on the mare. Then he led her out of the field and closed the gate. He used a low stone wall to jump up on Blossom's broad back; then I stood on the wall: he caught me by one hand and hauled me up in front of him. It wasn't very comfortable. We plodded up the lane to Fernhill, then down to 'the cottage', where he let me off on a grassy bank, by the hill. I was afraid I would end up underneath the horse, but that was just a normal risk for a boy in Middleton.

It must have been the following year that Robin took me along on a trip to the blacksmith's forge at Cheriton. Blossom's shoes on her rear hoofs were worn and one of them was coming loose. We were on our way by mid-morning. It was a peaceful late spring day. I sat up on the seat, next to Robin, enjoying the jerky motion of the cart, as the horse clumped steadily along past Fernhill Top, its loose shoe clanging whenever it hit a stone.

We travelled past the farms at Fernhill, then across the moor to Sluxton farm, taking the cart-track through the fields to the south of the orchard, then around the east side of the farm buildings. Soon, we were swaying along a stony hillside track, amongst stunted gorse bushes. A few sheep grazed on the short wiry grass, dotted with celandines and daisies.

As we passed above Whitemoor farmhouse and mill, Robin told me it was haunted by a White Lady. A lark was singing high up in the blue sky. Robin asked, "Coust th' see 'n, by?" I couldn't. Soon afterwards, we diverted to visit West Cathan farm, perched precariously on the side of Hardings Down, where Robin stopped for a cup of tea and to pay his respects to the Hughes sisters who farmed there.

From there, we rounded the east side of Hardings Down, crossed the main Llangennith road; then we travelled along the east side of Llanmadoc Down. The roadway sloped down along the side of the hill to Cheriton, where we made a hairpin turn into the blacksmith's yard. A few geese marched solemnly past, followed by their goslings; and chickens scattered as we turned in. A pleasant woman, the blacksmith's wife, greeted us and told us her husband was at work in the forge, which was attached to the far end of their cottage.

The blacksmith was a stocky, cheerful middle-aged man. We found him in the forge, sweat dripping from his brow, as he wrestled with an iron rim for a cart-wheel. He told us he had a lot of work to do, but realising how far we had come, he would fit us in that afternoon. This meant we would have to wait a couple of hours before he could attend to us. When the blacksmith's wife called him into the cottage for his dinner, we strolled down the sloping roadway which zigzagged into the hamlet of Cheriton.

It was a pretty little place, but quite boring for us because there was hardly anyone about, let alone children of my age. Robin was able to buy us a couple of lettuce-and-cheese sandwiches and a cup of tea at a small shop the blacksmith had recommended. We sat on a grassy bank at the roadside and munched hungrily. Afterwards, Robin wandered around the seemingly deserted hamlet, looking for anyone he could yarn with to pass the time. He exchanged a few greetings here and there; then, we went back to the forge and waited patiently.

Finally, the blacksmith was ready to examine the horse's hooves to decide which shoes needed replacing. We unhitched Blossom from the cart and led her close to the door of the forge. The front shoes were fine, but the two on the rear had to be replaced, so the blacksmith removed them both, prying the nails out with a large set of pincers. It took a few taps with a hammer and cold-chisel to free one of them. Each one was tossed on the scrap pile, with a clang.

Each new shoe had to be dealt with, separately. First it was selected from a rack of prefabricated shoes and measured against the hoof; then it was placed in the furnace with a long pair of tongs. It was heated until it turned first red, then gold; then it was removed and pounded on the anvil with a heavy hammer. After that, it was partly cooled by being dipped into a tub of water, so the blacksmith could set it in place, while gripping the mare's upturned hoof between his knees. It was an impressive performance.

I alternately sat or stood on the dirt floor of the forge, watching this painstaking process. Three times the smith went through the routine with the first shoe alone, all the while bemoaning the problems he encountered. It made me feel somewhat depressed. *Is he trying to do the impossible?* I wondered. It sounded like it. Finally he nailed the troublesome shoe in place. I was amazed that the horse felt no pain from the nails.

The second shoe went a little easier, requiring only one re-heat. I was over-awed by the huge set of bellows, fixed in place so that the blacksmith could operate them with one hand. They made the ones we had at home seem puny. The whole process must have taken almost an hour. Blossom was quite placid through it all, almost as if she realised that all the fuss and palaver was for her own good.

It must have been after three o'clock when we finally set out for home. It took us about an hour-and-a-half to get back to Middleton. The return journey was by a different route: I asked Robin which way we were going. We must have travelled through Burry Green to Henllys farm, then turned towards Kings Hall farm. It was unfamiliar country to me, until we had almost reached Kinmoor.

As Blossom clumped along, I wondered whether she was entirely comfortable in her new footwear. She stumbled once in a while, perhaps from the unaccustomed weight or thickness of her new shoes. Long before we arrived home, I was becoming tired and hungry, looking forward to my tea. But first, we had to unhitch the cart in the farmyard; drop the shafts on the ground; and remove all the harness, except for the bridle. Then we led the tired mare to water at the chute near Stan and May Beynon's farm buildings, at Riverside.

After she had drunk her fill, we led Blossom to the stable, where Robin removed her bridle, then gave her a good ration of oats and some hay. It had been a long day for her. Getting her new shoes had taken the best part of a day for us—another reason why those new-fangled tractors were becoming increasingly popular.

[Endnote1: A batkin was a metal draw-bar used to transfer the pulling power of the chains from a horse's collar to a single point, as when ploughing. For one horse, only one batkin was needed; but for two horses, a grouping of three was necessary.]

[Endnote2: In bygone days, there had been a blacksmith's forge at Middleton. A hitching-stone was still in evidence near the front of Middleton Lodge farmhouse.]

17

The Gale

Now the great winds shoreward blow;
Now the salt tides seaward flow;
Now the wild white horses play,
Champ and chafe and toss in the spray.

Matthew Arnold

IT was in the spring of 1947 that we had one of the wildest gales ever to hit the South Gower coast. There had been several wild blows, following the most severe winter in memory. In late April, the Mumbles lifeboat had lost all eight of its crew members, while trying to rescue the crew of a ship which had run aground near Porthcawl.

The gale had already lasted for a couple of days. On the Saturday, when my father, Joffre, came home at noon for his dinner, he said it was still blowing so wild that he'd only been able to work around the farm buildings, tending to the needs of the animals and tidying up about the yard.

Ever restless when he was indoors, at about half-past three Joff decided he needed to fetch a few things from the Post Office—like the Saturday *Evening Post*, a cottage loaf (if there were any left) and a bag of hard-boils for his "sweet tooth". My mother, Joyce, told him, "You don't need to go out in this weather, Joffre. Be sensible!" But he said, "It isn't raining, that's the main thing."

For some reason, Joff decided I might as well go along too. Mam protested again, but Joff said I might have to join the "rocket crew" some day, so I'd better get used to a gale. I laced up my boots as fast as I could. At the tender age of seven I hadn't given much thought to joining the "rocket crew", but if that was going to get me out of the house, I'd consider it.

As we marched down the unpaved, stony road towards the school, we were only partly sheltered from the wind. It was strong alright—I'd never seen the broken cumulus clouds scudding across the sky so fast; yet there was a solid ceiling of grey above them. The fields and hillside were water-logged, but the rain had passed.

Just opposite the school gate, my father spotted a rusted tin for roasting meat, trapped in a gorse bush. "Fetch that, Cyril," he told me. I didn't know why he wanted a rusty meat-tin, but I brought it to him. He took it and heaved it upwards in the air as hard as he could. Suddenly, the wind took over; the meat tin whirled upwards and off in the general direction of Talgarths Well, passing to the south side of our cottage. I stared in wonder as it blew on, out of sight. Who knows where it ended up—it might have flown as far as Llandewi!

We walked past the Post Office, out to The Green. We didn't meet a soul on the road, but being out in that gale felt invigorating. Joff decided we might as well go as far as the Worms Head Hotel and see how strong the wind really was. As we passed Bowen Richards's farmyard, we admired the large ash tree that grew horizontally there, about four feet above the ground. It was a wise tree! Standing upright, it could never have survived to such a mature age.

We strode down the narrow lane in the lee of the hotel, but as soon as we took a step past the end of the stone wall, into the open, it was a battle to stay on our feet. In many a gale, one had to lean at forty-five degrees into the wind. On that day, we would have had to lie down and roll over and over to travel any further. I don't think the Coastguards and their families could have moved from their houses. Probably, they had to share their supplies by going in and out of each other's back doors.

Peering from the shelter of the stone wall, we could see that Rhossili Bay, being relatively shallow, was one continuous expanse of foaming water from Worms Head to Burry Holms. Beyond that there were myriads of "white horses". It was wild, all right. I understood how sailing ships must have had little hope when they were caught off the rugged Gower coast in those conditions.

Our curiosity satisfied, we retraced our steps to the Post Office, picking up a few items. Soon we were back at 'the cottage'. It was comforting to know that the "pine-end" was a good three feet of solid limestone, as we listened to the wind roaring and gusting around our whitewashed, thatch-roofed home, sometimes threatening to suck our coal-fire right up the chimney.

The next morning the winds had subsided to just a blustery, though sullen, day. On his way to pick up the Sunday newspapers, Joff heard that the storm had washed whole schools of Conger eels into Mewslade Bay. Twenty-two-year-old Eric Gibbs had hauled a huge eel—a good six feet long and weighing exactly a half-hundredweight—all the way up from the bay. It caused such a stir that they weighed it on uncle Len's balance scales at Middleton Hall, before feeding it to his pig.

After doing justice to our Sunday dinner, we set off for the bay to see for ourselves. On the way down Mewslade Lane, we met Eric's uncle, Jack Gibbs (who farmed at Mewslade View with his sister Annie), plodding homeward with three or four large eels draped over his shoulders. They looked quite lifeless, but they were as thick as a man's arm and four or five feet long. He was carrying a potato-sack with several smaller eels in it. "There's t ... t ... tousands of 'um", Jack assured us, with his habitual stutter. "Th ... they pigs'll eat um qu ... quick enough."

Jack was a small, but feisty old-timer. His dark eyes were deep-set in a swarthy, bony face. He always wore the characteristic garb of the older generation—cloth cap, collarless flannel shirt, dark waistcoat and jacket, corded trousers or breeches, studded boots and leather gaiters that protected his shins. He plodded on up the lane with his heavy load, taking each step in his characteristic hesitant manner.

We continued down to the bay, where we could see that the wild winter seas had ravaged the sand from the beach, leaving exposed rocks with shallow pools around them. There were masses of brown kelp, some clinging to sodden pieces of driftwood. As we walked out towards the roaring, misty-white tide, we saw that many of the pools were occupied by Conger eels—but most were lifeless. It wasn't the Mewslade Bay I knew—it seemed like some mysterious, gloomy primordial environment.

Joff began to pull eels from one of the larger pools. He hauled them out by the tail and whacked them over the head with a short piece of driftwood, if there was any sign of life. I helped him get them into a potato-sack. I gingerly pulled a couple of small ones out of a pool, though I didn't like the slimy feel of them.

"They eat eels in London," Joff informed me. I didn't believe him. I helped him stuff my couple of small ones into the sack, which soon became too heavy for me to carry. Then he draped a couple of larger ones, which were just about dead, over his shoulder.

All I could do was help support the bottom of the heavy sack which Joff held by the neck with one iron-hard hand; otherwise, I wouldn't be contributing anything on the way home. "They'll be good for feeding the pig," Joff reminded me, as we began the uphill plod to Middleton.

[Endnote1: According to Eric Gibbs, that fifty-six-pound eel he dragged up from Mewslade, was weighed at 'the bank'. (Ernie Beynon independently verified the weight.) Len fed the eel to his sow, which ate the whole thing. The next day, Len saw Eric and told him: "That damned eel has killed my sow!" When Eric asked how, Len explained: "Well, the sow is just lying there—won't move!" Eric replied: "Well you wouldn't move either, if you ate a half-hundredweight of eel."]

[Endnote2: One plausible theory for the phenomenon that occurred at Mewslade Bay, in 1947, is suggested by Ernie Beynon. Conger eels are known to colonise submerged wrecks. It is possible that a drifting mine or other explosive device, could have been detonated during the gale. The stunning effect of an explosion would explain why the eels were so lifeless.]

18

Fun at Fernhill Top

If a man can take any pleasure in recalling the thought of kindnesses done …

Catullus

IT was a cool, dry day in the Easter holidays. After dinner, I decided to pay a visit to one of our nearest neighbours. "Uncle Tom" Williams and "aunty Olwyn" kept a small farm at Fernhill Top. I knew I could always count on a welcome because our families had been neighbours and friends through the hard times of the war years. Furthermore, Olwyn and my mother were second cousins.

Olwyn had been born and raised at Fernhill Top. Her mother, "auntie Min", was a cousin of my maternal grandmother. Olwyn was a plump, big-boned woman with a round, pleasant face. I always thought she would make an ideal (Mrs.) Father Christmas. Her husband, Tom, was a small, mild-natured man with a ready grin and a chuckle, who had migrated to Gower from the Brecon area.

Their elder daughter, Sylvia, was about a year younger than I, while Cynthia (always called "Sis" at home) was soon to start at the village school. Around the end of the war, our mothers had sometimes taken us to Mewslade bay to paddle and build sandcastles. Sometimes, I joined the Williams family for a picnic on the "flat rocks" at Fall Bay, after they first spent a couple of hours working in their field in the lower Vile. On those occasions, we kids used small nets to fish for shrimp or whitebait in the rock-pools.

At Fernhill Top, Tom and Olwyn had three or four small, rough fields on the shoulder of the hill, where they grazed a horse, a half a dozen cows and a few sheep. They also had a couple of small fields at Kinmoor, where they usually grew some potatoes, even though the soil was dark and rather peaty. In addition, they had some old cowsheds and a field next to Brook Cottage, which they used for grazing. They had one fertile field near the bottom of Mewslade Lane and one or two others in the Vile.

Soon after I arrived, "aunty Ol" had us playing some outdoor games. When we tired of playing hopscotch on the gravel road, she brought out a length of one-inch sisal rope, tied one end to the farm gate, stretched the rope out across the roadway and began to turn it so that all three of us kids could skip at the same time. It was great exercise for growing youngsters, even if it wasn't as exciting as a game of football. We had to interrupt the fun for the occasional tractor passing by, but that was a minor inconvenience.

Next, a length of rabbit-netting was tied across the road. A couple of children's tennis rackets were produced and we tried to learn to play tennis on the bumpy, gravel road. To add to the confusion, the Williams's sheepdog, which they called Pup, insisted on joining in with great enthusiasm. Pup loved to chase and chew tennis balls until they were punctured. No amount of yelling seemed to keep him out of the game.

Meanwhile, "uncle Tom" was going about his farm chores, in and out of the farm buildings, which included a stable, cowshed and a storage-shed with a loft. Then, he needed to siphon some washing-water from a rain-filled tub. Using a length of rubber tubing, he demonstrated how this was done. It seemed almost magical; but I found it wasn't as easy as it looked when I tried it.

A short while later, "aunty Ol" disappeared into the house to begin cooking something for our tea. The girls went with her to help, but I preferred to explore the farm sheds. In the loft, I discovered some broken seed-potato boxes. Placing together some pieces of broken wood, I got the idea of trying to build a model battleship.

Tom readily provided a hammer, a box of small nails and a sharp knife. I worked busily for more than an hour, breaking and shaping pieces of flat wood, then nailing them together in layers to build a superstructure for my ship. The gun turrets proved particularly challenging; but by improvising with spent Swan match-sticks and some small blocks of wood, a rudimentary ship was completed—though I knew it would not have won any prizes.

Soon, Tom let me know it was teatime. Olwyn was an excellent cook, whether it was Irish stew or a roast. For dessert, there would be apple pie with fresh cream, or some of her delicious Devonshire splits. Clutching my battleship, I headed for the warmth of the farmhouse kitchen. The day was already beginning to fade.

After tea, Tom lit the oil-lamps. While Sylvia was helping her mother with the washing up, he showed me a real hunting knife, complete with a goatskin sheath. Seeing how much I admired the knife, Tom told me I could borrow it if I would like to. It was as exciting as any Christmas present I had ever received. I couldn't wait for the day when I could fit it on my belt and go off hunting—for foxes or badgers, perhaps even arctic wolves!

When everything was finally cleared away and the dishes had been washed, it was time for Ludo and Snakes-and-Ladders, followed by some card games. We first played Snap and then Fish, which Tom seemed to particularly enjoy. Little Cynthia could join in the board games, but wasn't yet able to manage the cards, so Tom solved her frustration by sitting her on his knee to help him. Soon, the cosy living room was echoing with our shouts and laughter. Tom would chuckle at our mistakes, but he always gave us another chance. What a kind man! I was proud to call him "uncle", although he was not a direct relative.

Suddenly, it was half-past eight. It was time to go home. Before I left, I learnt that Tom's nephew, Trevor, would be coming to stay for the next few weeks. I knew they would be spending a lot of time entertaining him and taking him to the fields and the bays. I couldn't help feeling envious. Lucky Trevor!

It was quite dark by now, but there was enough light from the stars for a country boy to find his way along the rough, stony road and, at the same time, watch out for the stray ponies that frequented the hillside and often wandered onto the roads after dusk. When I looked up at the sky, I could identify the famous formation known as The Plough: it was the only one I knew. I wondered how the Earth, the Moon and the Sun could all be part of the "milky way" when it was obviously so far away.

Proudly carrying Tom's hunting knife, I hurried homeward. Gorse bushes could take on strange shapes in the gloom: it didn't pay to let one's imagination run riot. I didn't waste time. As I jogged past the gate that led to Talgarths Well, I could see the dark silhouette of 'the cottage'. There were no lights because the windows were all on the south-easterly face of the house, but I knew I was as good as home.

19

Mr. Hughes's Tobacco

What a pleasant thing it is to be thankful.

Anglican Prayer Book

JOHN Hughes was a retired gentleman, who lived in a bungalow in Rhossili Lane about halfway between the Post Office and The Green. He was a dapper, humourless man, who was married, but otherwise seemed quite reclusive. He was not "one of the village". He had the pasty, yellowish complexion and sunken eyes of a chain-smoker. I didn't know what his vocation in life had been, though I was told he'd been raised in Porteynon. He and his wife, both of them frail people, hardly left their bungalow, peculiarly named The Little House.

Even as seven-year-olds, Ron Beynon and I would cringe slightly whenever we saw the sparse, well-dressed figure in a trilby hat ambling towards us, as we wandered out along Rhossili Lane. Sometimes, Mr. Hughes (as we were obliged to address him) would be leaning against the cemented stone wall opposite his house, as if casually admiring the magnificent, unbroken view from Thurba Head around to Worms Head—but we came to know that he was usually waiting for a victim. As we approached him, he would seem hardly to notice us. We, however, had learnt not to be fooled by appearances.

On one particular day in 1948, Ron and I were only ten yards away from him as we headed towards The Green. There was no hint that Mr. Hughes was aware of our approach as he leant against the wall, staring fixedly towards Thurba. We had already edged over to the other side of the road, hoping to sidle past, unnoticed. We were beginning to feel optimistic that Mr. Hughes would completely ignore our passing, as he usually did when he needed no favours.

A few more steps ... then Mr. Hughes suddenly turned and faced us directly. With the help of his thin brown walking-stick, he shuffled diagonally across the road towards us with unmistakable purpose in his short, frail strides. We immediately knew we were trapped, but we also knew we could do little about it.

With no smile and the barest of pleasantries—he didn't appear to know our names or even whose sons we were—Mr. Hughes addressed us in a voice not much stronger than a hoarse whisper: "Boys, go to the Post-Office and bring me an ounce of tobacco; they know what kind I like." He held out a thin hand with a shilling and a silver thruppenny-bit in it. Ron reluctantly accepted the proffered coins. We had been pressed into service—once again!

Without enthusiasm, we turned and retraced the one hundred yards to the Post Office, which also served as the main grocery store and newsagent for our parish. This was an unfruitful diversion from whatever adventure awaited us at Rhossili End. It was already late morning; we hoped there wouldn't be two or three housewives ahead of us, with long grocery lists. If there were, we'd just have to wait politely, if impatiently.

The Postmaster, Will Williams, was a stocky energetic elderly gentleman who always wore a light-brown, full-length shopkeeper's coat. His sparse greying hair clung to the circumference of his rounded head. Finally, he turned to us, his pale grey eyes peering beneath a broad furrowed brow, over the top of his reading glasses. He asked in his gravelly, warm voice: "What can I do for you two, today?" We knew that he loved to tease us, so we hoped he was in a rush that morning.

We told him we needed an ounce of pipe tobacco for Mr. Hughes. "Ah, yes," he says. He selected a sealed packet from one of the shelves. He gave it to me, taking the money from Ron at the same time. We turned to go out through the tall twin wooden doors. "Just a minute, boys, there's some change!" Mr. Williams handed Ron a penny ha'penny.

As we made our way out towards The Green once more, we allowed ourselves to feel some optimism. Perhaps Mr. Hughes would say, "You can have the change, boys." Frankly, we didn't have much use for money, at our age—it just seemed to weigh down our pockets—but it would make us feel rewarded for our involuntary service.

We need not have been concerned about being burdened with heavy copper coins. With barely a word, Mr. Hughes took the tobacco I held out for him; then he stretched out his thin hand for the change. Ron handed it over. We knew better than to try hiding a penny or even a ha'penny. Mr. Hughes knew the prices of tobacco and cigarettes, exactly!

20

A Child of the Village

Alas! 'tis true I have gone here and there ...

William Shakespeare

MY mother often recounted examples of my inclination to wander, rather than be content to stay at home. From when I was only about eighteen-months old, my uncles would take me to the fields with them. One mild spring day, after hoeing potatoes all morning, they returned to the farmhouse for their dinner. She asked them, "Where's Cyril?" They looked at each other, but none of them could answer. "Uh mus' be still 'n the field," they finally agreed. My father immediately set off for the field (alongside the Chapel) and found me happily crawling among the potato rows, entertaining myself by throwing dirt and small stones in the air. To hear my parents tell it, the only time I ever complained was when I was put to bed.

After we moved to 'the cottage' in 1942, I could not be kept at home. My mother tried tying the gate—but I would climb over the wall. In desperation, she tried hiding my shoes, but I found a pair of Wellingtons, which had belonged to a much older cousin. They were far too big for me; they fitted me more like a pair of fisherman's waders. But my mother next saw me, trudging wearily home—not at dinnertime, not at teatime, but at sunset. After that, she gave up: she just made sure I got a good breakfast, because she never knew when I'd come home.

It was common for my father to come looking for me at dusk (which could be as late as ten o'clock in the summer). From about six o'clock, I could invariably be found in the vicinity of 'the bank', often joining in any impromptu sports activity until it was too dark to see the ball; or listening to the older men, perched like wise old crows on the fallen elm branch, telling their tales of yore. As they saw my father approaching, some of them would say "Hide theesel', by! Joff's comin'!" When I complained about having to go home, Will Morris would say, "Thee better bring thy cottage down an' put 'n in our rickyard, by."

Some of the regulars who liked to sit and yarn on the double-tiered fallen branch of the giant elm tree, which dominated 'the bank', included Will Morris, Stan Beynon, Enoch Beynon, Wilfred Beynon, Ingram Chalk, Jack Thomas and Joseph Richards. Other old-timers who often stopped by for a half hour or so, included Will Jones, Phil Jones, Bill Beynon, George Beynon, Alf Bevan and Jack Richards. They were almost all Middleton men.

Sometimes, two or three of us kids would hang about, idly listening to the old-timers' gossip. But we risked getting teased; or worse, being targeted by trickster Stan Beynon, who prided himself on the accuracy and distance he could spit—then, he'd look up at the overhanging branches of the elm tree and blame the starlings. However, we youngsters were observant enough to know that the starlings did not seem to frequent the elm tree; they preferred the small ash grove on the other side of the village hall.

I would often get a sandwich at teatime from aunty Doreen at Middleton Hall. Occasionally, I would receive similar charity from Sally Beynon at the The Ship farm, even though she had eight offspring of her own to feed. Sometimes, it was a piece of delicious fruitcake from dear old Jinny Morris, who loved to get us kids into her kitchen for a yarn. A couple of times, I shared a simple supper of bread, farm butter and cheese with those kind old-timers, "little Johnny" and "aunty Mag". They must have seen how weak and hungry I looked some evenings as I trudged homeward, past High Priest.

Rhossili was free of serious crime. The only frequent misdemeanour, which was considered fair game by us boys, was to steal apples and sometimes cherries or gooseberries, from farmers' orchards. Otherwise, helping ourselves to a snack of tender young carrots or peas, as we wandered through the fields, was hardly a cause for concern to anyone. Sometimes, we couldn't resist the ripe, black sloes growing wild in the hedges, in spite of their bitterness. Delicious blackberries were a favourite snack, in late summer.

As we got a little older (perhaps nine or ten), there were times when Ron Beynon and I, knowing that Davies's bread van would be outside the Lower Shop about 5:00 PM, would scrape together seven-pence-ha'penny between us to buy a fresh, doughy, round "batch", which we would tear up with our soiled hands and consume hungrily. That way, we didn't need to bother about going home for our tea.

From as young as seven, I would get an occasional day or two of work with local farmers, during school holidays. As I got older, this work became several weeks at a time. These farmers included Tom Williams, Ingram Chalk, Alf Bevan, Sid Thomas, Bevan Tucker, Jack Richards, Sid Thomas, Gordon Thomas and Chris Beynon. Over the years, the work involved loading hay and corn, picking and weighing potatoes, weeding, planting, hoeing, fencing, dipping sheep, cleaning out cowsheds and sketching registered Friesian calves.

Ron Beynon and I would often make up our own work projects. If it wasn't trying to mend something on the farm or rounding up someone's animals, it would be preparing for the next annual event, such as Guy Fawkes night. We would collect just about anything that we reckoned was no further use, to build a bonfire on the hill across the road from 'the cottage'. We thought this endeavour might help persuade my parents to spend a little extra on fireworks. Occasionally, Howard Chalk or the Williams family from Fernhill Top would join us to enjoy the blaze.

Village children, especially in Middleton, would be tolerated just about anywhere on most farm properties. That is not to say that we were never a nuisance; we often earned an exasperated "Dang thee, by!" from one or other of the farmers. At various times, through following the threshing-machine, helping with farm-work, visiting school-friends or just wandering, I enjoyed the hospitality of farmhouse kitchens from East Pilton to Rhossili farm, and from Sluxton to Great Pitton. Playing with pals, visiting extended family members or accompanying my parents to work introduced me to almost everyone else's kitchen, at one time or another.

There is an old saying that it takes a village to raise a child. There's no doubt that I was influenced by most of the people in Middleton and beyond. It was a no-nonsense environment, where kids were not spoiled, yet there was a sense of safety and confidence under the watchful gaze of familiar faces. As I grew up, we youngsters suffered no serious mishaps involving animals, machinery, traffic or coastal hazards.

That was not entirely due to luck.

21

Threshing Time

... Praise Him for our harvest store,
He hath filled the garner-floor ...

H.W. Baker

IT is a warm Friday evening at the end of September: there is a sense of anticipation in Middleton. We young boys (Howard Chalk, Ron Beynon and I) hear a distant rumble. We run towards the Lower Shop to meet the huge steam engine towing the threshing-machine, as it clanks and puffs along the main road. It has been calling at farms at Pitton Cross and Pitton, before coming to Middleton. This impressive equipment belongs to the Greenings of Killay. The driver, a slightly-built, hawk-faced man, pulls on the cord that operates the steam whistle. The ear-piercing blast is meant to announce his arrival, or perhaps to impress the youngsters he sees tearing madly towards him, in short trousers and hobnailed boots.

Which farm will be first in Middleton? The farmers already know, but we walk and jog alongside the strange, fascinating canopied steam engine, watching the engine driver on his high steel platform as he shovels coal into the fire. We stare in awe at the size of the huge fly-wheel and the steering chains connected to the front axle. The smell of burnt coke and steam is much more exciting than the smell of tractor fuel or horse-dung.

The engine turns up School Lane, past Jessamine farm; then it slowly turns right and plods its way up the short lane behind the stonewalled farm buildings that are shared between Middleton Hall farm and Alf Bevan's Middleton farm; then into "the meadow" and, with yet another right turn, it progresses carefully down the slope into the rickyard of Middleton Hall farm. It stops only when the threshing-machine is close alongside a large oblong mow of wheat-sheaves.

The farmer, uncle Len, talks with the engine driver, then the engine is detached from the threshing-machine. The engine puffs and hisses as it plods around to a position about ten yards behind the thresher. Next, a drive-belt, which was rolled up on the engine's platform, is stretched out and looped around the drive-wheel of the steam engine and then to a smaller drive-wheel on the thresher. A twist is made in the belt, so that it won't slide off too easily, then the engine is carefully backed up a foot or two, until there is enough tension in the belt that it won't slip. The engine driver provides large wooden blocks for the wheels of the engine and the thresher to ensure the belt tension is maintained.

There has been quite a lot of work involved in setting up. By now, it's almost six o'clock, so they won't be starting tonight, the driver advises uncle Len. "Aye, aye", he replies, "Better t' get a good start, first thing 'n the mornin'." The steam engine sighs and releases a cloud of steam, as the coal-fire dies.

By the time I wake up, get dressed, eat some breakfast (at my mother's insistence) and pelt down School Lane to the farm, it is already after nine o'clock. As I rush into the farmyard, I can hear the rhythmic moaning and groaning of the thresher, as it chews up the intermittent supply of corn sheaves. The rickyard is an amazing sight: it seems that every farmer from Middleton and Fernhill is here; they include Ingram Chalk, Harry Morris, Jack Richards, Tom Williams, Alf Bevan, Reg Howells, Wilfred Beynon and his two oldest sons, Reggie and Ernie, as well as my father, Joffre and uncles Robin and Phil.

There are three men on the large mow, pitching sheaves to each other and then onto the thresher. There are a couple of men on top of the thresher; one is cutting the binder-twine on the wheat-sheaves with a sharp penknife, while the other one is feeding the sheaves into the hungry throat of the thresher, where the "drum" begins the process of tearing the grain away from the straw. The monstrous machine groans and moans rhythmically while swallowing each sheaf, as though its throat is parched.

The thresher is spitting out straw from its four huge tongues as if it doesn't like the taste. Two men are collecting the straw with their pitchforks and carrying it to where another man is starting to build a strawrick. One man is tending to the corn sacks where the grain pours out in a never-ending stream, making sure that none is spilt. Two others are carrying the full sacks of grain (which must weigh at least a hundredweight and a half) off to the loft in one of the farm buildings, where it will be kept dry and well aired. They have to carry the sacks up a steep wooden staircase to the loft.

Howard, Ron and I are fascinated. It's men's work alright: we boys can only watch and try not to get in the way. We wander around to all points of the action, observing the men—trying to help whenever we get a chance. The men are mostly tolerant of our curiosity, but are impatient to get on with their jobs.

Once things are moving well, the men are reluctant to stop, but they have been working since about eight o'clock, so shortly after ten, aunty Doreen and some of the other farmers' wives bring a couple of large cans of hot tea and some home cooking from the farmhouse. There are scones with fresh butter and jam, Welsh-cakes, fruitcake and apple pie. It is strangely quiet when the engine driver stops the thresher. The steam engine continues to huff and puff, as steam escapes.

The men exchange a few opinions and stories as they eat, gulping down the hot tea gratefully. Someone tells a yarn about an unfortunate farm-dog somewhere in Gower, which somehow got on top of the thresher and fell into the drum: it was chewed up into small pieces. We youngsters shiver, feeling glad we don't need to be anywhere near that part of the threshing-machine.

A shrill blast on the steam whistle signals the engine driver is ready to go again. Feeling refreshed, the men meander back to their positions and the driver engages the drive-wheel. Another hour-and-a-half of hard work and it's time for dinner. Some men walk home; some have brought sandwiches, some go into the farmhouse for a bite. There is plenty more tea for everyone. We youngsters usually go home for food, but for me Middleton Hall is almost the same as home.

By late afternoon, two corn-mows have almost disappeared and been replaced by a sizeable strawrick. We boys are thinking about doing something else for a change, so we wander off to other parts of the farm, get into an argument and fight among ourselves. Soon, we get bored and drift off to our homes—Ron to The Ship farm, Howard to Hampstead, me to 'the cottage'.

Tomorrow, we would follow the threshing-machine to the next farm and have the same fun all over again.

22

Post-war Hazards

How are the mighty fallen, and the weapons of war perished!

The Bible: 2 Samuel 1:27

EXCEPT when a fleeing German bomber disgorged its load of seventeen or eighteen bombs across the backbone of Rhossili Down, and when another German plane was shot down somewhere off Porteynon Bay, our village was far removed from the mayhem of the war. Even so, several hazardous situations occurred in the aftermath.

A year or so after the end of the war, my maternal grandparents, visiting from Gorseinon, took me to paddle at Rhossili Bay. I hadn't learnt to swim at the time, but the bay was very shallow and quite safe for children. There were quite a lot of people on the beach, though they were easily swallowed up by its vastness. As the tide went out, a strange object could be seen sitting on the wet sands. Several kids gathered around it in curiosity. One of the older kids said it was a mine. It was taller than I and had tapered horns about six inches long, sticking out in all directions.

The partly rusted mine had a few markings on it, but we couldn't tell whether it was German or British. We walked around it, poked at it and tugged at the horns to see if we could move it. We even tried to climb up on it; but mainly it was just an alien object to stand and gape at. Eventually, at the bidding of our elders, we left it alone. A few days later, I heard that the Coastguards had called in a disposal unit. They blew it up on the sands when no one was around.

By the end of the war, Britain had developed the first operational jet plane. This was the Vampire; a beautiful single-engine, twin-tailed fighter. The RAF frequently indulged in target practice over the Bristol Channel. 'The cottage' was one house that offered a grandstand view of the proceedings. It was exciting to watch the action on a clear, sunny day. A target drogue, which resembled an oversized wind-sock, was towed by an old RAF bomber or transport plane. The fighters would dive steeply past it. We could clearly hear the chatter of the machine guns, but because of the slow speed of sound, it always seemed as though they had fired their guns too late.

Sometimes, the planes fired live rockets—if only accidentally. A couple of years after the war, aunty Ceinwen was hanging out her washing on her clothes-line, which was located in the rough field adjacent to her house at Hoarstone, when a rocket slammed into the field about thirty yards from her. It gave her quite a shock. It had been a misfire by one of the fighter pilots. There was some kind of investigation, but I heard no more about it. After all, it was an accident and no harm had been done.

Another incident occurred in the early spring of 1955. Wandering down to Mewslade Bay, I found a strange-looking canister which had been washed into the bay by heavy tides. It was left trapped in a small pool. It was about ten inches in diameter, but only about fifteen inches long, with a pointed cone at one end. From the many wartime films we'd seen at the village hall, starring the likes of Kenneth Moore and Richard Todd, I thought it might be a depth charge or per-haps a shell for creating a smokescreen at sea. I pondered it on a couple of visits to Mewslade before I finally decided to phone the local policeman, PC Kirkham, who had succeeded Tom Mabbett at Porteynon. He said that no one else had reported it, as far as he knew. He asked me to meet him at the Lower Shop.

By the time he arrived and we walked back down to Mewslade Bay, the calm tide was almost in and the shell was concealed by shallow water. "'S'alright," I volunteered, "I know exactly where 'tis; I'll paddle in an' carry it out." I knew the water in Mewslade was very clear, so removing my shoes and socks, and rolling up the legs of my jeans, I waded in to find the shell in knee-deep water. Carefully lifting it, I cradled it in my arms and slowly walked out, watching not to stumble over submerged stones.

PC Kirkham seemed quite puzzled by the shell, but he thought that we should put it somewhere safe, and he would report it to the proper authorities. We hid it on the Thurba side of the dry-stone wall, near the stile. I heard no more about it, until I saw the policeman's son, Peter, on the school-bus. His Dad had told him I had been very brave.

Those war films certainly taught us how to deal with tricky situations.

23

Brinsel Wood to Windy Walls

I know not why I am so sad; I cannot get out of my head a fairy-tale of olden times.

Heinrich Heine

UNCLE Phil married Evelyn Williams in the February, 1942, and brought her to live at the family farm. Middleton Hall was becoming quite overcrowded by then, especially when either aunty Peggy's husband, Wilfred Pugh, or uncle Oliver, were home on leave from the army. Fortunately, my parents and I were able to move up to 'the cottage' a few months later. In December of the same year, my cousin Clive became the newest addition to the Jones family at Middleton Hall, though he was born at a maternity hospital in Neath.

Before the end of the following year, with Clive's sister, Mary, already on the way, Phil and Evelyn obtained the tenancy of their own home. It was a quaint, slate-roofed cottage, set in a small, natural woodland known as Brinsel Wood. The isolated cottage was located closer to Horton than to Scurlage. Brinsel could be reached either from the narrow paved road between Horton and Oxwich, or from Scurlage via Berry Lane, then by a cart-track across the fields.

Even so, Phil continued working for farmer George (Dodi) Thomas at Rhossili. He usually travelled to work by catching the early bus. He was well-versed in working with horses; in his prime, he was about as strong as a horse. Once, I travelled with him by horse and cart, taking the shortcut through Margam Lane. Standing on the seat of the cart, I was tall enough to pick apples from the overhanging branches of a tree belonging to a house halfway along the lane. (I wasn't aware that the house had been the birthplace of my maternal grandmother, Sarah Jane Powell (nee Richards)).

I stayed at Brinsel cottage for a few days when I was about six. It was quite like a fairytale setting, inviting the imagination to run riot. Surrounded by natural woodland, it had bluebells, toadstool rings, rabbits, field-mice, moles, weasels, stoats, foxes—all the ingredients to spark childhood curiosity and imagination. Fortunately, the cottage did not have the reputation of being haunted. With my younger cousins, I explored much of the wood, mainly trying to sneak up on rabbits, but the family's sheepdog usually gave the game away. At night, while falling asleep under the steeply-sloping roof of the cottage, we could hear the hoots of owls and the occasional barking of foxes.

Uncle Phil kept a couple of pigs and a number of chickens, as was customary for farm-workers at that time. The chickens had to be guarded carefully from foxes, which were quite partial to poultry as a change from their regular diet of young rabbits and field-mice. There were game-birds, such as pheasants, which were raised and released by the Penrice Estate, but they were well-protected from would-be poachers by several hired gamekeepers: two of the well-known ones were Mr. Woodward and Mr. Gibson.

Nearby were a couple of chestnut trees, the fruit of which served as a late-evening snack when roasted in the embers in front of the fire grate. The garden area included a few apple trees. Blackberries grew in abundance in nearby hedges in late summer. They made a change from rhubarb, gooseberries and apples as pie-fillings.

Clive and Mary loved their lonely cottage, where they had a wonderful, natural playground. Whenever there was a snowfall, it was stunningly beautiful. They could follow the tracks of birds and wild creatures in the snow. However, the time came when Clive had to start school. Aunty Evelyn would take him to Rhossili School every day on the half-past eight bus, returning to fetch him each afternoon. This was time-consuming and expensive, so by the time Mary was ready to start school, the family took the opportunity to rent Windy Walls, a private house located on the brow of Rhossili Down, directly above the school.

Windy Walls was a relatively modern house compared to the other cottages strewn along School Lane. It was a stoutly built, slate-roofed house with brick walls. It had high ceilings and large rooms, but there was no plumbing or electricity and it had to be heated by a coal-burning stove. Clive and Mary now had a large, gorse-covered hillside to play on, instead of their magical woods. It must have taken a lot of adjustment for them, but children didn't complain very much in those days. They also had to contend with the arrival of a baby brother, Royston. Sadly though, Roy was stricken with meningitis in infancy, leaving him impaired for the rest of his life. He was never able to attend school.

When the family moved to Windy Walls, they became our nearest neighbours. There was a pathway across the hill from 'the cottage', so I was able to be on hand to help with unloading their possessions. They had hired a flat-bed lorry from one of the farmers or haulage contractors. As the last of their furniture was unloaded, a field-mouse scurried along the boards of the lorry. Naturally, I gave chase. Just as it was disappearing through a gap between two boards, I grabbed its tail and hauled it up. The tiny creature quickly twisted around and bit my finger, so I promptly dropped it. It made its escape to a new home on the hillside.

The move was a good one for Phil and his family, in many respects. Now, they had much better access to daily grocery shopping and to George Thomas's farm, where Phil was employed for most of his working life. Phil and Evelyn always maintained a close association with St. Mary's church, where Phil served as a warden for many years. He was a long-time, enthusiastic member of the "rocket crew"; and performed wartime lookout duties at Thurba Head.

Several years later, in the early 1950s, Phil and Evelyn had the opportunity to move down to one of the ten-year-old agricultural workers' cottages when the original tenant, Sid James, moved away from the village. They became next-door neighbours of Ron and Gwyneth Densley. It would be Clive's home for more than half a century.

The new location halved the walking distance to the village shops, so it was easier to carry their groceries home. The whole family was also able to benefit from the modern amenities of electricity and indoor plumbing. Above all, they now had independence from private landlords and "tied" cottages.

Even so, I suspected it wasn't only the children who missed the magical setting of Brinsel Wood.

24

Working Men's Independence

The house of everyone is to him as his castle and fortress.

Sir Edward Coke

THE War Agricultural Committee was responsible for the development of the first independent houses for farm-workers about 1944. They were well built, semidetached brick houses. There was one pair each at Middleton, Overton and Reynoldston. It was not until 1949 that the Gower RDC, acting on the policies of the post-war Labour government, built eight prefabricated, two-storey, semidetached Council-houses at Scurlage. These were followed, in the early 1950s, by a second phase—several pairs of brick homes at Scurlage and one pair at Burry Green.

These were important steps in providing modern housing for workers and their families, and also in providing alternatives to "tied" cottages and farm-houses, which could sometimes seem like a form of enslavement. There was potential for tremendous, perhaps unbearable, psychological pressure on a working man and his family. It would be bad enough to be out of work, but to face being put out of one's home at the same time must have been quite terrifying. The first tenants of the workers' houses in Middleton were Ron Densley and Sid James. Both had come to Gower, seeking agricultural employment, in the 1930s.

Aunty Margaret (better known as Peggy) met her husband, Wilfred Pugh, before the start of the war, when he was working on one of the local farms. He, along with his brother, Cuthbert, had come to Gower from Radnor in 1936, having been hired at the annual Brecon Agricultural Fair. Wilfred's first job was at Kennexstone farm. Even so, when war broke out he was called up for National Service and joined an artillery regiment—the Royal Regiment of Wales.

Peggy and Wilfred were married in 1940, but while Wilfred was in the army, Peggy continued to live at Middleton Hall. Their first child, Patricia, was born in 1942 at 'the cottage', probably because ailing sixty-five-year-old Granny Jones was the only other woman at Middleton Hall. All of Peggy's four sisters had migrated to England; the last one, Gladys, only a few months previously. Their first son, Alan, was born in 1945. It must have been a great relief to Peggy when the war finally ended and Wilfred was demobbed.

For a few years, they lived at Corner House, the farmhouse at the bottom of Pitton Cross hill, where Wilfred worked for farmer Bevan Tucker. It was very much a "tied" situation. In 1949, however, the Pugh family became the first occupants of the new prefabricated Council-houses at Scurlage. By that time, Wilfred and Peggy already had four young children—Pat, Alan, Janet and Ken. At Scurlage, there would be two more additions to their family—Jennifer and Chris. The four oldest children continued to attend Rhossili School until 1954, before moving on to Nelson. From the time they moved to Scurlage, though, Wilfred was free to change his job without having to move house; moreover, modern plumbing was a distinct luxury in southwest Gower.

Aunty Peggy was one of those people who always seemed cheerful. Uncle Wilfred was a fine-boned quiet man with a ready smile for a visitor. I could always count on a warm welcome from both of them. Shortly after they moved into their brand new home, where they had a modern kitchen, a bathroom and an endless supply of hot water, Peggy urged me to come and enjoy a hot bath. I was ten years old when I first experienced this luxury. At 'the cottage' we would not enjoy electric light, let alone a modern bathroom, for several more years. Therefore, I caught the bus to Scurlage on several occasions, just to enjoy a foretaste of modern conveniences. These visits also served to keep me in touch with my aunty, uncle and cousins.

When uncle Oliver was demobbed at the end of the war, he came home to live and work at the family farm at Middleton Hall. In his time with the British army, he had been evacuated from Dunkirk. Later in the war, he was wounded in Greece. He was an easygoing, handsome man with wavy blond hair and clear blue eyes. He always had some amusing yarn to spin and he loved kids. Around the age of six or seven, I often accompanied him to the fields by horse and cart.

Sometimes when I knew we were headed for one of the fields in the lower Vile, I wondered why he preferred to take the main road (Rhossili Lane) instead of just going directly down the Vile Lane, from 'the bank'. Then, he would pull up the horse and cart (with a "Whoa!") outside the gates of Broad Park, which was the largest guesthouse in the village.

After a couple of minutes, a dark-haired, brown-eyed young woman with a happy smile on her face, would hurry down the driveway. Oliver would hand the reins to me, before climbing down from the cart. The two of them would engage in intense conversation for several minutes, probably arranging to meet after they had both finished work. In the meantime, I would be trying to show old Blossom who was boss, as she decided to help herself to a snack from the tufts of grass along the edge of the road, taking me and the cart wherever she wanted.

After what seemed like a very long five minutes, the young couple would steal a quick kiss and wave goodbye. Looking a little flushed, Oliver would climb back on the cart. With another wave and a cluck of his tongue at Blossom, we'd be on our way again. The vivacious young woman was Kathleen Grove, who would soon become my aunty. Of course, this boy-girl stuff seemed a terrible waste of time to me.

It was when the second phase of the Council-houses was completed, that Oliver and Kathleen also moved to a new Council-house at Scurlage. By then, they already had two small children, Lyndon and Delyth. Before that, they lived with Kathleen's parents, George Grove (a First World War veteran) and his wife Nell, at Pitton Mill.

Other Rhossili families to be housed in the new Council-houses—which became their permanent homes—were those of farm-workers Jim Price, Cuthbert Pugh and Bert Proctor. The modern Council-houses were not restricted to farm-workers' families—tenants were employed in a variety of occupations, such as working on the buses or in the building trades.

To some, there was a stigma attached to living in this working-class housing development, which was referred to as "the Council-houses", but a good community was forged over the years. Scurlage was a particularly convenient location for bus services, as well as recreational facilities, even though it lacked its own church and village hall. A journey into Swansea was shorter and more direct (in comparison with Rhossili, Horton or Porteynon). The South Gower football, cricket and tennis facilities were convenient for sports-minded youngsters.

[Endnote: In addition to the South Gower sports facilities, Scurlage eventually gained a modern public-house (appropriately named The Countryman); plus a seasonal holiday camp and a couple of small shops. Today, it has more to offer its residents than most of the long-established villages in southwest Gower.]

25

Fetching Firewood from Fall

No man is born into the world, whose work is not born with him ...

James Russell Lowell

THE firewood supply for the village school, as well as 'the cottage', has become depleted. By Sunday, there is an urgent need for replenishment. After breakfast (which is about 9:00 AM on Sundays), my father, Joff, is preparing for the long walk to Fall Bay. There has been stormy weather for most of the past week, so driftwood should be plentiful; but it will be important to select from those pieces which have been thrown well up on the rocks by the powerful waves—they will have had more chance to dry out. Water-logged wood can be two or three times its dry weight.

Joff asks me if I want to go along. You can be sure I do. With his long working hours, I get little chance to spend time with my father. Even so, on the long walk to Fall, there will be more silence than conversation. My father is usually preoccupied with his thoughts. Unfortunately, he expects me to somehow know all the things which I really need him to be telling me—and I don't know all the questions I should be asking him.

The last of the March gales has abated. It is a mild but breezy day, with the sun not quite breaking through the heavy layer of grey/white cumulus clouds. My energy seems to increase, as we walk. We cross the main road at 'the bank', passing under the branches of the giant elm tree that is a Middleton landmark. At The Ship farm, my friend Ron asks whether I want to explore around the rickyard and sheds: I stop briefly to explain that I have to help my father this morning. Then, I run to catch up with him as he marches off down the Vile Lane.

We don't expect to meet anyone in the Vile on a Sunday morning and we aren't disappointed. Lewis Castle is just about in sight when Joff points out a dead badger lying beside the cart-tracks that run along the side of one of Wilfred Beynon's fields. It is not clear what has caused the badger's demise, but it is quite large and the only one I would ever see in the Vile, though their scrapes were sometimes seen along the cliff-top areas. My father tells me that men who hunt badgers are advised to use cane shin-pads, as a badger will only release its bite when it thinks it feels a bone snap.

We climb carefully down the decaying wooden ladder leaning against the retaining wall of Jack Richards's field. It has some missing rungs; it probably won't last too much longer. Halfway down the steep, grassy slope, we examine a fine example of a lime-kiln. Joff mentions the need for lime for fields, as well as houses. I can't quite grasp the amount of time and effort (let alone the process required) to extract the lime.

Arriving at the breezy, foam-flecked rim of the bay, we survey the sullen, restless sea. The waves are still powerful, pounding on the rocks at the foot of Lewis Castle, but the tide is only halfway in. Good, plenty of time to find driftwood! We scramble over and around the light-grey boulders, avoiding salty rock pools, collecting more wood than we can carry. The debris strewn over the rocks includes a broken hatch cover, pieces of a barrel, a short length of hawser, battered cork floats, even husks of coconuts, while a couple of leafless tree branches lie on the sand. A huge log drifts back and forth amongst a mass of seaweed, in the surf.

We select the driest, straightest pieces of wood we can find to carry on our shoulders, bearing in mind the long uphill march to 'the cottage'. My father puts together a bundle for me: I tell him I can manage another couple of pieces. He helps me to set the bundle on my left shoulder; then he picks up his own assortment of larger timbers, planks and a thick piece of tree branch.

First we struggle up the short, but difficult path from the beach. I have to drop two or three of my pieces of wood, but I go back for them. Next, there is a tough plod up the steep grassy slope to the short wooden ladder, placed to help surmount the limestone wall into Jack Richards's small field, where the helms of the early potato crop are already sprouting through the fertile soil. I climb the ladder precariously, one hand controlling my bundle, the other reaching for the rungs.

After that, walking through the gently sloping terrain of the Vile is quite pleasant, except for the increasing discomfort of timber pressing on my bony shoulder. From previous trips, I know how to duck my head to allow the bundle to swing over to my other shoulder, without putting it down.

Halfway back to Middleton, my father suggests a short rest. The badger is still there, white teeth showing in a permanent snarl. We put down our bundles, so we can rearrange them. Loading up again, I make sure that my shoulder is in contact with a smooth, rounded branch. Now I'm confident I can make it all the way home.

We pause briefly to exchange a few pleasantries with "Little Johnny" Beynon, outside his whitewashed cottage, known as High Priest. He and his wife, Margaret Anne, have just returned from church and they have picked up their Sunday newspapers at The Green, on their way home. My father will need to fetch his—the *People* and the *Sunday Express*—after he has had his Sunday dinner. One of the papers is running a weekly serial, *Forever Amber* (an historical romance), which my mother and most of the other women in the village, are following closely.

Although I feel weary, I have a sense of achievement as we finally reach 'the cottage'. We stack the wood in the shed. There is enough to last at least three weeks. Without my help, there would be only enough for a fortnight. Though he will still need to do a lot of wood-chopping with his axe and billhook, Joff is pleased with me today. I seem to have inherited some of his physical toughness and stamina.

We have worked up a good appetite for our Sunday dinner. We go into the house to find my mother rushing around in a pinafore and sandals. She has just finished roasting a freshly-shot rabbit in the oven of our newly-acquired Rayburn stove. Though it's still just a coal-fire, it's a lot cleaner and much better for cooking than the old open grate. There are also boiled potatoes and swede, mashed up together with milk and butter, and boiled Savoy cabbage. "You must be hungry, Cyril", Mam says.

I ask for the rabbit's kidneys. They will be my reward.

26

The Bays

I must go down to the seas again,
to the lonely sea and the sky.

John Masefield

OUR parish was blessed with three remarkable bays, each with its own golden sand beach, but with quite different characteristics. All three beaches were about equally accessible (or perhaps, equally difficult to access) from Middleton.

Rhossili Bay was always the most popular with day-trippers, because it was the easiest to find and there were good parking facilities. However, the southwest aspect and vast expanse of the bay exposed it to the prevailing winds, so there was no shelter from the elements. On most days, it was decidedly draughty on the cliff-tops, but the views of the bay, the hill and Worms Head, were magnificent.

People (mostly visitors) picnicked on the drier areas of the vast expanse of flat sands, which varied from a firm surface in some parts of the beach to soft, sinking sand in others. On occasion, in the mid-1940s, hockey matches were arranged where local enthusiasts like Reggie, Len and Ernie Beynon; Eric Gibbs; Margaret Bevan; Ann Harding; Edward, Betty and Dora Roberts; Josephine Richards; and Belinda Beynon played challenge matches against visiting teams, including students from Swansea U.C.

Rhossili Bay was always safe for bathers. It was almost entirely flat and predictable, at least as far as Hillend. As we grew up, we local youngsters valued the beach more for dragnet fishing than anything else. Sometimes our wanderings would take us to "the warren" or the fields known as Parsonage, near the Old Rectory, then down onto the sands to examine the *Helvetia* wreck. Sometimes we'd jog as far as the mysterious Burry Holms; then, as we returned towards the two-hundred-foot high cliffs at the Rhossili End, we would exploit the echo, shouting each other's names or mild obscenities.

When we did join the day-trippers for some bathing, we felt quite insignificant, lost in the crowd of strangers which was in turn swallowed up by the vastness of the bay. The long, often chilly, walk to the water was followed by difficulty in doing much more than paddling, especially on calm days. It could take ages to struggle out to where the water was chest deep. Even when there was surf, the waves had little power.

Fall Bay was an entirely different proposition. The magnificent sandy cove, sheltered by the majestic Lewis Castle on the east and Tears Point on the west, had a unique character. Although it was not favoured by our parents for family picnics because of the very steep and hazardous access, it offered all manner of attractions to the beach enthusiast.

There was a hard (though sloping) surface on which to play games when the tide was out. In contrast to the other bays, there were often powerful waves for bodysurfing as the tide flowed in. There was golden, powdery sand above the high water mark where the youthful could indulge in horseplay, while older people could relax, sunbathe or take a nap. There was shelter from sudden showers in the lee of the rock outcrops, in Mary's Hole or in the small caves.

To my mind, the originators of the Fall Bay "gang" were Dudley Thomas and his cousin, Colin Davies. Dudley's parents, Glynn and Mollie, leased the loft of Wilfred Beynon's barn at Sheep Green, so they could drive from Swansea to spend almost every summer weekend, as well as their annual holidays, in Middleton.

They usually walked down to Fall Bay around one o'clock on summer weekends and holidays. They often saw me hanging around 'the bank', while most of the other kids had disappeared into their homes for dinner. Eventually, they asked if I would like to go to the bay with them. You bet I would! I already had swimming trunks because my mother and her neighbours would sometimes take us kids down to Mewslade to paddle and picnic. That was fun, but what Fall Bay had to offer was ten times better.

Local siblings Edward, Dora and Betty Roberts, were also founding members of the "gang". Other locals or visitors were always welcome. In particular, there was the Thomas family's good friend, Horace Lamb and his equally good-natured wife, Shirley, who were regular visitors from Worcester. Then there was the multi-talented Ron Harris, a gifted humorist and athlete, who loved body-surfing and beach games, such as volleyball or quoits.

Ron was also a talented ballroom dancer and tap dancer. Well-known for his guest performances on BBC radio in various comedy programs, Ron eventually did a few silent skits on BBC Wales TV. (Indeed, he was exploring the type of humour that would become hugely popular many years later with Rowan Atkinson's "Mr. Bean".)

Ron was usually accompanied by his quiet, flame-haired wife and their vivacious daughter, Noir. One of his favourite pastimes—when he had tired of practising his gymnastics, which included walking across the beach on his hands—was to form a torso out of sand so that he could demonstrate simulated surgical procedures, with vital body organs represented by stones, seaweed and small pieces of driftwood. He would prepare the "patient" beforehand; then invite an audience to observe the delicate operation.

Eventually, Dudley's fiancé, June Lloyd, Edward's fiancé, Josie Pariser, and Margaret Bevan (when she came home to visit her parents) ensured that the fun and games on the beach never became dull. Another occasional visitor was art teacher, Haydn Jenkins, whose parents had purchased a retirement cottage at Fernhill Top. Sometimes when the boisterous Dudley would issue the challenge: "Anyone coming for a dip?" there would be as many as a dozen of us joining him in the waves. When the tide was out, a group of us might set off to explore the caves between Fall and Mewslade.

From the age of seven, I was privileged to join the "gang" on many a summer afternoon. We bodysurfed, canoed, did a little mackerel fishing, explored caves and played a variety of games on the beach. There was volleyball or quoits (similar to volleyball, but using a rubber quoit); sometimes we played a little football, but more often we played beach cricket, inspired by radio broadcasts of the test exploits of Compton, Hutton, Bedser, Lock, Laker, Bailey and others. News of the latest test cricket scores was eagerly sought from anyone (even strangers) who had just arrived at the bay. Portable radios were not available until the late 1950s.

While most local kids didn't share my fanaticism for the sea, Colin Dye, who was a regular summer visitor to his grandparents, at High Priest, was always ready for an afternoon at the bay. Locals Howard Chalk, Brian (Butch) Beynon, Mary Bevan, Clive Jones and Peter Greening (from Killay) could be persuaded to come along for a dip when the weather was warm enough. Howard had learnt to become a very good swimmer at his boarding school. But none were as desperate as I, to get into the surf.

Those summer weekends hold treasured memories. I experienced Fall Bay in all its moods. I learnt to swim (after almost drowning a couple of times) by observing the experts who were about a decade older than I. Then I learnt how to bodysurf, too. It's something you never forget (like riding a bike) once you've mastered it. Timing was all-important.

Once in a while there would be a surfing expedition to Rhossili Bay, but the waves did not have the same power on the open, flat beach: it was essential to use one of the rigid wooden surf-boards with a curved-up front, which was far too awkward for a youngster. Fortunately, Fall was the home base of our "gang". Over the years, I learnt valuable lessons in dealing with strong currents, powerful waves, undertow and backwash.

Of course, there were many laughs and quite a bit of horseplay. There were unexpected dousings with buckets of seawater, as well as some unintentional misfortunes. One warm afternoon, Dudley, Horace Lamb and I were returning to the beach from an unfruitful mackerel-fishing expedition in *The Feather*. Horace was concerned about carrying his pipe and tobacco ashore from where we dropped anchor. No problem: I took his tobacco pouch in one hand, dived in and swam ashore. I had assumed the plastic pouch was waterproof; while he had assumed I would be able hold it above the water.

Mewslade Bay was preferred by most locals, especially those who lived in Pitton. Overall, it had the easiest access, though it was still a long, tiring plod home up the spectacular Mewslade valley, at the end of the afternoon. Sometimes our parents, grandparents or other relatives would take us kids to Mewslade for a summer afternoon of paddling and picnicking. They would dress us (kids) in swimsuits, but they would just pull up their skirts or trouser-legs and paddle. None of my parents' generation could swim, except for my uncle, Jack Powell, who had served in the Navy—and he always brought an inner-tube to float on.

On these occasions, a variety of sandwiches, perhaps some combination of tomato, lettuce and cheese, was washed down with a cup of pop. This would usually be followed by some biscuits or a slice of fruitcake and another cup of pop. There was usually an orange or apple for a snack when we got hungry from building sandcastles. By the time we headed for home for our tea, our parents would be thirsting for a cup of their favourite hot brew.

In a very real sense, I grew up in the bays, always finding them more fascinating than the farmyards or fields. I never ceased to be awed by the majesty of the limestone cliffs, stretching from the Coastguard houses around to Tears Point and on to Thurba Head. Add to this, the golden expanses of sand; the caves; the grassy cliff-tops; the flora and fauna; and the ever-changing sea.

Where else in the world?

27

Body of Knowledge

I must go down to the seas again, for the call of the running tide
Is a wild call and a clear call that may not be denied.

John Masefield

SOMETIMES people answer the questions "What do you do?" or "What are you?" by stating their most passionate hobby or sport, rather than the job they are earning a living at. Many work to earn money so they can spend their leisure time doing what they love most. There are weekend sailors, hang-gliders, mountaineers, cavers, etc. In my case, the many afternoons I spent at Fall Bay resulted in a lifelong passion for bodysurfing.

I discovered that bodysurfing was just a way of enjoying the surf in the most relaxed and intimate manner. Being completely immersed most of the time (with zero visibility) requires a certain level of trust and nerve. For me, it was an ultimate form of relaxation which happened to include the important benefit of aerobic exercise, and development of the ability to survive in rough seas and ocean currents.

At its best, Fall Bay was close to being a perfect beach for bodysurfing: the important ingredients necessary to achieve ideal conditions were a flowing tide; a horseshoe cove; a sloping, sandy beach; and an on-shore wind. Those factors affected the wave height, strength and run.

When the surf was strong, Edward Roberts, Dudley Thomas and Ron Harris would compete enthusiastically to see who could get the longest run out of a wave. A good wave would leave them high and dry on the sand (face down, arms outstretched) before they would open their eyes or take a breath. There was sometimes only a finger's length in it and they would accuse each other of cheating. I would observe one or other of them give a push off the sand with a toe or knee to gain an extra inch or two. It was all just boisterous good fun. I imitated them and learnt well.

I saw that there were two effective techniques for catching a wave. Standing in water up to waist height, as the wave approached, a "jack-knife start" could be used. This involved a vertical launch, as if on a springboard, followed by jack-knifing the upper body into a horizontal position with arms outstretched. Then, as the wave broke, the lower body had to become horizontal, also. Then, it was necessary to flutter-kick as hard as possible, so as to catch the wave's momentum and dive down the face of the wave.

The "crawl start" had to be used in deeper water. As the wave approached, one needed to begin swimming towards shore, using a fast crawl stroke to keep pace with the wave. If the timing was right, I found that a wave would propel me forward so strongly that I became airborne, albeit briefly, as the wave broke.

Sooner or later, a wave would leave the bodysurfer floundering in its wake. Until then, an exciting roar would resound in the submerged surfer's ears. If the beach was gravelly, the roar was much louder. The overall objective of a bodysurfer was to stay with the tongue of the wave until the latest possible moment. I learnt, from watching Ron Harris, that the anticlimactic moment could be delayed somewhat by using a double-footed dolphin kick. I suspected that was how he won most of the impromptu surfing contests.

Even returning from the beach to look for another strong wave was exciting. As an option to repeatedly diving underneath oncoming surf, I could float on my back, either feet-first or headfirst, towards oncoming waves. I found that floating feet-first into a good-sized wave that was about to break could result in a back-somersault which left me standing on my feet (facing seaward) after the wave had passed. Floating headfirst was a little more uncertain: a powerful wave that had already broken would try to bury me in the sand; one that was just breaking would turn me over, head down, into a forward somersault.

Wave height is one of the critical variables for bodysurfing. I found that a wave needed to be a minimum of about three feet from trough to peak; anything smaller would not have much power. Waves between four and six feet high gave the best performance. Above six feet, the waves tended to become unmanageable for a bodysurfer, depending on the steepness of the face of the wave.

When the waves were not too strong, my surfing mentors would sometimes try out some new-fangled thin, laminated-wood surfboards, which were curved up at the front end, like a snow-sleigh. I soon found that it was impossible for a little person to use these boards effectively because the lower half of the body needed to be free to kick and steer. I instinctively disliked them and was pleased to note that my elders needed to try them out at Rhossili Bay (where the waves were weaker) to see if they provided any advantage. (Nevertheless, they were the precursor of the boogie-board.)

Of course, there were hazards in enjoying all that the surf had to offer, but I learnt how to deal with them. For example, when facing a large, breaking wave, there were two options: I could either stand in front of the wave (letting it bowl me over) or dive hard towards the base so as to pass underneath it. If there was hesitation in the latter option, a strong wave might pick me up and turn me over with it, which could leave me worse off than if I just stood there.

Sometimes a strong wave, which I had mistimed or tried to duck under, would press me down onto the sand and keep me there for a few seconds (though it seemed longer). This, I discovered, was a time to relax and enjoy being under the water until the wave had left me behind, when it was easy to bob up to the surface.

On a few occasions, in chest-deep water, I experienced undertow which was too strong for me to handle. It was only by trial and error that I learnt that it was best not to fight it. I learnt to allow it to carry me out; sometimes I had to wait patiently to catch a ride in on a "seventh wave", but it was never too long. In the worst case, if the current had ever carried me off towards Mewslade, I reasoned that the best course of action would be to swim with it, until I could escape (by swimming diagonally) into Mewslade Bay. Fortunately, this circumstance never occurred, as it would have been a long, chilly walk back to Fall, clad only in my swimming-trunks. Also, hypothermia could have become a problem if I'd had to remain in the water for more than about forty-five minutes.

I also learnt that waves move on the surface of the water, while the water itself merely moves vertically (up and down); hence a wave could not push me along, until it had broken. If I got myself trapped between a breaking wave and the rocks, the best chance of avoiding injury was to dive below the surface.

I learnt that heavy surf, even if breaking onto pure sand, could present serious dangers. For example, if the beach was steep and the waves were high, resulting in a strong backwash, the wave may be breaking into only a foot or so of water. In such situations, there was potential for being "spiked" against the sandy bottom, resulting in a neck or shoulder injury.

Undetected objects were another physical threat. There were sometimes size-able pieces of wood being transported by the tide; also, people's legs or unex-pected rocks could be problematic. It made good sense to surf with both arms extended, as in a dive. I learnt to surf with one outstretched hand down to defend against rocks; and the other one up to detect fellow bathers or floating debris.

To survive in a strong current or rip-tide, I reasoned that it would be best to swim diagonally across the flow, so as not to oppose it. My father sometimes spoke of dreadful whirlpools. Although I never experienced this particular phenomenon, I determined that the best survival technique must be to dive downwards into the whirlpool and swim out the side for at least twenty yards, before returning to the surface.

In general, I realised that the best defences against the various hazards of the sea were to dive below the surface or swim with the current, both of which were contrary to most people's natural instincts. The healthy respect I developed for the sea equipped me to read the conditions when visiting unfamiliar beaches. In particular, I would observe the mood of the tide, the direction and strength of the wind, the location rocks and other obstacles, the backwash and the behaviour of the locals.

While I enjoyed a number of sporting activities, bodysurfing would become the most fulfilling and lasting, as a lifelong passion. I learnt to enjoy many things to do with the sea, from fishing to snorkelling to sailing, but bodysurfing stands out—perhaps because it satisfied my particular psychological needs for physical challenge, independence and a moderate amount of risk.

[Endnote: I have heard tennis-great, John McEnroe, speak of his passion for bodysurfing. He mentioned a sandy, horseshoe cove at the Mexican resort of Ixtapa as being one of his favourite destinations. My favourite is Puerto Cruz beach on the northwest shore of Margarita Island, off the coast of Venezuela.]

28

Hunting and Shooting

There is a passion for hunting something,
deeply implanted in the human breast.

Charles Dickens

IN the 1940s our Sunday dinner was a roasted rabbit, as often as not. Almost every farmer owned a shotgun, but others would feel free to hunt on almost any farmlands, at dawn or at dusk. Rabbits were such a constant pest that farmers welcomed any help in reducing their numbers.

Some of the young men, like Ernie Beynon and Jim Morse (a farm manager in training at Jessamine farm) loved to hunt rabbits on Sunday mornings. Sometimes they would sell one for sixpence, which was little more than the price of a 12-bore cartridge, if it had quite a lot of lead pellets in it. My father, who could not afford a shotgun or the time for hunting, was often able to buy a rabbit on his way to pick up the Sunday newspapers at The Green. If he bought two, we could look forward to rabbit stew for one of our evening meals, in midweek.

Of course, it was my mother who did most of the work involved in gutting, skinning and roasting the rabbits. Often my father would help remove the skin, which could be stubborn. Then, shotgun pellets might need to be dug out of the flesh with a sharp knife.

Until 1953, when the deadly disease of myxomatosis struck, rabbits devoured such crops as cabbages and carrots. "The warren"—the sandy, rabbit-infested area above Rhossili Bay, along the cart-track to the fields at Parsonage—was so over-run that such crops couldn't be contemplated in the adjacent fields. The farmer, Wilfred Beynon, would grow mostly potatoes or corn. On the positive side, rabbits were a plentiful source of meat until the myxomatosis epidemic, which all but wiped them out. After that, people seemed to suffer a permanent loss of appetite for rabbits, whether plentiful or not.

My fascination with hunting was signalled by the time I was eight when I was allowed to play with "uncle Tom" Williams's folding 4-10 poacher's gun and a real hunting knife. Soon, I was prowling the fields between Fernhill Top and Talgarths Well, doing imaginary battle with arctic wolves or any other wild animals which dared to invade my imagination. On one of these expeditions, I was accompanied by Tom's eldest daughter, Sylvia, who was about a year younger than I. She was my "Maid Marion" and I did all I could to impress her with my prowess at tracking and stalking wild animals.

Perhaps it was fortunate that Alf Bevan's cows had been moved to safer pastures. After failing to find wolves or black bears in the small fields behind Professor Lee's bungalow at Talgarths Well, we ended up at Bunkers Hill, just below Hoarstone. Sylvia was carrying the knife, safe in its goatskin sheath.

When we saw old Mr. Bennett emerging from his bungalow, I slipped the folded gun into some ferns growing at the side of the lane, so he wouldn't see it. He didn't seem to notice my guilty demeanour. After he had gone, I decided we should visit aunty Ceinwen at Hoarstone, where I was always certain of a warm welcome.

It was the middle of the afternoon, so aunty Ceinwen was all alone. She invited us in for a glass of water. As we sat opposite her near the fireplace, Sylvia still cradling the hunting knife, I calmly announced that I had real bullets for the gun. Poor aunty Ceinwen suddenly looked slightly pale, but she was able to compose herself almost as quickly, as she was quite familiar with my fertile imagination.

As a ten-year-old, I began to experiment with trapping rabbits with wire snares. My snares, mostly placed in uncle Len's fields around the Chapel, presented little problem to the rabbits. The hedges were pockmarked with old and new burrows. I learnt to carefully place a wire loop, supported by a small, cleft stick, directly in the "run" outside a burrow, then anchor the tail of the loop to a strong wooden peg, hammered into the ground.

However, the rabbits always seemed to use their other entrances to come and go, or they knocked over the wire loops, or they pulled my pegs out of the ground. Often I wouldn't get around to checking my wires for several days, particularly if the weather was bad; or I would forget where some of them were.

At The Ship farm, Ernie Beynon kept a hutch with three or four restless, healthy-looking ferrets. With his younger brother, Ron, I was sometimes able to tag along on a ferreting expedition to "the warren". Selecting one of the ferrets, Ernie would sew a couple of stitches in its lips and release it into one of the numerous rabbit-holes, after first placing nets over as many bolt-holes as possible.

Then, he'd stand ready with a shotgun. Although this method could produce a few rabbits at any time of day, I soon learnt that if anything went wrong—especially if the thread in the ferret's lips came undone, there could be a lot of shovelling to retrieve it. The sandy soil helped make this unwelcome work easier.

Being far too young to use a 12-bore shotgun, I was delighted when rare opportunities arose to accompany uncle Oliver on a hunting trip. Oliver had been evacuated from Dunkirk then he had served in Greece, where he had been wounded. He was a good shot. On one occasion, we walked down through the Vile on a Saturday afternoon—not the best time to see many rabbits. Perhaps he was hoping to get a shot at a game-bird, though they were scarce in the Vile. On the way home, perhaps in frustration, he decided to test his aim on a flock of seagulls, which were themselves hunting for worms on some freshly ploughed ground. The seagulls were not a protected species then. One shot killed five seagulls outright: a sixth had to be put out of its misery.

On another occasion, a couple of years later, I was invited to stay overnight at Oliver's Council-house in Scurlage. He woke me at 6:00 AM on a Sunday morning to go after rabbits in some of the fields adjacent to Berry Lane. We dressed quietly, speaking in whispers so as not to disturb aunty Kathleen and my little cousins, Lyndon and Delyth. It was a dull, drizzly morning. As the mist gradually lifted, we sneaked up to hedges and stiles and peeked over. This time, although the rabbits were not as plentiful as we hoped, he was able to bag a couple. As we walked home for breakfast, I felt I was already a seasoned hunter.

At the age of fourteen, I saved about eleven pounds to buy a new air-rifle from Atkinson's Sports, in Oxford Street, Swansea. It was quite powerful, very accurate at thirty yards and could tickle cows at about a hundred yards. It was my pride and joy for a few years. My pal, Alan Button, also had an air-rifle, so on Saturday mornings or school holidays, we'd take a stroll through some of the fields or rough-lands for a spot of target practice; just small birds or inanimate objects.

I still had access to "uncle Tom's" 4-10 shotgun but I was almost fifteen before I bought a box of cartridges from Atkinson's Sports shop, in Swansea. I arrived home from town, hardly able to wait for the next day to test my prowess.

In testing my gun on inanimate targets, however, I soon found that its range (with any degree of accuracy) was woeful. If I hit anything with this gun, it would have to be from a distance of about ten yards.

One cool, grey November afternoon, I searched some fields around Kings Hall farm. Nothing stirred; there was no sign of any kind of game. I was beginning to think of going home when, with a sudden flurry of flapping wings, a whole family of partridges (about seven or eight of them), got up just a couple of yards in front of me. Though startled, I coolly took aim into the thick of the bunch. *I'm bound to hit something*, I thought. Just before they reached the hedge, about 15 yards from me, I squeezed the trigger. There was a resounding silence—I hadn't cocked the gun! By now, the flock had dipped over the hedge and were gone.

It wasn't until the following summer that I came up with an idea worthy of my ancient gun. Across the lane from uncle Will's house at Hoarstone, was a steep cultivated field which belonged to Middleton Hall farm. As a small boy, I had accompanied uncle Robin, as he ploughed this particular field with our carthorse, Blossom. At the bottom of the field was an abandoned laneway with hedges on both sides, which ran along the boundary with Donald Button's corn fields. There was a line of medium-sized trees along the west side of the laneway.

I remembered I had seen a lot of birds, including wild pigeons, around those trees. So, one beautiful August evening, after tea, I walked over to the secluded laneway, cradling the little shotgun. In less than half an hour, I saw that wild pigeons, fattened by gleanings from the recently harvested wheat-fields, returned to these trees before dusk to roost. I decided this looked like a good spot to hunt game-birds; well pigeons, at least. For the next few weeks, it became a habit.

Standing in the narrow laneway, I would wait for the pigeons to appear. I could almost set my clock by their regularity. About eight o'clock they'd begin to arrive in ones and twos, and perch on the branches right over my head. They were well within the range of my ancient, feeble shotgun, and firing straight up meant that I didn't need to allow for trajectory. The pigeons were indeed "sitting ducks".

Although the startled birds would disperse whenever the gun went off, they could be counted on to return within ten minutes. All I had to do was wait. When a bird dropped, I'd pick it up and decapitate it, so that the blood could drain. I found that pigeons lost their heads very easily, with just a quick twist and a pull.

Sometimes I shot just a couple of birds, sometimes more, but I rarely missed from point-blank range. I had found a target the ancient gun could hit. I would proudly take my bag of headless birds home and hang them in the shed to drain the last of their blood. The following day, I'd remind my mother to roast them. But that was where the hard work began. The pigeons had to be feathered and cleaned out, just like any game-bird, but they were bony, and their meat was dark and meagre.

Not surprisingly, after several of these hunting trips, pigeons began to seem less attractive. Perhaps a decade earlier, during the war, I might have found a demand for the birds; but I wasn't interested in shooting them just for target practice. I soon stopped these hunting expeditions altogether.

29

The Fishing Trip

How poor are they that have not patience.

Shakespeare

IT is a fine evening in early July. My father has arrived home from yet another day of hard work on the farm. That's nothing unusual, except that he asks if I want to go fishing after tea. I'm puzzled. "But Dad," I say, "We haven't got a fishing rod." He assures me he knows where he can get one. He offers no further explanation.

It's about seven o'clock as we walk empty-handed down School Lane and take the Vile Lane towards Fall Bay. As we pass by 'the bank' at Middleton, a few old-timers, wearing collarless flannel shirts, waistcoats and cloth caps, look at us inquisitively. "Where't thee gwain t', Joff?" one of them asks, but my father tells them nothing. They are well-meaning, but discovering other people's business is the main pastime for some of them.

When we get to Lewis Castle, we turn left towards Mewslade, walking along the inside of the grey limestone wall separating Jack Richards's fields from the cliff. Just inside a low wall, as if by magic, we find a long fishing rod, complete with line and tackle, lying hidden in the grass. The owner, Alec Thomas, a good friend of my father, has described the location perfectly.

Armed with the borrowed rod and line, and solemnly observed by a few of Jack's Friesian milking cows, we scramble over the dry-stone wall, then down a steep grassy gully between two towering limestone cliffs, to the gnarled, sea-splashed rocks, below. On the rocky ledges of the inaccessible cliffs, on either side of the gully, seagulls are tending to their young. Wheeling and crying overhead, they make plenty of noise at the sight of two suspicious-looking humans.

The tide is well in: there is a gentle swell, aided by a light breeze. The water is a beautiful translucent green as it rises and falls between the rock formations, making gurgling and rushing sounds alternately. Perfect. I feel the urge to jump into the water and practise my dog-paddle, but I know it would be chilly here, in the shadow of Lewis Castle, even if I had brought my swimming trunks. Anyway, we're here to fish.

I'm anxious to learn how to cast for mackerel, but my father tells me to wait. I sit dutifully on a rock to his left, so I won't get in the way when he casts. Twenty minutes later, there is no sign of a bite. It's too early in the season for mackerel, and this is not a good spot for bass, even if they would take a spinner. Let's face it; there are no hungry fish around this evening.

I ask for a turn to cast. My father says he'll just try a couple more times, first. No luck. Then there is a sudden jerk on the line, as he winds in—a large horse-mackerel, perhaps? No, the spinner has caught fast in a submerged rock. My father tugs this way and that. After about five or ten minutes he finally frees the spinner and winds in.

"Well," he says, "We'd better head home, now: it'll be nearly dark by the time we get there." I feel disappointed, but I can tell he doesn't want us to risk getting the spinner caught in the rocks again. The long day is beginning to catch up with him, at last. I'll just have to look forward to the next time.

We retrace our steps to the wall, replace the fishing rod in its hiding place, and begin the long march home. My father walks with long, swinging strides. I alternately walk and jog, to keep abreast of him. We arrive back at 'the cottage' just as empty-handed as when we left. "There was no fish about, Mam" I tell my mother. "Never mind," she says, encouragingly, "Better luck next time, isn't it?"

Joff remarks wryly that there'll be no fish-and-chips for our tea, tomorrow. "Well," says Joyce, "There's a tin of corned beef in the pantry. I'll make a few chips to go with that … and some peas from the garden."

I realise it might be quite a while before the next fishing trip.

30

Fisherman's Choice

Gaze upon the rolling deep
(Fish is plentiful and cheap)

Edward Lear

THERE was always a wide range of sea-fishing available at Rhossili for those who were prepared to put in the physical effort. One could choose between fishing off the rocks, off the beach, from a small boat or with a dragnet. Each choice was likely to be associated with exposure to the elements and/or hazardous conditions. Ambling along the bank of a river and picking a shady spot to relax and work with your favourite lure or fly, was far different from fishing off the beaches or rock-ledges.

The real fishermen were those who fished for salmon-bass off the rocks at the base of the cliffs or from the sands at Rhossili Bay. In either case, they may have first taken the trouble to make the long walk to the Worms Head causeway at low tide to search for soft crab to use as bait. Those fishing off the beach would pay their lines out, as the tide came in, leaving multiple baited hooks suspended above the sandy bottom. They would pace around on the beach, subject to the discomfort of sudden gusts of wind and sharp, drenching showers, waiting patiently for the bells at the tips of their rods to signal a catch.

Other bass-fishers, especially the locals, but also some fishing fanatics who were frequent visitors, had their favourite spots on the rocks at the base of steep cliffs, like Thurba Head, Kitchen Corner or Worms Head. They would usually wait until the tide was almost full in, before beginning to fish. They would need to do some walking, climbing and scrambling to reach their favourite perches—and they would need to watch for those "seventh waves" as they swelled up over the rocks—but for the experienced fishermen, the reward was a delicious pan of fried fish.

There was more than a hint of rivalry among the keen fishermen of every generation. Locals like Fred Marks, Harold Jones, Alec Thomas and George Beynon were proud of their catches, in much the same way that Johnny Beynon (Meadowside) and "aunty Mag" (High Priest) competed for crabs and lobsters.

Those who preferred fishing from a boat were usually interested in making sure they caught a good supply of fish, in return for their investment. They had the advantage of being able to try their luck at varying distances from the shore, so they would rarely be unsuccessful. Their main concern was in handling the boat, while keeping a weather eye open—especially when passing through "the dangers" off Tears Point.

Before the war, several rowboats had been parked around the "flat rocks" in the shelter of Tears Point. Johnny Beynon (Fernhill; later, Meadowside) had even built a small wooden boathouse. After war broke out, small boats were considered a potential means of transport by spies, while the old boathouse was a potential means of unauthorised shelter. Both the boat and the boathouse were therefore demolished.

It was about 1948 before another small boat appeared in the area. This was a sleek, two-man canoe, jointly owned by Dudley Thomas and Edward Roberts. When not being used for recreation (including mackerel fishing) by the Fall Bay "gang", it was parked high and dry in a rocky cove between the flat rocks and the bay. About 1953, after Edward returned from his two-year National Service, he, Dudley and Ernie Beynon jointly purchased a small, second-hand clinker-built rowboat, named *The Feather*, which they powered with an outboard motor. It was kept parked on the flat rocks, protected by a tarpaulin. When the seagulls were seen "beating" above the surface of the water out towards "the dangers", the little boat would quickly be put into the water. Ernie, who was a dedicated non-swimmer, would always take along an inflated inner-tube as a sensible precaution.

On occasion, a small boat could be useful for rescuing people from the deceptive tides swirling through the Shipway between Kitchen Corner and Sound. Edward Roberts was instrumental in saving a man who had become trapped by the rising tide, as he tried to return from Worms Head. Edward received a hero's write-up in the *Evening Post*, though I daresay it seemed a fairly routine operation to him.

By the late 1950s, several other fishermen, some from the Swansea area, had boats parked on the flat rocks or on the grassy slope above. My friend, Alan Button, and my cousin-in-law, Joe Niwa from Hoarstone, shared a boat and an outboard motor for several years.

When the harvest mackerel followed the whitebait in, usually in August and early September, many of the young men would dust off their ancient rods and head for the flat rocks at Fall Bay. It was time for "spinning": no bait was required, just the silver spinners that mackerel would readily mistake for whitebait. They'd spend two or three hours, around high tide, repeatedly casting and reeling in their spinners from the flat rocks, while watching to see what others caught. There was little chance of boredom.

No great skill was required: on a good evening, they would be heading home at dusk with between a dozen and a score of mackerel each. (On rare occasions, as many as fifty or sixty mackerel might be caught.) Sometimes, a tope shark would show up and scare the mackerel away. Then the land-lubbers would search for large stones to hurl at the intruder. As well as mackerel, pollock, whiting and mullet were often attracted to the silver spinners.

I loved to tag along with the young men on their fishing expeditions on summer evenings. This usually meant the flat rocks or the more awkward ones around the corner of Tears Point; but sometimes it was Kitchen Corner, under Rhossili cliffs. Plodding homeward at dusk along the path that followed the rim of Fall Bay could be a little nerve-racking. It was certainly important to make sure you didn't trip over a projecting rock.

On one occasion, I was with uncle Oliver and a couple of other men on "the ledges" near Kitchen Corner. There were a few mackerel out there in the translucent green water as it swelled up and down about six feet, but they were not biting very often. Some of Oliver's fishing tackle was "all 'n a caffle": I was trying to untangle it.

I was sitting well back on the rocks to my uncle's right, but when he tried to make one really big cast, the spinner caught in my scalp at the back of my head. Oliver realised something was wrong when I yelped, and his line broke. After that, there was some careful attention to removing the three-pronged hook. No damage was done—"Just a scratch," the men said. The next day, I had almost forgotten about it—at least until my mother insisted on brushing my hair.

Dragnet fishing appealed to those of us who were not patient with a rod, line and tackle (except perhaps when the harvest mackerel were in), but who nevertheless enjoyed a feed of fish. It was basically an unskilled operation. Whatever fish were about would get caught; there was usually enough for everyone in the fishing party to get a share. When the net became heavy with schools of skate or because there was a lot of seaweed about, it was best to pack up and try again, the next week.

Rhossili Bay, with its expanse of level sand and shallow water, was ideal for operating a dragnet. Furthermore it was populated with several varieties of flat-fish. Even when paddling in the water, one would often feel a fish wriggle away, underfoot. The only skill in dragnet fishing was to recognise good fishing weather and to know when there might be more luck under the cliffs than out in the open bay, opposite the Old Rectory. It was just a matter of commonsense that a spring tide was far better than a neap tide; also, that fishing should commence a couple of hours after high-tide.

A dragnet was about fifty yards long and six feet high: it had about a one-inch mesh. The net had a six foot pole at each end, so it could be dragged parallel to the beach. One man on the shallow end (no more than knee deep) dragged his pole steadily along, while it took two people to drag the pole at the deep end, in water about chest height (which allowed for the swell of the waves). After dragging parallel to the beach for about a hundred yards, the inside man would stop, while the outside men would pull around in a semicircle, toward the beach. Then, with a little extra help from those on the beach, the net and its contents would be dragged clear of the water's edge.

On summer evenings when the water had been warmed during the day, we could fish as the tide ebbed, from almost halfway out until low tide. Then, we faced the less pleasant work of changing out of our wet clothes in the chilly, early-morning darkness. There was the work of cleaning the net, rolling it up, and carrying it up the steep pathway to a waiting tractor and trailer.

A bad night was when we found a lot of seaweed in the water; then, the net would become almost too heavy to pull in. On other occasions, there could be large shoals of skate about. These close relatives of the stingray would hook their long, barbed tails into the net, causing a lot of unrewarding work, especially as we regarded these fish to be good only for feeding to pigs; therefore, we rarely bothered to carry any home. The fact that there was a market for them in some London restaurants left us unimpressed.

Dragnet fishing offered plenty of opportunity for everyone in the party to make a significant contribution to the effort. It had quite a social aspect to it: sometimes, women would participate. Most of the time, the catch would be at least sufficient for everyone involved to take home enough for a tasty meal for their family.

[Endnote: On my later visits to Rhossili, my father and I would sometimes join uncle Oliver and his son, Lyndon, in some late afternoon dragnetting at Rhossili or Porteynon bays. Carrying a wet, rolled-up net from Rhossili sands all the way to The Green, was a good test of stamina for me. On other occasions, I took the opportunity to join Alan Button and Joe Niwa on a summer's evening of dinghy fishing in Fall Bay.]

31

Community Activities

Man seeketh in society comfort, use, and protection …

Francis Bacon

IN some sense, community activities are not easy to define. Such activities may be either organised or informal. They may involve a majority of the community or just a few who share a particular interest. Among the organised activities in our parish, there were both seasonal and annual events; for example, whist-drives in the winter months, Saturday dances in the summer months, as well as annual Sunday-school outings and Harvest Suppers.

There were also weekly activities of various kinds, which lasted for a few years, perhaps even a decade, but the most persistent and fruitful of them must have been the Women's Institute (WI). It was inclined to be cliquish, and was never attended by a majority of the women in Rhossili on a continuous basis; however, most of the women did participate in it at one time or another, over the years. The WI met once a week in the village hall to hone or learn all sorts of domestic skills. Occasionally, they would produce a very good play with a cast of local stars: there was always a good turnout for such events.

During the war, and from time to time afterwards, public dances were organised in the village hall. Around the end of the war, I was able to peep through the door at a Saturday night dance. My father finally fetched me from 'the bank' at about 10:00 PM. I couldn't wait to describe the mayhem I had seen: "They put their arms out like this … then they put their legs out like that … it was a hell of a dance!" I told my parents. Evidently I was attempting to describe the "Hokey-Pokey" which was a big favourite at the time. A few years later "the Conga" became another big favourite. It was usually performed late in the festivities. It was common for young tearaways like Eric Gibbs to lead the line of Conga dancers out of the hall and all around 'the bank'.

The dance music for both public and private events was provided by a trio of farmer/musicians from the Llandewi/Horton area. They were Ron Parry (accordion), Don James (accordion, saxophone), and Curtis Grove (percussion). For private parties, Ron would perform alone; indeed, he was just as well known in Rhossili as many of the parishioners.

A few fastidious adults and families attended either St. Mary's Church or the Methodist Chapel on a regular basis. The two groups would usually keep quite separate from each other. For us kids, there was a choice of Sunday-school at the Chapel or the Church. Since my father had been raised in the Anglican faith, while my mother had a Welsh chapel background, I was one who felt free to switch back and forth, as one or the other flourished. Some years, there was a jointly-organised Sunday-school outing, as if a sort of truce had been called. On one occasion, I believe, there was even a joint Christmas party.

The annual events, which were very well attended, included the Harvest Supper at the village hall, followed by a brief concert involving some entertainment, such as the ubiquitous Ron Parry, or a few skits organised by locals. There were also well-attended thanksgiving services at both the Church and Chapel. Then there were the (separate) annual Christmas parties held in the village hall, when Sunday-school attendees would receive their well-earned gifts from Father Christmas, himself. On several occasions, the Methodist Chapel produce a children's Christmas pageant, directed by Mrs. Gwendolen Thomas, usually focused on the Nativity.

In the late 1940s and early 1950s, there was a mid-week film night through the autumn, winter and spring months, when black and white feature films were shown at the village hall. A poster would advise the main features for the following four or five weeks. The supporting feature was usually a long-running half-hour serial: often it was a western, where the good guys seemed to be always galloping after the bad guys, repeatedly passing the same clump of rocks. One year it was a menacing suspense called *Perils of Chinatown*, involving good and evil Chinese characters, dressed in gown-like tunics, baggy pants and slippers.

These film nights, before any television sets appeared in the community, were a tremendous recreation for the farm-workers' families, especially for the hard-working housewives who had the opportunity to see all the wonderful film actors and actresses of that era—stars like James Mason, Vivien Leigh, Olivia de Havilland, Ray Milland, Maureen O'Sullivan, Bette Davis, Deborah Kerr, Margaret Rutherford, Glynis Johns, Clark Gable, Gary Cooper, Errol Flynn, Kenneth Moore, Richard Todd, John Gregson, Lawrence Olivier, Greer Garson, Shirley Temple and many others. Without doubt, it was the golden age of "the movies".

Our parish was honoured with a special showing of the film *Scott and the Antarctic* (1948) at our village hall in acknowledgement of the achievements and heroism of Edgar Evans, who was a resourceful Petty Officer in the Royal Navy. The hall was packed out. The ever-popular John Mills played the part of Captain Scott.

Any kind of adventure, western or war film was a treat for me, but there was one film which made a lasting impression, even though I was no more than seven or eight years old when I saw it. A youthful Victor Mature played the role of a primitive, but brave prehistoric man in *One Million BC* (1940). For months afterwards, I fought imaginary dinosaurs on the hill behind 'the cottage' with only a sharpened wooden stick, while enduring unexpected earthquakes and defeating rival cavemen in hand-to-hand combat.

For young boys, romantic films were inevitably tedious, but comedy films were always popular. In the mid-1950s, we youngsters had to catch the bus to Porteynon, if we wanted to see any films. A Laurel and Hardy film was often the supporting feature; otherwise, it might be Charlie Chaplin, The Marx Brothers or Abbot and Costello.

There were occasional variety shows in the village hall, which might include a troupe of young dancing girls from Swansea, a singer or two, a juggler, a comedian and a conjurer. In volunteering as an assistant to a conjurer, I became acutely aware of the technique he used for one of the card-tricks. Of course, what the conjurer was telling me to do (under his breath) was quite different from what he was saying aloud to the audience.

When there was a hypnotist, children were excluded. However, we would always hear a blow-by-blow account of events, the following day. On one occasion, Eric Gibbs was instructed to give himself a false name for twenty-four hours after the show. The next day, everyone he met asked Eric his name—it must have set some kind of record—but Eric continued to give the same (incorrect) answer, the whole day. However, knowing Eric was quite a trickster, we weren't quite sure whether he was really under the hypnotist's control, or just "playing along".

Almost two years before the end of the war, a company of Boy Scouts was formed by Fred Hunter, a temporary resident from Swansea. Recruits included Ian

Hunter, Ernie Beynon, Len Beynon, Reggie Beynon, Vivian Williams and Malcolm Shepherd. It lasted about four years. A little later, (about 1944) a well-organised company of Girl Guides was started by the tireless Mrs. Mary Roberts, assisted by her daughter, Dora, and Kathleen Williams. Many of the village girls, including Ann Harding, Mary Beynon, Heather Chappell, Norma Chappell, Enid Beynon, Muriel and Anne Dorling, Marlene Shepherd and Mair James, joined the Guides over the next few years; those who were a little younger, were recruited as Brownies. This lasted about eight years.

Mischievous Middleton boys, like John Bevan, Ron Beynon and I, were all too aware that the village hall was a hive of activity for the girls on Friday nights. We kept a weather eye open for any Guides who might leave the hall on tracking exercises. The lead party would leave chalk marks on telephone poles, or form arrows on the road with small stones. It was all too tempting for us to add a few signs of our own; but we made sure we weren't caught.

From about 1952, a few Rhossili boys, including Peter Crozier, Alan Button, Brian Beynon and I, would catch the bus to Horton one night a week to participate in the thriving Wolf Cub pack there. Other Cubs came from Llandewi, Scurlage and Porteynon. The Cubs were organised by Horton business Bernard Hastie; the pack leader (Akela) was easygoing John Bevan, also of Horton. Some of the Wolf Cub "six" leaders were Mike Roberts, Geoff Evans and Ron Nuttall. This activity lasted for just a couple of years, for us Rhossili boys.

There was a very successful Young Farmers' Club operating at the village hall for a number of years in the 1950s. One year we almost won the Glamorgan YFC championship in a wide range of competitions held at Singleton Park in Swansea. There were weekly meetings in Rhossili village hall throughout the autumn, winter and spring months. There were occasional coach trips to socialise with other YFCs in West Glamorgan. There were even seven-a-side rugby tournaments on several occasions.

Informal arenas also contributed much to a sense of community. There were such essential institutions as the village shops. There were three in Rhossili, by 1950—the Post Office, the Lower Shop and The Green. For the farm-worker, a trip to the Post Office after tea to fetch the daily order of bread and the *Evening Post*, was an opportunity to be updated about the local news.

The Postmaster, Gower Rural District Councillor Will Williams, was a man of good education and long experience in local government, who could always be counted on for good advice, whether solicited or not.

There was also the popular men's perch on the fallen branch at 'the bank', which provided an opportunity to exchange information and opinion on a wide range of issues and personalities. Then, there were the pick-up football, cricket and touch rugby games, which included any male participants who could handle the pace of the activity.

Very few families owned a car, so people made good use of the double-decker bus service to go to town. They socialised informally at the bus-stops, as well as on the buses.

[Endnote: There was no public-house until about 1970, when the Worms Head Hotel was finally granted a public licence. Previously, all applications had been effectively opposed by a broad coalition of village elders representing Church, Chapel and secular communities, but with a common set of values. Their moral argument was infallible, but the effect was to make Rhossili seem quite dead at times.

When the public-house was finally opened, it became quite a vibrant centre for the community for about a decade, especially in the summer months. Older farm-workers and their visiting offspring mingled with the younger generation of farmers and their wives. *It feels good to be home*, I thought, whenever I visited Rhossili in the 1970s. But it was perhaps too little, too late. By the mid-1980s, there were few locals who were making use of the public-house as a meeting place for families.

Either the novelty had worn off, or a warm lounge and a TV set were more appealing.]

32

Sports Mad

The essence of education is the education of the body ...

Benjamin Disraeli

FROM a tender age, I was fascinated by the idea of playing football in proper boots, shorts and jersey—kicking, heading and scoring spectacular goals. Rugby also appealed greatly—passing, catching, kicking, tackling and diving over the line to score a try. As a boy, I'd play imaginary matches on my own (involving two teams) of either football or rugby, on the patch of grass between our cottage and the road. I could engineer these desperately hard fought contests with a tennis ball (if I was lucky) or just about anything else I could kick or throw in the air. My interest in sports was always focused very much on participation, rather than as a spectator.

At about six years of age, I took part in my first "real match". It was in The Ship farm's triangular field, opposite Meadowside. About twenty of the young men of the village, including my father and uncles Oliver and Len, gathered for a prearranged evening match—perhaps it was Middleton against the rest, or married men against single men. They had put up some goalposts and even sticks for corner flags. I was still trying to comprehend the positional aspects of the game. I had heard of "right wing" and "inside right" and "outside right". I assumed that these were three different positions; therefore, there must be seven forwards on each team.

Watching from the side of the field, it looked as if both teams were somewhat short of forwards. I couldn't understand why they didn't ask if any of us kids wanted to join in. After a while, I decided to take matters into my own hands. I just joined in with one of the teams and played on the left side. Soon the hard leather football was lobbed towards me. I stood my ground and it bounced off

127

the top of my head in the general direction I was facing. Several of the men howled with laughter. That only made me redouble my efforts, getting in a few kicks, as well.

In 1948, the South Gower football club was formed. My uncles Len and Oliver were among the Rhossili players in those early days, but the mantle soon passed to young stars like Ernie and Len Beynon. The green shirts were like working shirts; they were quite loose and had full collars with open v-necks, which could be laced up. Each player took his own shirt home for laundering. Uncle Len was proud of his number 9 shirt, but it was his young wife, Doreen, who had to wash it.

As I grew up and heard the football results every Saturday on the radio, I began to take an interest in the professional leagues. The football annuals I received at Christmas or on my birthdays increased my knowledge of heroes like Wilf Mannion, Roy Paul, Trevor Ford, Stanley Matthews, Tom Finney, Jack Kelsey and many others.

From about the age of eleven, I occasionally managed to get to the Vetch Field to watch the Swans play. Every time, I would daydream that one of the Swansea Town players would not appear, and somehow, I would have the opportunity to fill in. However, the only time I participated at all was on one rare occasion when my father found time to take me to a match at the Vetch Field. My attention must have lapsed just as the Swans' right-back, Rory Keane—with the opposing left-winger bearing down on him—booted the ball safely into touch. We were standing a few rows from the front; the ball smacked the side of my face. I wasn't hurt, just embarrassed because I'd got caught looking the other way. A couple of minutes later, Rory was able to come over and ask my father, "Is he alright?"

Only once, in my mid-teens, did I get to see Wales play an international match; but on that occasion, I saw the superb young Duncan Edwards of Manchester United, as well as Fulham's Johnny Haynes and Preston's Tom Finney, all playing for England. England won rather comfortably, as Wales were so short of talent that they needed to play the Swansea Town centre-forward, Des Palmer, with his troublesome hamstring heavily strapped. I must have been about fifteen at the time, but I was lacking in social skills and didn't find it easy to fit in with the rest of the locals on this unusual venture. Fortunately, one of our neighbours, Ron Densley, invited me to join him, his son John, and one or two others, in finding our way around the strange city of Cardiff, both before and after the match.

Inter-village football matches for the under-16s were organised by word of mouth. If we didn't have nets, we settled for goalposts; if we didn't have goalposts, we settled for coats on the ground. For these informal matches, referees were rarely available: no hardworking adult could be expected to devote his time to such trivialities. Critical decisions were usually resolved by the loudest voices; or sometimes with fists. In the early 1950s, informal matches were arranged by "South Gower juniors" against other villages like Penmaen/Parkmill or teams as far away as Llansamlet. Brian Jones of East Pilton, Bernard Cottey of Overton, and Ivor Leyshon of Reynoldston (all about three years older than I) were the teenage stars I admired in those days. I was disappointed that none of them went on to become South Gower football players—though the last two loved to play cricket for South Gower.

Sometimes, hastily arranged football matches went wrong. On one occasion, about 1953, someone tried to organise a match at Parkmill. It was at short notice, so we could only muster about seven players from the South Gower area to catch the bus to the Gower Inn. We climbed up the steep hillside opposite the inn, only to find a small, irregular, mole-hilled field at the top; furthermore, only three boys had showed up for the other team. Two of us had to play for the opposition in this make-shift match, which was hardly more than a kick-around. Another forgettable occasion saw us catching the bus to Fairwood Common, then marching for about a mile easterly along a paved road, only to find that no opposing team members had turned up. We were able to buy cups of tea, biscuits and sandwiches in a Nissen-hut café, while we waited a couple of hours for the next Rhossili bus that came through Killay.

In 1955, Rhossili teenage boys played a round-robin tournament against Porteynon/Horton, Scurlage/Llandewi, and Reynoldston/Knelston. The whole thing was planned on the school-bus as we travelled noisily homeward, each day. Winston Morris of Reynoldston thought we should have a trophy to play for, so having exhausted all other possibilities, he found a diminutive silver-coloured plastic ornament, shaped like the real FA cup, complete with handles. I don't know whether Winston's mother ever missed the ornament, but it spent several years in a place of honour in my room at 'the cottage'. Rhossili had a lot of strong young boys, so we could usually field a team, even without those who had little interest in football or were just unavailable. Our team included Alan Button, Brian Beynon, Fred MacVitie, Russell Jones, Howard Chalk, Norman Parker, John Morris and even young Ed Tucker.

All our local matches were played at the Scurlage sports ground. We never thought about refreshments until after the game was over. Sometimes, after a hard-fought match, we'd be waiting for the Rhossili bus when dear old Nellie Coghlan would come out of her cottage with a jug of lemonade and some cups.

Her brother, Frank, would chat with us. When the jug was empty, Nellie would go into the house and fetch some more. If she was out of lemonade, the kind soul would offer us water.

At grammar school, there was pressure to play rugby rather than football; however, the limited opportunities, plus the reluctance to stay after school (which would have made a long day even longer), meant that I didn't develop strong rugby skills. Even so, I still managed to play well enough to score a try in a one-off match at Scurlage between a South Gower team and a team from the Pennard/Bishopston area. At sixteen, I was one of the youngest players. I scored the first try, before being taken to Swansea Hospital with a snapped collarbone.

In Rhossili, a high standard in competitive sports was set by Len Beynon. Len played football, rugby, field hockey, cricket and tennis with almost equal aplomb. Those of my generation who followed in his sporting footsteps, could set their standards by him. Keen players in my era included Ernie Beynon (football, cricket), Edward Roberts (hockey, cricket), Ted Chappell (tennis), Roger Harding (rugby), Brian Jones (rugby, cricket), Howard Chalk (rugby), Russell Jones (rugby), Brian Beynon (rugby), Leo Harding (rugby), John Morris (football, cricket), Edward Tucker (rugby), John Dorling (rugby league), Colin Jones (football, rugby, cricket) and Geoff Beynon (rugby). On the girls' side, Dora Roberts, Ann Harding, Heather and Norma Chappell stood out in field hockey and tennis.

Len Beynon made a huge contribution to the successful star-studded South Gower team of the early 1950s. Before that, he had been instrumental in organising hockey matches on the firm sands of Rhossili Bay against various guest teams. In the summer, he and his brother, Ernie, would prepare a cricket pitch in the field opposite the Post Office. A full set of equipment was stored at The Ship farm through the winter months. Ernie and Len not only excelled at sports, but they were also willing to put their time and energy into organising them.

Whenever Len was on leave from National Service or from his subsequent teaching job in Wiltshire, he would still catch the bus to Scurlage a couple of hours before a home match to prepare the pitch. He'd mark all the lines, place the corner flags and hang the goal-nets. He took the trouble to raise the level of the game by making everything as professional as possible. I played only one or two matches with Len, for South Gower. I felt glad I wouldn't need to stop one of his shots with my head. Without doubt, Len was one of the hardest kickers of the old leather football, even including the professionals.

There were three sports enthusiasts in the village from whom I learnt valuable, lifetime lessons in my favourite sports. The mercurial teenage rugby player, Roger

Harding, when he was home from private school, would sometimes wander up to Middleton with a rugby ball. He would soon attract a few of us youngsters to learn some rugby skills from him. It was an interesting change from football. He showed us a side-step that would not have disgraced the great Gerald Davies (though it was two decades before his time).

Then there was Ernie Beynon. He would take the time to explain football tactics to me when I was in my early teens. On one occasion, I was on the way down to 'the bank' when I met him just opposite The Barn at Sheep Green. Right there, Ernie picked up a few small pebbles and placed them to demonstrate South Gower's successful 4-2-4 formation. Ernie was one of the centre-backs (though they called them twin centre-halves, at that time). From then on I became an ardent football tactician and coach, as well as a player.

It was Ron Densley, a local farm-worker, who encouraged my interest in boxing. Ron, who originated from the village of Llanfrynach, near Brecon, came to work in Rhossili as a young man, before the war. He married Gwyneth Butler from Reynoldston and they subsequently lived at Morawel for more than half a century.

Ron had some practical experience as a pugilist, and he loved the sport. I don't know how he discovered that I was interested, but he gave me about a dozen lessons in his front parlour which I would never forget. I sometimes borrowed Ron's set of gloves to spar with my friend Alan Button in Tom Williams's cowsheds, next to Brook Cottage. But Alan never realised I was getting lessons from Ron.

[Endnote: Over the years, I was able to make good use of the examples and advice of my mentors. Although I didn't participate in formal sports at grammar school, I was always involved with local football or rugby teams. While still in my teenage years, I was proud to represent Swansea U.C. at football and the University of Wales at boxing.]

33

The Countryman

How blessed is he, who leads a country life ...

John Dryden

WILFRED and Sally Beynon of The Ship farm raised seven children. Their second son, Ernie, was born in 1930, a decade before me. He experienced, indeed embraced, just about every aspect of country life during the time of transition from the old to the modern Rhossili.

In 1944, Ernie left Rhossili School to work on his family's farm. By contrast, his brother, Len, (about one-and-a-half years his junior) was more studious, earning the privilege of a grammar school and university education. But Ernie had been introduced to the rigours of farm-work long before he left school. He experienced, first-hand, the transition from horse-drawn equipment to tractors.

He developed a lifelong passion for horses not only as working animals, but also for riding and breeding. He also became an ardent shepherd, learning much about that family tradition from his father.

For recreation, Ernie went crabbing, shooting and ferreting. He liked to fish off the rocks with a rod; or at Rhossili Bay with a dragnet. From about 1953, he shared a small dinghy, named *The Feather* with local man, Edward Roberts, and Swansea man, Dudley Thomas. But unlike his two companions, Ernie was not a swimmer; he always insisted on wearing an inflated inner-tube as a life-jacket. This could make *The Feather* seem a little crowded at times.

Despite Ernie's participation in just about everything that life in Rhossili had to offer a young man, that was the one omission that I could identify—he never learnt to swim in the tide. But in that respect, he was absolutely typical of the older generations. Our fathers would wade chest-deep in the breakers to haul on a dragnet at Rhossili Bay; our mothers would raise their skirts to paddle at Mewslade or collect laver-bread at Fall, but they would never consider learning to swim.

Ernie's younger brother, Ron, and I would sometimes admire the restless ferrets, which Ernie kept in a secure hutch in one of the farm sheds known as "the picnic rooms"—a title which harked back to the days when The Ship had been a public-house. Ernie used them to help control the rabbit population in "the warren", adjacent to his father's fields at Parsonage, around the Old Rectory. This was much more exciting than setting wires. He could also practice his marksmanship with a 12-bore shotgun on any rabbits which escaped the nets. He soon put this skill to good use as he began to make a big contribution towards controlling the fox population in southwest Gower.

Another lifelong passion he developed was for the country tradition of hunting game-birds such as woodcock, partridge and pheasant, in the late autumn and winter. In the late 1940s and early 1950s, he kept lurchers (a whippet and sheepdog crossbreed). These dogs were aggressive in running down rabbits and flushing out game-birds. The first of these he named Roper; the later one was Mick. They were well-known in Middleton, being so different from the other farmdogs.

To some of the veteran hunters and fishers, like Fred Marks and Harold Jones, Ernie must have seemed something of a "young upstart"; but he had an easygoing nature, always ready to listen and learn from others. Furthermore, he must have learnt much about crabbing and fishing from observing his great-uncles, "Johnny, Fernhill" (later known as "Johnny, Meadowside") and "Little Johnny, High Priest", (who was also a renowned rabbit-catcher and grower of prize garden vegetables), even though they were generally reluctant to reveal their secrets.

About the end of the war, I became aware of an elite cohort of enviable young men and women, who indulged in sports in the most skilful yet sportsmanlike manner. In retrospect, they seemed quite Victorian in their values. This elite group included Ernie and Len Beynon; Margaret Bevan; Edward, Dora and Betty Roberts; Teddy, Heather and Norma Chappell; David Tucker and Ann Harding. They formed formidable hockey, tennis and cricket teams. Occasionally, I watched some of them practise at Professor Stephen Lee's tennis court near Talgarths Well. On one occasion, I found my way to Rhossili Bay and saw them play hockey against a visiting team, perhaps from Swansea U.C.

What made Ernie extraordinary was that, of all this charismatic group of young people, he was the only one who had to work long days on the farm—yet he could still find the energy to enjoy a vibrant social life and compete with his contemporaries at a variety of sports and pastimes.

Ernie enjoyed team sports, especially cricket and football, but also hockey and tennis. He developed a keen interest in most of these sports before he was a teenager. By the time I was old enough to know him well, he was already in his midteens. For the next decade, he would often join in the football and cricket games on 'the bank'. When there were just two or three of us youngsters hanging around, he liked to help us sharpen our fielding skills with a game of French cricket.

Social life was a strongpoint with Ernie. He was an active and good-natured participant in all the social events in the village. These included volunteering for visiting conjurers or hypnotists, and taking part in locally produced plays and concerts. He also enjoyed social evenings, parties and dances. In the 1940s, he and other teenagers would ride, sometimes share, their bicycles to get to dances in neighbouring villages like Porteynon or Llandewi; or walk across the moor to Llangennith. In the winter months, he was a regular participant at the whist-drives which were popular in all the villages.

In more formal activities, Ernie joined the Scouts which were active for a few years, after the war ended. There was a healthy rivalry with the Girl Guides. The Guides were big, strong girls who could (and did) surprise the Scouts at tug-of-war. Though he was wiry and tough, Ernie did not have quite the same physical strength of many of his heavier-built contemporaries when it came to farmwork—all the more reason to wonder at his energy and enthusiasm for so many social and sporting activities.

Although he was too young to be officially involved in any of the wartime auxiliary services, Ernie eventually became a member of the "rocket crew"—a family tradition—about 1951, applying his characteristic enthusiasm to help the Rhossili crew win many competitive events. By then, he was in his prime—lean but muscular. Sure-footed on the cliffs and crabbing-grounds, he walked with a long, loping, efficient stride. He had a keen eye for tracking anything that moved, whether it was a cricket-ball, a lobster or a game-bird.

Of all the skills and attributes Ernie possessed, the one that stands out in my memory is that he was always a friendly, non-threatening figure to us youngsters. Some of his contemporaries, such as his older brother, Reggie, Gordon Thomas and Eric Gibbs (who were inclined to be mischievous) could make us younger boys feel nervous, on occasion; but Ernie was more likely to provide some blunt advice. In my mid-teens, I developed a habit of walking with shoulders hunched, while focusing on my shoes, in deep thought. Ernie told me, more than once: "Thee walk like thee got the weight of the world on thee shoulders, by."

[Endnote: By his mid-twenties, Ernie was competing in sheep-dog trials at the Gower Show and other venues up the Swansea valleys, mainly for the pleasure of "having a go"—but sometimes he won. He still continues to actively pursue his interests in horses and sheep, as well as hunting and crabbing. He raised four children, all of whom share his enthusiasm for the country life. His son, Nicky, has won the Welsh shearing championship a record seven times, and has represented Great Britain in international competitions. Ernie's two oldest grandsons have been successful in junior competitions.]

Rhossili End and Worms Head (ca. 1940).
[A view from above the field known as Hawk Walls. The Vanguard
Motors building is prominent.]

Aunty Evelyn with daughter, Mary, and baby son, Royston, at Windy
Walls (ca. 1950).
[The photographer was eight-year-old Clive.]

Carefree days before the war: Oliver Jones snags another drowned hare
(ca. 1938).

[The exact location was a closely-guarded secret.]

Cutting corn at Sandylands with a Hornsby reaper-and-binder (ca. 1925).

[L to R: Will Jones (on binder), Francis Jones (holding the scythe), and Arthur Jones(holding the oil-can).]

Granny Jones being persuaded to pose at the front door of Middleton Hall (ca. 1935).

[Daughter, Gladys is in the background. She moved to Manchester in 1942.]

Phil Richards of Higher Pitton exhibits the essentials of the traditional countryman's lifestyle (ca. 1930).

A crabbing-stick can never be too long. Johnny (Meadowside) posing at Sound (ca 1950).

[The Shipway can be seen in the background.]

Rhossili School (ca. 1930).
[The extensions are the infants' cloakroom and the coal-sheds.]

Joffre Jones and Blodwen Beynon receive "best pupil" awards (ca. 1927).
[Teachers Ada Thomas and Lily Button look on proudly.]

Some of the Jones children pose under a hayrick at Middleton Hall farm
(ca. 1922).

[L to R: Joffre, Margaret (Peggy), Clifford, unknown neighbour (possibly
Blodwen Beynon), and Oliver.]

Julie and Marie Niwa at Hoarstone with their grandfather's horse (ca.
1952).

[They were last of seven generations of our family to live there.]

Mrs. Mary Roberts with some of her Girl Guides (ca. 1950).

[L to R: Jean Davies, Anne Dorling, Mair James, Mrs. Roberts, Enid Beynon, and Muriel Dorling.]

Arthur Thomas ("The Overlander") in Australian Army uniform (ca. 1940).

[Arthur served in both world wars.]

Village girls (ca. 1960).
[L to R: Christine Hinton, Pamela Jones, and Thelma Jones.]

Frances Niwa (nee Jones) lived her whole life at Hoarstone (1930–1973).
[She experienced all the hardships of the "old Rhossili"; followed by the
benefits of technological progress.]

Rhossili girls' hockey enthusiasts, ready to face-off against a visiting team (ca. 1945).

[Back row: Betty Roberts, Kathleen Williams, Dora Roberts, Josephine Richards, Belinda Beynon
Front row: Valerie Jones, Jean Davies, unidentified youngster, Margaret Bevan.]

Rhossili men's hockey team prepares to play a match against a visiting team (ca. 1947).

[The group includes: Coach Heinz (a German POW), Stan Walters, Len Beynon, Enoch Beynon, Eric Gibbs, Edgar (Archie) Beynon, Ernie Beynon, Bill Beynon, Reggie Beynon, Ivor Pullen, Edward Roberts, and "Bonzo".]

Young cousins at Mewslade (ca. 1949).
[L to R: David Winfield, Pamela Jones, and The Author.]

A happy bunch of (mostly) junior members of the Fall Bay "gang"(ca. 1947).
[L to R: Persistent dog, Edward Roberts, the author, Margaret Bevan, Ann Harding, Dudley Thomas, Peter Greening, Gwenifer Thomas, Mary Bevan, Howard Chalk.]

Beach athletes keep fit at Fall Bay by playing "volleyball" with a rubber quoit (ca. 1953).
[L to R: Dudley Thomas and Edward Roberts vs Ron Harris and Betty Roberts.]

The original Fall Bay rugby club (ca. 1946).
[L to R: Russell Rees, Dudley Thomas, David Phelps, Ron Harris (at rear), Colin Wales,
Glynn Thomas (coach), Edward Roberts, Haydn Jenkins.]

Will Jones and DPs take a break from planting seed potatoes at Donald Button's Lower Pitton farm (ca. 1945).

John Bevan enjoying a new-model Ferguson tractor and planter (ca. 1954).

[Technology had revolutionized farm-work, making it more enjoyable.]

Members of the Swansea U.C. Boxing Club pose with the dazed and blood-spattered author (1960).

[L to R: Neville Britton, Andrew (Nobby) Clark, The Author, Peter Ellery, and Des Jones.]

Royal Observer Corps recruits at ROC camp at RAF Tangmere (1957).

[L to R: The Author, Howard Chalk, and Alan Button.]

34

Hereford Foray

Breathes there the man, with soul so dead,
Who never to himself hath said,
This is my own, my native land!
Whose heart hath ne'er within him burn'd,
As home his footsteps he hath turn'd
From wandering on a foreign strand!

Sir Walter Scott

DURING the summer holidays of 1950, I had the opportunity to spend about ten days with my father's brother, Clifford, and his wife, Clara, in the beautiful countryside at Staunton-on-Wye, near Hereford. Although their house was beside a main road, there were no other buildings within at least a quarter of a mile in any direction. Their Tudor-style cottage was surrounded by woods and fertile fields.

They arranged for a family friend, a lorry driver named Bill Ferris, to meet me in Swansea. The flat-bed lorry (owned by SWR of Landore) was carrying several heavy rolls of steel from Margam to a manufacturing plant in Birmingham. After a two-hour journey, through Brecon and the border country of the Wye valley, we arrived at my uncle's house, where Bill often stopped for a tea-break.

We reached uncle Clifford's house about teatime, where I received a warm welcome from aunty Clara and my cousins, Frank and David. I knew I would be well looked after. David, who was a couple of years older than I, and much taller and stronger, took me out for a long walk after tea, to show me the surrounding landmarks and countryside.

A couple of days later, David said we should take part in a rabbit hunt, as a nearby farmer was cutting corn. We arrived at the field in the late afternoon when it was already more than half cut. A group of children, ranging from about eight to sixteen years old, were scanning the ever-diminishing square of uncut corn in the centre of the field.

Suddenly, a full grown rabbit broke cover and sprinted straight for the hedge, a distance of about fifty yards. Immediately, the group of youngsters gave chase. *They're wasting their time*, I thought, *the rabbit will be safely in the hedge long before they can even get close*. Nevertheless, the youngsters chased and shouted with enthusiasm. The rabbit was only a couple of yards from the hedge when it suddenly pulled up, turned sharply to its left and began to race parallel to the edge of the field. It had become disorientated by the hullabaloo.

This looked like fun. Now I was ready to join in the hunt, but I had been left a long way behind. I started to run after the crowd, but I could not gain on the leaders; if anything, I was falling further behind. After running a quarter of the way around the field, I stopped. I felt inadequate. In the meantime, the rabbit had run almost halfway round the field without getting caught. I began to wonder whether the rabbit could stay ahead until it reached the spot where I was standing.

I started to jog in the opposite direction, so as to meet the scared bunny. The frontrunners in the crowd were gaining ground. Could the rabbit keep going until it reached me? The rabbit was stumbling badly and when it saw me it seemed to finally give up. Its legs, already weak from fear, became paralysed. It ground almost to a halt. With a yell, I dived onto the poor creature, pinning it down and claiming my prize.

The other hunters pulled up in disbelief. They didn't say too much, but I knew they were frustrated and doubted whether I deserved the rabbit. David found a short stick and, while I held the rabbit by the back legs, he whacked it sharply on the back of its head to put it out of its misery; then, we proudly carried it home to aunty Clara. Rabbit hunting, Hereford-style, was great fun!

A couple of days later, we visited another larger cornfield. However, for some reason this one didn't produce any rabbits. There was, though, a boy about a year older than I, who decided to demonstrate his superiority. I suppose he saw me as a trespasser.

After some taunting, he informed me that he was going to give me a beating. I had no desire to fight, but when he grabbed hold of me I quickly put him on his back and sat astride him: Gower farm boys were no weaklings. Infuriated, he began to describe just how much damage he was going to do when I let him get up, as I must do sooner or later.

Regrettably, the only acceptable solution to my predicament (that I could think of at the time) was to make sure he didn't want to fight any more. Using both fists as clubs, I gave him a good beating while he lay on his back, before allowing him to get up. Bruised and tearful, he ran off towards his cottage.

I carried on playing in the fields with the other kids. Suddenly, someone yelled that the boy's mother was coming, so I should run. Perhaps I should have, because I found myself confronted by a short, stocky woman, armed with a walking stick. After berating me at length, she laid into me with her staff, whacking me hard across my left bicep. I still didn't retreat, so she turned and marched her son, none too gently, towards their home.

Over the weekend, I forgot about the incident, except when I touched my bruised arm. On the following Monday morning, about one week into my stay, David (just starting high school at Kington) had to catch the school-bus. I walked with him to the bus-stop. When the bus came to a halt, I saw that it was already about two-thirds full.

As the bus stood there for a few minutes, I saw that some of the kids were chattering about something. They spoke to David; then a couple of them opened a window and yelled "Well done, Joe Louis!" (Retrospectively, I would have preferred them to call me Tommy Farr, but at the time I was both puzzled and embarrassed.)

When he came home from school that day, David explained that the boy I had beaten up was the son of an unpopular farm foreman. The boy was developing into a nasty young bully, who was terrorising some of the smaller children, so there was little sympathy for him. He would take a long time to live down his defeat. Nevertheless, I didn't go to the school-bus stop any more.

A few days later, the lorry that was to take me back to Swansea arrived. I had mixed feelings as I left my cousins and the beautiful farming country behind. The driver had a couple of detours to make, but we reached Swansea in good time. About two hours later, I was back in Middleton. *England is really a strange kind of country*, I thought, *they hunt rabbits differently from us; and some of them don't seem to like foreigners.*

[Endnote: My cousin, David, became a career policeman (now retired). He patrolled on a DMW (Deemster) police motorbike in the *Heartbeat* era of the 1960s. It seems that the boy I battled with became well known to the local police, in adulthood.]

35

Fighting and Bullying

He which hath no stomach for this fight,
Let him depart ...

Shakespeare

FROM a very young age it seemed natural for us boys to wrestle, to try our strength against each other or to sometimes quarrel and fight; yet ongoing or systematic bullying was virtually non-existent. Only one or two of the boys of my generation ever exhibited such characteristics. Even so, I always felt insecure around youths who were more than a couple of years older than I, especially those that seemed to have a mischievous nature.

Young boys around the same age, such as Howard Chalk, Ron Beynon and I, often took a swing at each other, in childish attempts to settle perceived grievances. However, when someone was significantly different from the crowd, systematic verbal and physical abuse could raise its ugly head. One is usually acutely aware of one's personal experiences in these matters: I experienced both sides of the coin.

It was a couple of years after the war had ended. Two uncles who were still single were living at Middleton Hall, as well as uncle Len and his new wife, Doreen. Although my parents had moved to 'the cottage' about five years earlier, I often found myself sharing meals and sometimes even staying overnight at the farm. On this particular occasion, I had to share a bed with my two uncles. This was just part of the rough and tumble of farm life, but I didn't like being stuck in the middle of the bed while my two large uncles slumbered on either side. They didn't snore—well, not too loudly—but I felt trapped; worst of all, I felt too warm. I was no complainer, so all I could do was stay put and try to sleep.

I woke earlier than usual, scrambled out of the bed and got dressed, already looking forward to my own bed at 'the cottage', the next night. What I didn't realise was that I had contracted an itchy skin disease, known as scabies. It wasn't as dangerous as measles or chicken pox, but it was highly contagious. I had to be quarantined from other children in the village for three whole weeks.

Three weeks seemed an interminably long time to a seven-year-old boy, who loved to be in the thick of things; but even worse, many of the other kids were not sympathetic. If, on their way home from school, they spotted me at the farm-house, they would chant "Scabies! Scabies!" I still liked to spend time at the farm, but I quickly learnt to retreat into the house whenever I saw the schoolchildren approaching.

Then there was the other side of the coin. In 1948, a skinny, bespectacled boy about a year younger than I, who was an only child, moved from the London area to Rhossili. His parents ran the Broad Park guesthouse for more than five years. His father also freelanced as an accountant, sometimes working for an auction-eering firm or keeping the books for the Grass Drier Cooperative at Scurlage.

This boy did not take to the more physical sports or to farming chores; but he was very intelligent and imaginative—great fun to be with. In school holidays or at weekends, I often spent an afternoon at Broad Park, enjoying his fleet of Dinky cars or playing board games. Yet, because he had a different personality from most of us farm boys and also sounded very different with his English prep-school accent, a few of us began to harass him with name-calling at school.

On one occasion, a couple of the other boys assisted me in waylaying him on his way home. Three or four of us caught him and roughed him up, just below Brook Cottage. On later reflection, I could understand that he must have felt not only frightened, but perhaps worse, isolated.

Apparently, he made excuses not to come to school the next day—which was how his parents found out. His father had a word with my father; then my father marched me out to Broad Park and made me apologise. That was the end of the bullying. The boy and I soon resumed what would become a long-lasting friendship.

Secondary school was a much different proposition. Tussles were frequent and fights were fairly regular, while bullying could be an ongoing problem for the unfortunate few. On the more harmless side, on our long bus-ride home from school, most of the boys would get off the school-bus at The Towers while the bus delivered the Oxwich teenagers. The older boys would put us newcomers through a ritual which involved removing our pants and ridiculing our private parts. I did not consider this to be anything more than a minor embarrassment.

I observed (and on occasion, experienced) serious bullying from only one older boy. This boy's true colours were revealed in an inter-village football match, when he annoyed one the opposition team and then made the mistake of challenging him to a fight. Although the other boy was younger, he soon had our bully screaming for help. This should have taught him a lesson, but sadly he continued picking on younger or weaker boys until at least his late teens.

Up to the age of about twelve, it seemed to me that one must always anticipate a high probability of having to prove oneself against any newcomers of a similar age. There was one boy who was a regular summer visitor to our village because his grandparents had lived there all their lives. He was almost a year older than I, and therefore somewhat stronger. We became very good friends, mainly because of our common interest in sports. We sometimes corresponded during the winter months. Actually, we shared some great-grandparents through our maternal grandmothers, so we were third cousins.

When we finally disagreed over some minor issue, I realised I had little chance of out-punching him, so I decided to act first. Without warning, I took a wild swing at him, connecting with his ear. This, of course, made him instantly angry. I realised I was in trouble, but it was too late. He delivered a beautiful straight punch right between my eyes, followed by another one for good measure. I realised he wasn't only talented at athletics, football and cricket—he was good at boxing, too. I endured a couple of weeks of embarrassment and disgrace, with a black eye to boot, before I felt that the incident was forgotten in the village. By then, we were happy to resume our friendship and put the incident behind us.

It was perhaps the following summer that the two of us jogged down to Fall Bay one afternoon. It wasn't a great day for a swim; it was quite fine, but there was a light, chilly breeze and the tide was well out, almost flat calm.

We had just begun to walk towards Mewslade when we saw a group of five boys coming towards us. Alas, they were about our age and they looked rough and tough. They must be Welsh "townies" who had come down for the day or were camping somewhere nearby.

There was nothing to do but keep walking. If they had been English visitors, they would almost certainly have ignored us; but as we approached, our fears were confirmed by their accents. They were valley boys alright; so now, what? They confronted us with some probing questions, asking whether we would like to fight them and addressing us as "wus"—a clear sign that they were confident of their superiority. Well, we played it cool and to our relief, they decided to continue on their way.

After they had gone, my friend asked me what I thought we should have done if they had insisted on fighting. I said I supposed we would just have to fight: I hadn't thought of any other option. He said he had assumed we would have run as fast as we could, since there were five of them. Perhaps he forgot that I, though not lacking in stamina, wasn't as fast as he was.

A few years later, in 1957, I became at odds with another boy who was a regular summer visitor. He was a tall, strong boy. Although he was at least two years younger than I, he ignored my warnings. I challenged him to "meet me on Thursday and 'have it out' after I finish my day's work at the car-park". The word got around and there was great anticipation among the village boys.

Anyway, my opponent and I decided to meet earlier than we originally planned. I didn't dislike him and I was hoping he wouldn't show up. When he did, it put me in a no-win situation. After a brief wresting match, we both realised we didn't want this to get any worse, so we decided to shake hands and call it a day, just as the first of the would-be spectators began to arrive. I was about seventeen.

From then on, I resolved I would do my best to restrict the physical stuff to the boxing ring or the sports field.

36

Roping Horses ... and Pigeons

The best laid schemes o' mice an' men
Gang aft a-gley.

Robert Burns

MY friend, Ron Beynon, often came up with an idea about how to spend an afternoon in the school holidays or on weekends. On this occasion, in the Easter holidays, he suggested we should try to catch one of the many horses roaming the common lands. He had seen some on Pitton Cross common the previous afternoon, when he was returning from a trip to Swansea on the bus. I thought his suggestion had some merit, though it sounded a bit risky; besides, I was sure that neither of us really knew how we would go about achieving the objective. Even if we could catch one of those horses, it might be dangerous to try to ride it.

Ron borrowed a piece of sisal line about twenty feet long, from The Ship farm. We set off to walk to Pitton Cross common. As we trudged up Pitton Cross hill in our short trousers and well-worn jackets, the half-past two bus came flying around the bend. The driver, the legendary Jim Brockie, waved to us. We reached the open common and began to walk across it. Sure enough, there were about a dozen horses and ponies grazing there. As we walked towards them, we discussed a course of action: the first step would be to drive them into the confines of Kinmoor Lane. We hadn't yet thought of a second step.

We spread out and began to move the herd towards the lane. This should have been quite easy, but there was an aggressive young stallion which was determined not to be told where to go. Just as the herd was about to enter the lane, he snorted and wheeled away to gallop between me and the hedge of Will Tucker's field. He passed within about five yards of me; the rest of the herd followed. We were not pleased, but we knew we couldn't give up that easily.

156

On the third attempt, we got the herd headed into the lane. We followed, feeling some sense of success: but what to do next? As we plodded through the lane, with the herd about thirty yards in front of us, we racked our brains for a plan. We knew that ahead of us were the ruins of an old stone cottage and disused garden, where a few apple trees and gooseberry bushes still flourished.

Shortly before we reached the ruined cottage, we passed through what had once been a gateway in a garden hedge. Ron suddenly had a great idea: if one of us could drive the herd through the gateway, the other one could attempt to lasso one of the horses. We stopped and considered the situation. The horses had already passed through the gateway before us, so it was too late to implement the plan—or was it?

We decided on a scheme which just might work. Carrying the coiled-up rope, I jumped over the hedge into a field alongside the lane and jogged along until I was well past the herd. Meanwhile, Ron had retreated about a hundred yards back towards the common. When I got ahead of the horses, I scrambled back through the hedge into the lane and confronted them. The stallion did not seem too pleased to see me, but I advanced steadily, slapping my arms to my sides. The horses turned and began trotting back the way they had come.

I followed the horses until the last of them had retreated through the gateway in the garden hedge. Now, it was Ron's turn. When they reached him, he would reverse their direction once more. I crouched beside the hedge, on one side of the gateway. The horses would not be able to see me, as they came back towards me. As I crouched there, I hastily formed a loop at one end of the rope and made a simple slip knot. Already I could hear Ron "hallooing" as he forced the young stallion to reverse direction yet again.

Soon, I could hear the thud of hooves as the horses, now breaking into a trot, hastened towards my hiding place. I didn't have much hope of lassoing any of them; but at least I would try, then we could call it a day. The first group of three or four horses rushed past me before I could move; but I had seen just how they came through the gap. *Look out, here comes the next bunch!* I concentrated on timing my throw. Just as the next horse reached the gap, I optimistically lobbed the noose into the air in front of it. *Missed! No!* Suddenly the rope was slipping through my left hand and I quickly grabbed on with my right one, before it disappeared.

By dint of cunning and careful planning, we had captured a fine young mare. The loop had closed around her nose, just below the eyes, and this had been enough to hold her. Ron came running up, full of excitement. He loved horses almost as much as tractors. Now we had to decide what to do next. Without a bridle, we didn't feel it was safe to try to ride this strange horse, but if one of us led the horse, the other could ride it. Ron formed a halter by looping the rope behind the mare's ears, then back to the loop around her nose. He told me to climb up on the horse from a nearby bank, while he held her by the halter. *Whew!* The mare remained calm and obedient while Ron led her out of Kinmoor Lane and turned towards Fernhill farm.

We hadn't got too far, though, before we realised we were being followed. The aggressive young stallion was trailing us every step of the way, tossing his head and generally looking agitated. We pressed on, but with a growing sense of nervousness. Every few yards, I would twist around on the mare's back to take another look at the stallion. *Was he getting closer?* "Yes, I'm sure he is," I told Ron. In fact, he seemed to be breaking into a trot after us. He could catch up with us in a couple of minutes! *What should we do?* I decided it was time to slide off the mare's back; so we led the horse together. Still the stallion approached.

About this time, we both seemed to ask ourselves where we were headed with our captive. Neither of us really knew the answer to that one. I certainly couldn't take it home to 'the cottage', but neither would Ron's father appreciate him turning up at The Ship farm with someone else's mare. Stimulated by the presence of the stallion, we realised that we would just have to release our captive before we went home for our tea. Common sense told us that a couple of nine-year-olds didn't want to risk any serious confrontation with that stallion.

As we got abreast of Fernhill farm, we looked to see whether farmer Reg Howells was about. He would know how to deal with the persistent stallion. But the farmyard was deserted—not even Reg's dogs were around to help. We looked at each other, then reluctantly slipped our improvised halter off the mare's head. We watched as she turned and trotted off to join her possessive mate.

"What'll we do tomorrow, Ron?" I asked, as we carried our coiled rope homeward.

Lassoing adventures weren't entirely confined to horses. Once in a while, a racing pigeon would be blown off course and hang around for a few days, perchance to recover its strength and its bearings. We could always identify them by the rings and bands on their legs.

On one occasion, a particularly beautiful pigeon remained for several days in Jack Richards's rickyard, opposite The Ship farm. Late one afternoon, Ron and I decided we'd try to capture it. We knew the standard procedure for trapping birds. Ron found a deep wooden box in one of his dad's sheds. He also sneaked half a slice of white bread from his mother's kitchen. Now all we needed was a short stick and a lengthy piece of binder-twine.

With our trap set up, we made half a dozen attempts, but the pigeon escaped every time. This was not going to work—either the box was not dropping quickly enough or the pigeon was too alert. However, the wily bird kept returning for the bread, as though it was beginning to enjoy the game. There was no chance of trapping it, now. But was there another way?

After some discussion, we hit on the idea of a simple noose. We had noticed that the pigeon favoured one particular corner of the roof of a low brick building. From somewhere around The Ship farm, we borrowed a good length of thick cord, formed a noose at one end, then climbed up to the corner of the shed and draped the noose where the pigeon liked to perch. We added a few crumbs of bread for good measure. After five minutes or so, the pigeon alighted on the roof and strutted directly to the centre of the noose (as far as we could judge). I tugged the cord sharply: the startled bird flew up, as the noose fell off the shed. Two more attempts failed.

We were ready to give up, but the bird wasn't as smart as we thought. It still kept coming back to exactly the same spot on the corner of the roof. Right, one more shot, we agreed. We placed the noose carefully, making it a little smaller than before; then we hid behind the shed, holding the end of the cord and waiting patiently.

The pigeon landed, walked to the breadcrumbs and began to peck. It was my turn: I closed my eyes, counted 1, 2, 3, and tugged sharply on the cord. The pigeon ascended gracefully. *Oh no, missed again*, I thought, as the pigeon flew away. But the cord was ascending, too! We held firmly on to our end and slowly pulled the bird down to us—it was caught by one leg.

Ron and I kept our magnificent prize in captivity for a day or so, so we could show it off to as many of our friends as possible, then we let it go. We would have liked to learn more about racing pigeons, but there was no one we knew in our village who indulged in the sport.

37

Authority Figures

Even reproofs from authority ought to be grave, and not taunting.

Francis Bacon

TO a farm-worker's child growing up in the years around 1950, there was no shortage of authority figures. In reflecting on my own reactions to what seemed to be an overload of authority, I can certainly relate to the rebellious nature of young people of every generation.

From a youngster's viewpoint, the coastguards were the friendliest of all the formal authorities. Although they wore sombre uniforms, they seemed entirely benign to us and could only be heard barking orders during rocket practices or rescue operations. They never tried to control our access to the cliffs, the bays or Worms Head. We youngsters rewarded them by never getting into trouble, despite the many potential hazards along the rugged coastline.

Our local policeman, Tom Mabbet from Porteynon, was a rare visitor to the village. Whenever he appeared on his motorbike, the old-timers on 'the bank' would urge us boys to run and hide. They got a kick out of seeing us get nervous. Whenever we heard a motorbike coming up past the Lower Shop, we would run into Will Morris's rickyard. Despite our apprehensions, the only attention we ever received from Tom was a friendly smile or a wave of his gloved hand.

From when I was a small boy, my father had unintentionally encouraged my apprehensions by sometimes threatening to tell the policeman when I disobeyed him. This ended one day, before I was five, when he was trying to correct my behaviour at teatime. I said to him, in a mocking voice: "What now? Tell peace-man, is it?" My parents were "tickled pink" at my audacity, but they never used that threat again.

160

Our parents, of course, were the strictest authorities in our lives; but this was more than offset by the work they did to give us food, shelter, clothing, schooling, toys and entertainment. I knew of no children who did not seem to have plenty of respect and appreciation for their parents' efforts to provide for their needs.

Our schoolteachers were at least as influential as our parents in shaping our attitudes, work ethics, hopes and aspirations. Rhossili School was blessed with two excellent teachers, Lily Button and Ada Thomas—though it has to be admitted that the latter's forceful style may not have been ideally suited to the psyches of some of her pupils. She tested everyone's preparedness for the dreaded 11+ examination, well in advance of the actual event. No one was encouraged to attempt it unless they had a reasonable chance of success.

As we moved on to secondary education, we were perhaps not well prepared for the more impersonal relationships with our teachers. Hence, the air of authority intensified, but with a sense of diminished input from the student's perspective. There was no such thing as parent-teacher meetings in those days—not that many of us teenagers would have cared for the idea.

There is no doubt that we were taught to respect all adults, at least to their faces. On occasion, some farmers would discourage kids from playing on their properties. However, if they had an orchard, they would eventually pay for their unfriendliness. For others, revenge might be sought around Guy Fawkes when a fizzing banger might be placed on the doorstep (or in the keyhole), followed by a sharp knock on the door and a hasty retreat by the perpetrators. Sometimes these incidents almost resulted in a heart attack—not so much from the exploding firework as from the fit of anger which could follow.

On one occasion when a farmer's wife suspected me (amongst others) of stealing her apples, she told me that she would much prefer me to ask for some apples, rather than steal them. It took me a while to absorb this strange new concept; but a few weeks later, feeling a bit hungry by late afternoon, I decided I would give it a try instead of walking home to 'the cottage' for my tea.

Putting on my most innocent face, I knocked on the door and politely asked if there were some apples to spare. "Yes, certainly," said the farmer's wife, "I'll fetch some for you". She soon returned with a small brown paper bag crammed with rosy apples. I began to thank her and tell her I didn't need quite so many apples, but she said, "That's alright, Cyril ... that will be sixpence, please."

Sometimes, an adult could be victimised quite undeservedly. One of my friends found that he was strong enough to hold back retired Professor Lee's moped, so he made a habit of hanging on to the parcel rack, usually after the professor had stopped to pick up his pint bottle of milk from Jessamine farm. I participated once or twice in this mischief, though I felt that it was somehow breaking an unwritten code of conduct with regard to respect for our elders.

The influence of authority on our parents was less amusing. Authorities of all kinds affected their ability to provide for their families. From an early age I heard my parents discussing the Penrice Estate because that was where they paid their rent, every six months. The day-to-day administration of the estate was the responsibility of one Mr. Pritchard, initially, but then it became Mr. Sinnett until my parents purchased 'the cottage' in the late 1940s. There was always concern as to whether there would be enough money to pay the rent, after buying food, coal and other necessities.

Because of the hand-to-mouth existence of the married farm-workers, coupled with the absence of unemployment benefits, their employers had a disproportionate influence on them and their families. Fortunately, this was tempered to some extent by the ongoing shortage of farm-workers from the early 1930s. Farm-workers often had a choice of employers, which some exercised from time to time, unless they lived in "tied" accommodation.

Throughout the 1940s, our parents were subjected to severe rationing of food and clothing. Producing your own food from animals resulted in further regulations. Almost as late as 1950, popular Moor Corner farmer, Ron Parry, was fined for being too generous with the richness of the ice-cream that he sold door-to-door around southwest Gower. Of course, during the war years, our parents experienced even more rules and regulations. The men belonged to one or other of the local auxiliary services, and all adults were required to carry Identity Cards when travelling to and from town.

Our postmaster, Will Williams, served our interests on the Gower RDC throughout the 1940s. When he decided to retire, farmer Jack Richards JP took his place. Our parents could always count on good advice from either of them. The Parish Council included (at various times): Jack Bevan, Mansel Bevan, Alf Bevan, Jack Richards, Wilfred Beynon, Mary Roberts, Jim Brockie and Ingram Button. They exerted at least indirect influence over our lives, though as a child I was vague on the details. They addressed many matters on behalf of the parish, ranging from the issues related to the village school to communication with such organisations such as the Gower Society and the National Trust.

It was a reflection of the secularisation of our society that the religious leaders exerted virtually no authority. They did their best to encourage people to participate in all the traditional Christian activities, especially at Christmas, Easter and Thanksgiving. They did their best to encourage youngsters to attend Sunday-school by organising annual outings and Christmas parties. Nevertheless, it was largely through the influence of such conservative elders that the Parish Council managed to keep Rhossili without a public-house until the 1970s.

To the working people, the Gower Society was considered to consist of a bunch of do-gooders who often got their priorities wrong. They seemed to oppose any development by local people (including small farmers and farm-workers) who might want to make improvements to their properties. Further-more, by limiting the development of facilities, they seemed to discourage outsid-ers from enjoying the beauty of Gower. Nevertheless their sincere intention to do the right thing for Gower was not doubted. Most ordinary people just thought they were misguided.

The National Trust was an invisible body which posted signs and notices, tell-ing the natives what (or more likely, what not) to do. We were sometimes made to feel like outsiders in our own parish. In the early 1950s, I suddenly became aware that it was not only the Worms Head that was an official bird sanctuary, but so was all the rest of the parish coastline. Henceforth, there would be no gulls' eggs for breakfast in the early spring, even though there seemed to be no shortage of seagulls. There were permanent signs erected on posts around the cliff-lands, which laid down the law to those who had been born and raised to expect certain freedoms—even under the Penrice Estate. In other cultures, this would have been considered an unnatural and unfair restriction of indigenous rights. But no one objected. The locals may have sneered at it, but it was accepted peacefully.

The larger farmers in particular (but also many others) were sometimes at log-gerheads with the Gower Society and the National Trust because of their opposi-tion to the use of land for building or for grazing rights. The distaste for what was perceived as outside interference filtered through to the farm-workers, particu-larly when the Gower Society fought (with the support of some influential parish elders) to prevent the development of a Butlins holiday camp at the Llangennith end of Rhossili Bay, in the mid-1950s. After all, this project would have resulted in a variety of alternative employment opportunities for locals.

It seemed to the working people, and therefore to their children, that when one form of authority was not controlling their lives, then some other form was. Nevertheless, we youngsters were generally uncomplaining, preferring to seek out the wide range of opportunities that social and technological changes were bring-ing to us.

But the predictable result would be the (eventual) abandonment of Rhossili by virtually all the working-class families.

[Endnote: Over the past quarter century, the policies of the EU have increased its influence over rural communities. The fact that the EU sets a high priority on quality of life factors and heritage sites of all kinds would seem to lend tremendous support to the objectives of the Gower Society and the National Trust. When Gower was officially declared to be an Area of Outstanding Natural Beauty (AONB) in 1956, its long-term future was effectively predetermined.]

38

Kindness and Cruelty

Nothing can be more obvious than that all animals were created solely and exclusively for the use of man.

Thomas Love Peacock

ON and around the farms, animals were invariably accorded a degree of respect. Priority was given to their feed, water and general well-being. Farmers and farm-workers arose well before breakfast to "do the things". Yet in the end, the primary function of animals was to provide sources of labour and food for human beings. In contrast to today's values, the care and concern for the well-being of animals was never on a par with that of humans.

When a farm animal died, there was no fanfare: it was simply disposed of as quickly as possible. Smaller animals might be buried (sometimes covered over with quicklime) near a hedge, or a corner of a fallow field or garden, where they were unlikely to be disturbed by farm implements. Perhaps there would be a marker for a while. Larger animals, such as cows and horses, were usually taken away by Tomkins's lorry to be disposed of, with no money changing hands. If the animal was still alive, a flat fee of a couple of pounds might be paid to the farmer.

In the late 1940s there was a brown-and-white spaniel at Middleton Hall. One day, its neck swelled up enormously. It became obvious that it had been bitten by an adder. I think it was about May, when adders were particularly venomous. For a few days the dog was given bowls and bowls of milk, but to no avail. The swelling was getting worse and the dog was clearly suffering. Uncle Len took the poor spaniel and placed her near the stable wall; then he fetched his 12-bore shotgun. One shot from about a dozen yards was enough to put the poor animal out of its misery.

From as young as five years old, I and my pals, Ron and Howard, found that hanging on to a cow's tail was a great way to get around. The trick was to get the cow pointed in the direction you wanted to go. Wearing our hobnailed boots (made to measure by the village cobbler, Harry Gammon) it was even possible to crouch and "skate" down Sheep Green hill. Woe to any cows we caught wandering the hillside or roads, though little harm was done.

On the other hand, tying a tin can to a sheep's tail was not something to be proud of. My friend Ron was not in favour of this experiment, but I wouldn't listen. We were on the green in front of Rose Cottage when a stray sheep came wandering by. It wasn't difficult to find a discarded sardine tin and a piece of string. Ron held the sheep still while I did the tying. At first, the sheep just stood there, looking bemused at the contraption.

Carefully, like scientists involved in a ground-breaking experiment, we encouraged the sheep to take a few steps on the paved road. The can clinked on the surface of the road: the sheep's ears pricked up. The can clinked again; the sheep took a couple of quick steps. Clink-clink! Suddenly it sprinted down the road towards the Lower Shop. We never thought a sheep could move so fast.

Once we got over our amazement, we gave chase as fast as we could run; but by the time we got to the Lower Shop, the sheep was already out of sight down Mewslade Lane. As we jogged down the narrow lane, we met a family of summer visitors. The man asked if we were the ones who had tied the can to the sheep's tail. I must have looked as guilty as I felt, but I said that someone else had tied the can to the sheep and that we just wanted to catch the sheep to remove it. The last part was true, but I don't think he believed me. However, we never caught up with the sheep. Perhaps the man had been able to stop it and remove the can; we would never know.

Much later, in my mid-teens, I was alone one afternoon at 'the cottage' when I found one of our cats in a very bad state. The young tabby was crawling on its belly, moaning pitifully. I realised it must have found and eaten some kind of poison. What should I do? I couldn't leave it in that state. I was now the proud owner of a powerful air-rifle, but that was the only gun we had at the time. Perhaps I should have run to try to find a neighbour with a shotgun.

I slipped a piece of cardboard under the cat and dragged it out onto some fallow ground. I fetched a spade from the shed and dug a hole more than a foot deep. As gently as I could, I tipped the cat off the cardboard, into the hole. Then I fetched my air-rifle and slugs. I loaded it and pressed the muzzle to the centre of the cat's forehead. *This should do it*, I thought, as I pulled the trigger. To my horror, the cat jumped right out of the hole. It was about the most unpleasant moment of my life.

Pulling myself together, I realised I had to finish the job now, so I quickly reloaded. Then I held the gun to the cat's head and fired again. *The cat should at least be unconscious*, I thought, *and therefore feeling no pain*. But it was still moving. I reloaded and fired several more shots before I was satisfied that the cat was indeed dead, so I could push it into the hole and cover it over. Then, rather shakily, I returned to the house and waited for my parents to come home.

In 1953, when our family was temporarily relocated to Middleton Hall because of the major renovations taking place at 'the cottage', our cat (known only as "puss") was left to fend for itself. My mother, who was never a cruel person, would visit 'the cottage' at least once a week and put milk and food in a bowl for the cat, outside the back door. The cat was healthy and capable of obtaining its own food supply, for the most part.

Nevertheless, some female do-gooder, who had business at the school, found the hungry-looking cat wandering nearby and took steps to find out who it belonged to. My mother, who was the caretaker at the school, never denied it was her cat. The do-gooder threatened to report the situation to the RSPCA. The issue did not go far, but it caused my poor mother some distress.

I had learned that putting an animal out of its misery was not cruelty; while trying to treat animals as if they were humans was not necessarily kindness.

39

Rocket Practice

When I'm not thank'd at all, I'm thank'd enough,
I've done my duty and I've done no more.

Henry Fielding

RHOSSILI had a long history of shipwrecks. Of the more than thirty shipwrecks occurring along the Gower coast since about 1750, about half occurred around the coastline of the Parish of Rhossili, between Paviland and Burry Holms. Many of the village families had a proud tradition of serving in the "rocket crew", from its formation, in the late 19th century.

The Rhossili crew were always proud of their record, not only because of their involvement in some notable land-based rescues (including the *Roche Castle*, in 1937), but also because they won most of their competitions with neighbouring crews, such as Oxwich. When they didn't win, it was always due to some unforeseeable misfortune. They maintained a sharp edge with their teamwork by taking their practices seriously. During the mid-1950s they won the (all-Wales) Cambrian Cup on two occasions.

Most of the able-bodied working men in the village, including farmers, were involved. There were several representatives from some of the larger families. There were four brothers from the Jones family (Will, Phil, Joffre and Len); two from the Shepherd family (Doug and Les); and a large contingent from the Beynon family, including three sets of brothers (Reggie and Ernie; George and William; Enoch and Stanley) as well as Wilfred. When a new man joined the crew, he was assigned a numbered armband. If a crewman missed a practice, he must provide an explanation to the senior coastguard; if he missed two practices in a year, his armband could be allocated to some keen young man on the waiting list.

There were about half a dozen full-scale practices a year: the first was held in the early spring, about the middle of April. They were always held on Sunday mornings at about ten o'clock. It was indeed a fine sight to see most of the able-bodied men of the village performing with such discipline and teamwork. The weather usually cooperated, though it was often fresh and breezy on the open cliffs.

On one particular Sunday morning, in the spring of 1951, the weather was quite atrocious. There was a persistent drizzle, but worst of all, there was a chilly westerly wind with strong, unpredictable gusts. Since shipwrecks almost invariably occurred in bad weather, Chief Coastguard Dorling decided to press on with the practice.

Until the late 1940s, farmer Bowen Richards had hitched his tractor to the impressive wagon loaded with rescue equipment, and towed it from the "rocket house" located at the base of Rhossili Down, past the car-park and the Coastguard houses, to the practice site. But now, the modern, lighter equipment was stored in the new Coastguard Rescue Equipment building, next to the Coastguard houses. It just had to be loaded onto an ordinary farm trailer.

The crew, though not enjoying the drizzle, dutifully unloaded the boxes of essential equipment—the rocket mounting, rocket components, firing line, hawser, tripods, blocks and breeches-buoy. The rocket was assembled and cleared for action, but the difficult part still lay ahead. To complicate matters, a new type of rocket was to be used for the first time. Some tough decisions had to be made.

The target was the fake ship's mast near the edge of the cliff. Should they fire lower than usual, so as to avoid the worst effects of the wind? If so, the three men (Will Jones, Jack Gibbs and Ingram Chalk) who usually formed the "ship's crew" would not take their usual stations in the ditch near the base of the mast: for safety reasons, they would stay behind the rocket until after it was fired.

Should the rocket be aimed well to the west of the mast to allow for the strong, gusty wind? If the wind suddenly dropped, it might fly uselessly over the cliff edge; but if the wind gusted too strongly, it might fly along the cliff edge. It was an unacceptable risk to have the rocket fly in a direction where unobserved animals, or even humans, could be lurking.

After what seemed like an endless discussion to the crew members and the handful of onlookers, Coastguards Dorling, Payne, Parker and Number One (Alf Bevan), were ready to fire. The "ship's crew" waited with the main party, even though the rocket was aimed well to the west of the wooden mast. The crew stood in a disciplined line, well behind the rocket, with their backs to the stone wall of Bowen Richards's field. We spectators (mostly sons of the crew members) stood even further away.

"Fire, Number One!" Bang! This was the moment we boys held in awe. No matter how much warning we got, it still made us jump. The rocket roared off into the drizzle, the thin orange firing-line snaking out of the box at a furious pace. We could see that the line was curving well to the west side of the mast, before the rocket disappeared over the edge of the cliff.

It was a bad shot alright; the wind had suddenly lulled at the instant of firing, so it had missed the ship's mast (which only some seventy yards away) by about thirty yards. Nevertheless, it was decided to press on with the drill.

The "ship's crew" hustled over to the mast. Two of them prepared to mount a block at the top of the mast, while another retrieved the orange firing line, now lying lifelessly on the grass.

In a series of efficient operations, blocks and tackle were employed to pull out a thick hawser, which was then firmly anchored at both the "shore" end and the "ship" end. This supported the running-block and tackle for the breeches-buoy. Furthermore, guide ropes were set up such that the "shore party" could do all the pulling to move the breeches-buoy in either direction. To keep the breeches-buoy clear of the ground at the "shore" end, a sturdy tripod was erected, with a block at its apex to support the main hawser.

Half a dozen of the shore party moved the breeches-buoy smoothly, hauling in unison on the outward or inward line, as necessary. Usually, one of the "ship's crew" would ride in the buoy to simulate a rescue, but with today's wet, slippery conditions, they decided not to take chances. Meanwhile, several men were kept busy retrieving the firing line and rocket casing, which was dangling almost down to the bottom of the cliff.

Finally, it was time to wrap up, but that took some time to do. The firing line, the hawser and the guide ropes had to be re-coiled carefully in their boxes, in a prescribed figure-eight pattern. All the other equipment had to be properly stowed. Usually, there was a resuscitation practice before the men were dismissed, but it was cancelled that day because it was so wet.

The crew followed the tractor and trailer back to the Coastguard Station, where they received their fixed payment. It was already past noon. Then, most of them proceeded to The Green, where they picked up their Sunday newspapers and plodded homeward, knowing that their well-deserved Sunday dinners would await them.

That day, every man earned the ten shillings he received.

40

The Shepherds

A merry heart maketh a cheerful countenance.

The Bible: Proverbs 15:13

ALF Shepherd was the son of an itinerant railway worker, Joe Shepherd, who hailed from somewhere in the West Country of England. He was lean, big-boned and rugged-looking; he had large fleshy ears and a nose to match. Twenty-year-old Alf married eighteen-year-old Violet Richards of Fernhill Top in 1910; so they were still youngsters when they made their lifelong commitment. Violet was the sister of "aunty Mag" of High Priest, and "uncle Lem" and "aunty Min" of Fernhill Top. Another sibling, Albert, lived at Penclawdd.

"Aunty Vi" (as I knew her when she was in her middle-age) was a plump, cheerful woman with a round face which seemed to bear a perpetual smile. Alf, too, had a well-developed sense of humour which was reinforced from time to time by a deep, booming laugh. Their family home was West Pilton Cottage, a large slate-roofed farmhouse near West Pilton farm. It was one of the more isolated places in the village in the days when working-class families did not have cars; so all their shopping had to be carried home from the bus-stop at Pitton Cross. There was no electricity or indoor plumbing until about 1950.

Alf and Violet produced four sons, Leslie, Douglas, Raymond and Malcolm, and two daughters, Olive and Elvira. They were tall, big-boned people; the only exception being Olive, who was relatively petite. They were always a close-knit family, often loud and boisterous, yet jovial and friendly. They supported each other, first and foremost. They were not church-going people, but they were kind-hearted and enjoyed many years of happy times and family celebrations at their isolated home, as the children grew up during the pre-war years.

"Aunty Vi" was a first cousin of my maternal grandmother (nee Sarah Jane Richards), thus my mother always referred to her as "aunty". On more than one occasion, I accompanied my mother to join the Shepherds for a birthday or anniversary celebration. We would catch the bus to Pitton Cross, then walk across several fields. On one occasion, my maternal grandmother came with us. There was great joy between her and Violet, as they had not seen each other for quite a few years and probably would not meet again for several more. Burdened with families of their own, without telephones or personal transportation, many working people relied on chance meetings or rare opportunities to visit extended family members.

On such visits, I saw that Alf kept a large, well-tended garden, so that his family could grow quite a lot of their own vegetables and fruit. Runner-beans, peas, carrots and new potatoes were all considered important components of the basic diet. Alf liked to do a bit of fishing along the Pilton cliffs; he also snared rabbits. In spring, seagulls' eggs must have been plentiful. He also fattened up a pig, every year.

Not surprisingly, Alf's two oldest sons, Douglas and Leslie, developed a strong liking for market-gardening, which led them to operate a stall in the old Swansea Market for many years, after the war. They were also long-serving members of the "rocket crew". As a young man, Douglas was involved in the celebrated rescue of the *Roche Castle* which foundered off Paviland cliffs in 1937. They continued to serve until at least the mid-1950s.

Douglas married Sheila Alstedt in 1933. They lived and farmed at Sluxton from about 1940 to the mid-1950s. Sluxton farmhouse was the most isolated dwelling in the parish; it was actually closer to Llangennith, but there was a better roadway to Middleton. Their two daughters, Marlene and Gloria, had to make the long daily trek, first to Rhossili School; then later, to catch the school-bus at 'the bank'. They could find their way home across the moor-land on the dark winter evenings, with just the help of a torch. Often though, their father would meet them at Fernhill with the tractor and trailer.

A visit to Sluxton was always fun, whether for threshing or for a birthday tea-party. It was a lovely farm with a spacious orchard and garden. Near one of the farm buildings could be found the remains of an ancient motorcar, which must have been impressive in its day. It had solid tires, the windscreen opened outwards and upwards, and the two large doors opened the wrong way. It also had a running board on either side. The headlights were huge, supported by brackets mounted on the large, front wheel-wells. There was an over-sized brake-lever and short, orange-coloured indicators that popped out of slots in the door pillars. We kids were happy to spend an hour or two exploring the fascinating mechanical features of the grand old car.

Leslie Shepherd married Winifred Jones, who hailed from the little village of Landimore near Llanmadoc. She was a slim, raven-haired beauty, with fine features and a pale complexion. They lived in a semidetached farm-worker's cottage in Upper Pitton, where their next-door neighbour was Phil Richards, a lifelong resident of the area.

Les and Winnie raised a daughter, Beryl, born in 1941, who would one day continue the family tradition at the rebuilt Swansea Market. Their son, David, was not born until the mid-1950s. Whenever Winnie took Beryl to visit their relatives in Landimore, they would get off the bus at Knelston and walk the rest of the way—a distance of about three miles!

My mother would sometimes decide we should "take a walk down round Pitton and back up Bunkers Hill". If "aunty Win" was at home when we knocked on the door, we would be invited in for a cup of tea and a piece of cake or some biscuits. I was never bored by these visits, because she—and "uncle Les" too, if he were there—would always find something to tease me about, while enjoying a good chuckle.

Raymond Shepherd had served three years in the British Army, even before the war started. In 1939 he re-enlisted to serve for three more years. He was evacuated from Dunkirk; then served in other parts of the world. Fortunately, he suffered no serious wounds, though he did lose the tip of a finger, which had been jammed in a gun carriage. He also suffered from recurring nightmares. He was discharged in 1943. He married a Reynoldston girl (Joyce Jones) and lived in Swansea for a few years, but returned to work at Bevan Tucker's farm.

The oldest daughter, Olive, worked as a bus-conductress through the war years, but shortly afterwards, she took a factory job in the London area. There, she met her husband, Jack Kemp. They decided to set up home in Rhossili, where they purchased Dainsbury after the Williamses moved to Oxwich, and continued to run it as a bed-and-breakfast enterprise. Jack worked as a bus-driver. Eventually they built their own bungalow nearby, which they named Carissima.

The younger daughter, Elvira, married Harold Hinton early in the war years. Harold served throughout the war with the RAOC. After about five years' service, he was demobbed in 1945. At that time, he received the customary dark-blue demob suit and civilian Ration Book. Two daughters, Christine and Dawn, were born in 1943 and 1946. By contrast, it wasn't until the 1950s, that Alf's youngest boy, Malcolm, was called upon to do his National Service. Afterwards he commenced a long career with the police force in London.

In the meantime, when one Harry Long retired, Alf took over the important job of maintaining the hedges wherever they threatened to encroach on the paved roads. In the 1950s as we youngsters travelled to or from secondary school on the bus, we might first notice Alf's bicycle leaning against a grassy bank or half-hidden in a hedge; then perhaps a hundred yards or so further along the road, we'd see Alf. With his hat pushed to the back of his head, especially on warm days, he wielded a short stick in his left hand to support weeds and brambles while he hacked at them with a sharp hook. To deal with the stems of bushes, he would use a bill-hook. Sometimes we'd see him pedalling steadily homeward, no doubt looking forward to a fine evening meal—especially on the chilly, wet days.

It was fitting that West Pilton Cottage was among the first homes in Rhossili to boast a television set. It must have done wonders to break the monotony for Alf and Violet in their later years, after their children had left home. Around 1954, Les's daughter, Beryl, and I would sometimes get off the school-bus at Pitton Cross to view the modern-day phenomenon, even though we had to walk home afterwards. Though the picture was snowy, early programmes like *Bill and Ben* were quite fascinating. A couple of years later, Elvira's children, Christine and Dawn, sometimes with my sister, Thelma, would get off the school-bus to keep up with such fascinating serials as *Heidi*.

Throughout the 1950s, Elvira and Harold made a good living by converting their home, New Park Cottage, into tea-rooms, which provided home-cooked lunches and teas to day-trippers, visitors and (sometimes) locals. They were conveniently located adjacent to the bus terminus. Elvira was the proprietor, while Harold augmented the family income by following in his father-in-law's footsteps as the local roadman for a couple of decades.

Elvira was one of the stronger characters in the parish. She epitomised the jovial, generous nature of her family. It seemed as though she found something humorous in every situation. In a village where people were almost always kind to kids, she stood out as a warm-hearted woman. Once in a while, my mother would try to patronise Elvira's business by taking my sister and me there for a simple meal, but invariably Elvira would not accept payment. On the other hand, my mother would often help Elvira on busy Bank Holiday weekends.

Family loyalties remained strong.

[Endnote: Later on, my mother worked part-time for several years at Dainsbury (now Sunnyside), helping Elvira's older sister, Olive, and her husband Jack Kemp with their bed-and-breakfast enterprise.]

41

Sunday-school Outings

Ever let the fancy roam,
Pleasure never is at home.

John Keats

THE nearest we came to taking a family vacation was the annual Sunday-school outing. Those daytrips were sometimes jointly organised by the Church and Chapel. Almost all the families with children, plus a few other fun-loving souls of all ages, took advantage of this joyful experience. Everyone dressed well for these occasions: the men and boys in their best sports-clothes, the women and girls in flowery dresses or pleated skirts and blouses. The day would begin with a small crowd of excited families waiting on 'the bank' by half-past eight on a fine Saturday morning in May or June.

Mostly, the destination of these outings alternated between Barry and Porthcawl. Occasionally, it would be Tenby, "… for a change, like, isn't it?" Barry and Porthcawl were strongly favoured because of their permanent fairgrounds. By the time our bus (usually a double-decker) arrived at our destination, it would be about half-past eleven. This gave us the opportunity to take a walk around the town, stretching our legs after the two-and-half hour journey. The fairground didn't open until at least one o'clock, so kids tried hard to be patient while their parents found a café for the mandatory "cuppa" and a buttered scone—or fish-and-chips, if they felt hungry. Then we looked in a few shop windows, comparing the stores and their contents to what we had in Swansea, or took a walk along the promenade.

The fairground was like another world to us kids. We weren't used to such elaborate technological contraptions. There was just so much to see and experience in one small place. In a way, the excitement was like Christmas—full of magic for about half a day. There were carousels, bumper cars, the ever-popular Ghost Train and a Hall of Mirrors which not only made our mothers scream with laughter, but was hard to find our way out of.

Most importantly for us boys, there were the nerve-testing rides like the Ferris-wheel, the Roller-coaster and fast-whirling contraptions that pressed one's stomach and brains first one way, then the other. In between all this, we would tackle a sticky, pink candyfloss and an ice-cream or two. If our parents would allow us, we could come back at half-past four to see the death-defying motorcyclist ride the Wall of Death; but we had usually spent all our money by then.

Parents would try to drag out the time (and spending money) as much as possible, but most children had usually got through their allowance, plus a bit more, by about three-thirty. However, the bus didn't leave until about five o'clock. Our poor parents would try to draw us away from the rides, diverting out attention to other things and probably wishing the bus was leaving an hour earlier than planned. They would scrape their almost empty pockets for a couple of shillings to buy a last sandwich and cup of tea—well away from the fairground, of course.

On the long ride home, the adults would chat quietly to pass the time, perhaps wondering how they were going to pay for next week's groceries. Someone would start us kids singing songs, which we would then repeat endlessly. *If I Knew You Were Comin', I'd've Baked a Cake* was the big favourite in 1950. The adults were relieved when we eventually became diverted into excited chatter about our day of sheer pleasure.

Once we'd passed Scurlage, one or other of the men would pass his hat around to collect a tip for the driver, then he'd count the money so we'd all know how much had been collected.

One such trip stands out in my memory. I was about eleven. Through picking early potatoes for some of the farmers, I had saved a full three pounds. It was the most money I'd ever owned: it seemed like a small fortune, but I knew what I wanted to do with it. The upcoming Sunday-school trip was beckoning me to Barry fairground, though my parents had decided they wouldn't be able to go, this time.

When we arrived at Barry, I walked around the town impatiently, just killing time for the fairground to open. Finally, one o'clock came: some of the rides began to start up. One by one, I tried them all. I was like a man who has worked hard in the hot sun all day, thirsting for a long, cool drink. I visited the Roller-coaster about six times. I spent my last two shillings when the Wall of Death opened, at half-past four. Then, I was spent out. All I could do was wait for the bus to take me home. It was only then that I realised how hungry I was. I found enough pennies and ha'pennies in my pocket for a packet of crisps.

My parents were aware how much money I had saved, so when they asked me how much I had left, I had to admit it was all gone. I felt guilty because I knew it was more than half a week's wages for a farm-worker. Worse still, I hadn't even bought any real food—just a couple of ice-creams and a packet of crisps. My mother said if I'd managed to buy a decent meal it wouldn't seem so bad. She had a knack of being able to hit the nail on the head. Of course, this made me feel even worse; but I knew I had got fairgrounds out of my system, once and for all.

Tenby, by comparison with Barry and Porthcawl, offered less hectic and less artificial entertainment. There was no fairground to rob the imprudent of their hard-earned cash. Understandably, Tenby was much preferred by the adults. They could take a boat-trip to see the old monastery at Caldey Island; take a fishing trip for a couple of hours; or take a long walk around one of the most fascinating little seaside towns in Britain, stopping every couple of hours for a pot of tea and buttered scones, of course.

On one memorable journey back from Tenby, our modern-looking coach began to sputter as we reached the Loughor River. The driver was able to coax the bus along until we were most of the way up the north side of Cefn Bryn, where it finally sputtered to a halt. It was after 11:00 PM and there was no moon—only starlight to see by.

After a brief discussion with the driver, all the men and teenage boys filed out of the coach. We went around to the rear and put our shoulders into it. In the end, everyone had to get off the bus, except for the driver, but we managed to push the coach to the top of Cefn Bryn. From there, it began to roll slowly down the other side as the last of the men jumped back on board. A few grinds of the clutch and first gear, and we were on our way home.

42

'The Bank'

Yet meet we shall, and part, and meet again,
Where dead men meet on lips of living men.

Samuel Butler

MIDDLETON Bank was the figure-eight shaped area formed by the junctions of the Vile Lane and School Lane with the main road running between Pitton and Rhossili End. 'The bank' was the heart of Middleton and the hub of the parish of Rhossili. Almost within a stone's throw, but in opposite directions, were the two village shops—the Post Office, operated by Will Williams; and the Lower Shop, operated by Alf Richards—which competed to supply all the day-to-day grocery needs of the villagers, most of whom relied on their feet as a means of transportation. There were seven farm-houses within a fifty-yard radius; furthermore, the village hall had been built at 'the bank' in 1924.

The farmers who lived in the vicinity of 'the bank' in the mid-1940s included Jack Gibbs at Mewslade View, Ingram Chalk at Ivy Dene (lived at Hampstead), Will Morris at Middleton Lodge, Wilfred Beynon at The Ship, the Joneses at Middleton Hall, Stan Beynon at Riverside, Alf Bevan at Old Farmhouse and Jack Richards at Jessamine.

In my memory, 'the bank' is forever symbolised by the giant elm tree which grew in the corner of the small, rough field known as Broad Hay, stretching one of its huge branches across the main road to hover over Jessamine farmyard. Along the stone wall underneath the tree lay a heavy, forked limb—generally referred to as "the log"—which served as a two-tiered bench, where villagers could sit and talk for a while.

In the 1940s, unless the weather was wet or cold, old-timers would habitually gather on the fallen branch on weekday evenings to exchange yarns about the old days. Football enthusiasts would join in the continuous game that ebbed and flowed like a tide between the shed doors of Jessamine farm and Will Morris's Middleton Lodge farm, directly opposite. "The log" was perfectly placed for viewing the game, as well as criticising the players.

The other natural feature was the gurgling, sometimes swollen, brook that poured over the water chute outside Stan and May Beynon's farm buildings, then ran past Jack Richards's farmhouse before crossing under the road through a pair of eighteen-inch diameter, steel pipes. Whenever a ball got carried into one of the pipes, if it didn't come out at the downstream end, we would have to dam the stream and release it abruptly to try to wash it through. Stones, twigs and other debris ensured that this was not always a routine task.

From 'the bank' we kids were free to choose the direction of our next adventure—any one of half a dozen farmyards; or four or five routes to other parts of the village, via Rhossili Lane, School Lane, the Vile Lane, Mewslade Lane or down the main road to Pitton. Otherwise, we could indulge in a variety of games around the farm buildings, or some impromptu sports.

From 'the bank' it was possible to observe just about everyone who lived in Middleton and beyond. Farmers drove through the crossroads with their loaded carts or trailers, people waited for the bus, got off the bus, rode through on the bus (including the three bus-drivers who lived at Rhossili End).

Hard-working Sally Beynon might be seen beating the heck out of a pound of salty fresh farm butter on a butter-fist at the doorstep of The Ship farmhouse; while Jinny Morris fussed around Middleton Lodge farmyard, feeding the chickens and collecting fresh eggs from hidden nesting spots in the hayricks. There was industrious little May Beynon at Riverside, forever scurrying to take on her next chore, always finding things that needed to be done; and kind-hearted Myfi Bevan, always concerned about others, especially youngsters, who might get themselves into any kind of difficulty. They were the very heart of Middleton when I was a boy.

Other overworked housewives, clutching grocery lists and carrying large shopping-bags, hurried towards the Post Office or the Lower Shop, being careful not to reveal to one shopkeeper what they had bought (or were intending to buy) from the other one. Some would even leave their shopping bags or other belongings on the wall under the elm tree, knowing they'd be quite safe.

In the daytime, villagers would stop for a brief rest on the fallen branch on their way home from work or from the shops. They would exchange a few pleasantries or some gossip, before going on their way. "The log" was replaced in the late 1940s by a teakwood bench in memory of Professor Lee's son, Major John

Lee, who had been killed in the fighting at the Anzio beachhead in Italy, in early 1944. He was not a local man, but his parents had become permanent residents in the village, following their retirement.

Although Will Morris's farmhouse created a blind corner for cars approaching from Pitton, resulting in one or two close calls, no one was ever injured by traffic in this local sports arena. The shout would go up, "Car coming!" from whoever was first to see or hear the approaching vehicle. The game would part like The Red Sea: someone would grab the ball or trap it with his foot, until the all-clear was given. It was a remarkably efficient safety system.

At the base of the chimney of Middleton Hall, there was a pale patch of plaster, shaped like the rounded outline of an oversized set of cricket stumps. In the summer months, inspired by the exploits of test cricketers like Bedser, Lock, Laker and Loader, we bowled off-breaks, leg-breaks and googlies with style and skill from the bus-stop. Being a batsman was daunting with this kind of bowling to face, not to mention a handful of razor-sharp fielders just looking for a half-chance of making a catch. At other times we played touch rugby or French cricket on the area behind The Ship farm cowsheds, in front of the village hall. The main road was always included in our area of play.

Boys and men up to their mid-thirties, would join in, or exit, these games as they wished. We were like a large family in some respects. On one occasion, we had taken off our jackets to play football and tossed them onto the milk-stand set in the wall of Jessamine farmyard. When failing light finally forced an end to the game, I went to retrieve my jacket only to find that Roger Harding from The Tors in Pitton (who was three years older than I) was putting it on. Roger insisted that it was his jacket, but I knew it was mine. Suddenly, the penny dropped for both of us: by a circuitous route, I had acquired the hand-me-down jacket which Roger's mother had given away about a year earlier. Problem solved, we went our separate ways.

Will and Jinny Morris were endlessly patient with the continual hammering of the "football" on the double-doors of the old forge. Even Jack Richards, at the opposite end of the football pitch, made few complaints, except when his walls had been freshly whitewashed. The ball could be wet and/or dirty at times. The Ship farm was also affected on occasion, but then it was only the whitewashed walls of the cowsheds. The Joneses at Middleton Hall kept their walls a shade of grey roughcast (never whitewashed) since their house was not only subjected to fast bowlers, but also tennis practice, on occasion.

But 'the bank' wasn't always bustling with activity. One mild Saturday afternoon in the early 1950s, it was deserted as I sat alone on the memorial bench. All was quiet; there was no one around, though an occasional car-load of sightseers passed by. Then, farm-worker George Beynon rounded the corner of Will Morris's house, plodding homeward from his Saturday morning's work at Great Pitton farm. He stopped and sat down for a few minutes' rest. As we chatted, seven or eight cars of sightseers suddenly zipped past, one after the other, on their way to Rhossili End. With typical Gower humour, George dryly remarked, "Some'dy must've let that lot out of a sack, by."

The importance of 'the bank' as a meaningful, though informal, meeting place for the male population of the village cannot be exaggerated. There, we came to know and test each other's strengths, weaknesses and sporting skills.

[Endnote: Today, many of the features of 'the bank' have disappeared. These include the stream, Middleton Lodge farm, the giant elm tree and its fallen branch. However, the shed doors at Jessamine farm and the free space in front of the village hall are still there; so is the "cricket pitch" between the bus-stop and Middleton Hall.]

43

Culture Clash

I'm a labouring man, and know but little,
Or nothing at all …

Thomas Hardy

FOR hundreds of years, Gower has not been very "Welsh". Even as a child, I could detect hints of disdain for the "Welshies", as people of the industrial area to the north and west of Gower were sometimes referred to. The ordinary working people of Swansea were treated with the additional slur of being called "townies", whether they were "Welshies" or not. As my mother was born and raised in Gorseinon, this attitude did little to encourage harmony in my parents' marriage.

Many of the names of South Gower families such as Richards, Holland, Butler, Shepherd, Tanner, Bevan, Beynon, Button, Rosser, Nicholas, Chalk, Ace and Morris, reflected the fact of Norse, Norman-French and Flemish migrations to Gower. Of course, there would have been much intermarriage over the centuries, so that families with typical Welsh names such as Jones, Thomas or Williams often displayed such physical features as blond hair and blue eyes, which indicated the likelihood of Flemish or Norse ancestry.

Although I spent the first twenty-one years of my life in Rhossili, I was actually born at my maternal grandparents' semidetached Council-house at 13 Brynhyfryd Road, Gorseinon. For the birth of her first child, my mother wanted to be taken care of by her female relatives, as was common in those days. My maternal grandmother was born and raised in Horton, while my grandfather, Fred Powell, grew up in the Forest of Dean; but they had established their home in one of the industrial areas of west Glamorgan.

Foundries, coal-mines and steel-works were the primary employers in northeast Gower and beyond. The culture was dramatically different from South

Gower. Roughly one-third of the people spoke Welsh in their homes; it was partially understood by about a further one-third; while the remainder had only a weak comprehension. With the exception of the Penclawdd and Llanmorlais areas, there was little attention paid to the Welsh language in Gower, except on St. David's Day, when the national anthem was sung with fervour (at least, in the schools).

Grandpa Powell was a short, frail man, who had suffered quite severe head injuries from a mining accident. His pale complexion and sometimes hacking cough betrayed the onset of silicosis—a disease which plagued many veteran miners—yet he rarely missed a day's work at the pit-head or a Sunday morning at the Pentecostal chapel where he was a passionate member and lay preacher. I sometimes saw him arrive home from the mines, his face still blackened by coal dust. Like most of the colliers, he often wore a white scarf (perhaps because of its contrast to the coal-dust) and he covered his narrow, bald head with a cloth cap.

Grandpa (or Bampi, as my "Welshy" cousins called him) lived within easy walking distance of the local park where he was a member of the lawn-bowling club. Otherwise, his favourite pastime was gardening. It was amazing what he achieved in a garden about twenty feet wide and about forty-five feet long. He was meticulous about everything in it. There was a plot for strawberries, a row of loganberry bushes, a corner for rhubarb, a couple of rows of bean-sticks, a small cabbage patch, and a few short rows of lettuce, carrots and potatoes. He kept chickens in a small henhouse, feeding them with a mash made from boiled potato peelings and other scraps of food.

His only means of daily transportation was his "push-bike", which he kept in his garden tool-shed near the back-door of his house. He would slip on his shiny metal trouser-clips and pedal off to his shift at the mines or to a chapel meeting. Cycling was a common mode of local transportation for working-class people, so maintaining his bike was a necessary skill. Grandpa was also quite handy at carpentry; a talent which he put to use around his home. He also made children's toys, such as wooden tanks and railway engines as Christmas or birthday presents for those of his grandchildren who lived nearby.

Several times a year, I would accompany my mother on a visit to her parents' home. As few people owned a telephone, these visits were often unannounced; but there was always a warm welcome. Grandma Powell (who my cousins called Nana) was a robust, cheerful woman with a mischievous twinkle in her eyes and a grin to match. She was always happy to share whatever food she had in the pantry. If necessary, she would dash up to the local Co-op shop to buy something tasty for our tea.

My aunties, uncles and cousins spoke with strange, almost musical, accents. "Where iw gooyin', 'en?" or "'ow are iw?" they would ask (their voices dipping sharply in the middle of the question), so producing the characteristic sing-song effect. This was in sharp contrast to the South Gower dialect: "Where't thee gwain t'?" or "How art thee?" The emphasis was on the same syllables, but the tone was very different.

My favourite aunty was Joan. She was a skinny, attractive woman with a lively personality. In spite of a couple of difficult marriages, she never lost her wonderful sense of humour. Her oldest son was John; then there were the twins, Bronwen and Alan; then Philip and the youngest daughter, Carole. She also had one son by her second husband. As we got older, Philip and I found a common interest in boxing. In the late 1950s, we trained at Pengelly ABC, located at a farm in Loughor.

I had the benefit of experiencing two very different ways of life in South Wales. I enjoyed all my cousins on my mother's side of the family, yet I associated visits to Gorseinon with nauseatingly long journeys on double-decker buses; with a depressing smell of sulphur in the air; with coal-ash for footpaths; with the greasy smell of fish-and-chip shops; with streets, buildings, asphalt and vehicles of all kinds; and with crowds of people who were all strangers to me. This was a far cry from open spaces, fresh sea air, and knowing every person, house and field.

In the industrial areas, though, there were wonderful modern conveniences such as electricity and plumbing in the homes. There were also gas-cookers, which were excellent for cooking and baking when compared to lighting a coal-fire and trying to control the temperature of the oven alongside it. Then there was a variety of retail stores, including chemists, shoe-shops, clothing stores, fishmongers and butchers shops. At weekend markets, even before rationing was removed, cheap-jacks auctioned kitchenware or cuts of meat from the backs of their vans and lorries. All of this gave me my first glimpses of the benefits of free market competition and economies of scale.

Once a week, my cousins would receive pocket money to go to "the pictures" at the Lido cinema, in the town centre. It was an exciting experience for me, even though sitting in the first two rows made the films look as though everything was on a slope. Afterwards, we would share fish-and-chips wrapped in newspaper, then get a drink of Corona pop when we got home. This seemed like a nice life to me, but I still would not have wanted to swap it for my life in Middleton. My oldest cousin, Rowland, took good care of me in some after-dark dashes around the neighbourhood, as youngsters formed into "gangs" (no doubt influenced by what they had seen at the pictures), but I never saw any violence.

Late one Saturday afternoon, I tagged along with Rowland and another cousin, John Davies, to fetch some milk from a farm bordering the built-up area. As we approached the house, I saw an Alsatian tied up at the porch. The farmer was not at home. Being quite used to farm-dogs, I approached to pat its head. Without warning, the dog attacked, snapping at my arms and head. I was about ten years old, but I had the presence of mind to crawl out of the dog's reach. My cousins took me back home, where Grandma could put ointment on the bites on my arm and ear. I didn't go to the doctor. It was the weekend and, anyway, domestic dogs were not suspected of being rabid.

Visiting Gorseinon meant not only interacting with family members, but also being exposed to the values and ways of life of the working people in the industrial areas of my country. They lived a decidedly different kind of hand-to-mouth existence from farm-workers' families. They seemed to be in no hurry to own their own homes, for example; after all, they lived in street after street of identical, semidetached Council-houses. There were such delights as "the pictures", public-houses and fish-and-chip shops, as well as many other shops where they could spend their money.

In contrast to the strict sobriety of Grandpa Powell (or perhaps as a result of it), his two sons loved to drink. One of my uncles, a lifelong bachelor, worked at a foundry most of his working life. He would sweat pints in the intolerable heat all day; then, each night, he would do his utmost to replace the lost fluid with beer. The other uncle spent most of his free time in the local British Legion club, after he was demobbed from the Navy at the end of the war.

Even the passion for sports was different in the industrial areas. There was a strong preference for rugby, in contrast with the love of football that was so dominant in the South Gower villages. Rugby was variously thought of as an art-form, a relaxation for the well-educated or a kind of religion. There was a somewhat snobbish attitude towards those who were not rugby enthusiasts, especially if they preferred to play football.

In addition to their work, their homes and their families, the men of the Welsh valleys centred their lives round chapel, rugby or public-houses—or some combination of the three. The married farm-workers of South Gower led more isolated existences, were not as well-paid, and so enjoyed fewer choices.

[Endnote: No doubt I have benefited greatly from the "Welshy" side of my family. They had a great sense of cheerfulness and humour, regardless of difficult circumstances (not to mention poverty). This contrasted with the English-style sarcasm which often passed for humour in Gower.]

44

Winds of Change

The winds of change are the most powerful force on earth.

Author Unknown

The changes that would occur in southwest Gower during the second half of the 20th century resulted both directly and indirectly from technological innovation. Scientific advancement accelerated dramatically during the Second World War. By 1945, sophisticated rocketry, nuclear fission and the jet plane had been achieved by Germany, the USA and Britain, respectively.

The servicemen returning to their rural roots at the end of the war may have assumed that life in Gower would continue as it had before, but powerful forces had already been set in motion by the greatest conflict in all of history. Not only the far-reaching effects of technological advances, but also the evolution of the European Economic Community (propelled by the Marshall Plan) resulted from the cataclysmic war.

Technological advances would inevitably lead to economic growth, the globalisation of industries and services, increased standards of living for millions of people in many countries, and eventually to the notion of the "global village". In reaction to such rapid technological and economic development, the European Union would eventually see the need to place greater importance on the preservation of heritage sites and quality of life factors than on economic growth.

National politics, too, had a huge influence on the nature of change in the villages of rural Gower. The Education Act of 1944, emanating from the wartime Coalition Government, provided for the development of secondary education for all children, be it through Grammar Schools, Secondary Modern Schools or Secondary Technical (i.e. vocational) Schools. This effectively expanded educational opportunities for working-class children. New Secondary Modern Schools, like

Penclawdd, ensured some degree of further education for all—not just those who could pass the 11+ examination, or who could afford to attend private schools.

The post-war socialist regime of Clement Attlee had an unexpectedly severe effect on the feudal system that dominated large tracts of southwest Gower, including most of the parish of Rhossili. This was the break-up and sale of the Penrice Estate, which was initiated by the "death duties" which had to be paid when Lady Blythswood's daughter died, in the late 1940s. Lady Blythswood had signed over the Penrice Estate to her daughter, not anticipating that her daughter would pre-decease her. The resulting opportunity for many farmers (and even one or two farm-workers) to purchase their own properties at reasonable prices may have slowed down the forthcoming exodus from Rhossili.

In addition, the labour government's public housing programme resulted in about twenty semidetached Council-houses being built at Scurlage. Eventually, four or five families of Rhossili farm-workers moved there. Who would not wish to enjoy the benefits of modern plumbing? The Council-houses were govern-ment-owned; however, more than thirty years later, under a Tory government, the tenants would be given the opportunity to purchase them at very reasonable prices.

Many in Britain feared the communistic aspirations of the extreme left-wing of Attlee's labour party (Aneurin Bevin, for example) as the Labour government embarked on a massive programme of nationalisation of essential industries, including railways, coal-mines, steel-works, electric power and health services. There were also increased powers for various workers' unions. From about 1950, the development of the farm-workers' union (FWU) began to improve their working conditions, if only gradually.

The social benefits provided by Attlee's government included medical treat-ment, prescription drugs, hospitalisation, dental services, eye-glasses and child-allowances. All of this made it easier for my generation to benefit from free sec-ondary education.

During the 1950s, after Churchill's "new conservatives" had returned to power, free education continued up to the university level, with a grant increas-ing from about fifty pounds per term in 1950 to eighty pounds per term in 1958. This grant was to cover textbooks, board-and-lodging, etc. In 1958, "digs" in Swansea could be found for about three-pounds-ten a week, which left about two pounds a week for textbooks, beer and sundry expenses. At that time, a farm-worker's basic wage was about ten pounds a week.

By working in the summer months, a student did not need to incur any debt. The children of farm-workers were able to take their education as far as their ability permitted—though they still depended on the support of their parents to stay in grammar school until the age of eighteen.

This seemed like utopia for a working-class student. Furthermore, the compulsory two years of National Service, for which all young men became liable at the age of eighteen, could be deferred until after university was completed. All of this provided a real incentive for working-class youngsters to strive to qualify for university entrance.

While technological advances led to economic development, which led to job opportunities, free college education ensured that my generation were able to take advantage of those opportunities. This, in turn, facilitated the exodus of most of my generation from Rhossili. However, it should not be thought that previous generations of Gower people invariably stayed at home. They were involved in sailing ships; in military campaigns; and in migration to Australia, South Africa and the Americas, from as far back as the 1660s, when the "Gower Pilgrim Fathers" migrated to Massachusetts, USA (as described in *The Ilston Book*).

Not to be overlooked as a cause of change is the hard life endured by the small farmers, but even more-so by the farm-workers. I knew of no farm-worker who did not encourage his children to seek a different life. Those who could get a grammar school or university education became engineers, scientists, veterinarians, teachers, nurses or accountants. Otherwise, they used the good work ethics they had been brought up with, to obtain employment in retail businesses or service industries in Swansea.

In the end, it should not be forgotten that the advances in technology and economic development offered not only a variety of career opportunities, but also alternative lifestyles, leisure activities and sports. By contrast, growing up in Rhossili could feel like a rather limited (not to say, isolated) existence. There were no real library facilities. Those who were avid readers would make sure they met the mobile library at the appointed one-hour time-period, every second Wednesday morning. Then, one could peruse what limited choice of books they had on board.

There were no ready diversions at which to spend time on rainy or chilly days. There was no youth club, swimming pool or gymnasium. There were no organised sports for those under the age of eighteen. Some houses, such as 'the cottage', Windy Walls, Talgarths Well, the Fernhill farms and Hoarstone, did not have electricity until about 1950 (or later), while televisions only became affordable in the late 1950s—even though some had purchased them, earlier. At that time, working-class families still could not justify the cost of a telephone. What young person would not have wanted to experience what the urban communities had to offer?

The larger farmers would be justified in bemoaning the difficulties and changing times that they would face over the remainder of the century. But the families of the small farmers and the farm-workers (soon to become almost non-existent) would feel those changes even more drastically—though with less regret.

[Endnote1: "Death duties" were introduced before the end of the 19th century, but they were drastically increased by Attlee's post-war Labour government. This measure resulted in the break-up of several huge estates in England and Wales.]

[Endnote2: To understand the full impact of technology, it is perhaps useful to consider the modern conveniences enjoyed by today's residents, which the families of farm-workers and small farmers could not afford until at least the late 1950s—by which time their children had left home or were providing an additional source of family income. These include (in order of priority) electric stoves, washing machines, refrigerators, televisions, telephones and cars.

Central heating, double glazing, electronic calculators, VCRs, remote controls, PCs, video games, home entertainment centres, DVDs and cell-phones were hardly dreamt of, at that time.]

[Endnote3: The exodus of local youth, which began in earnest in the early 1960s, continued through the 1970s. There is no doubt that the majority of my generation left the village permanently in pursuit of career opportunities, only ever to return for brief visits. At least three of us have spent most of our adult lives in Canada; about six others have spent most of their time in Australia and New Zealand; about a dozen have enjoyed professional careers in England; many others have moved to the Swansea area to pursue careers in banking, accounting, retail, technology and teaching. Some live in nearby parishes. A few are, sadly, deceased.]

[Endnote4: Of an estimated one hundred and fifty Rhossili children born between 1930 and 1950, about fourteen are living in Rhossili today. About ten are still managing family farms. The other four are retirees (of whom only one or two were the children of farm-workers).]

45

Seasonal Pastimes for Youngsters

To every thing there is a season,
and a time to every purpose under the heaven:

The Bible: Ecclesiastes 3:1

IN the first decade of our lives, we kids enjoyed discovering and experiencing our rural, coastal environment. There were farm buildings, fields, animals, crops, wild life, wild plants and trees. Then there were games to be played; there were life skills to be learnt from parents and others; and the lessons and games we enjoyed at school and Sunday-school.

Even when our early fascination with spiders, flies, caterpillars, chrysalises, butterflies and dragonflies had waned, we wanted to know when to expect the cuckoo; when blackberries would be ripe and sloes would be (almost) edible; how to avoid gorse bushes, stinging nettles and thistles; and how to distinguish between tasty mushrooms and poisonous toadstools.

There were stoats, weasels, foxes, badgers, rabbits, hedge-hogs, newts, toads, grass-snakes, adders, magpies, crows, hawks, owls, bats and seagulls to contend with. We learnt where to find acorns, chestnuts, conkers and catkins; when to look for snowdrops, primroses, bluebells, daffodils, forget-me-nots, foxgloves, cowslips and a host of other wild flowers; and we learnt to distinguish between a buttercup and a celandine.

Most of this learning about our natural environment occurred in springtime, the season of renewal. There were the returning cuckoos, swifts and the swallows, as well as the loveliest of the wild flowers. It was a particularly busy time for our parents, with spring-cleaning to be done at home, and the planting and weeding of fields and gardens, which meant that adults were always glad of some help, even from unenthusiastic kids. Often we were coerced into doing chores by our no-nonsense parents, though most of us were still allowed plenty of play-time.

In May, the search would be on for birds' eggs. Most boys had a collection of them stored in a wooden box, well padded with cotton wool, which they would proudly display for any visiting friend or relative. Brian Jones, at East Pilton farm, had a collection that was the envy of all who viewed it. It included such rare trophies as the eggs of a kestrel, a rook, a cuckoo and some of the less common sea-birds that haunted the cliffs around Paviland. The eggs would be "blown" in the time-honoured way, by first making a pin-hole at the pointy end, then a slightly larger hole at the other one, so the contents could be carefully forced out.

Of course, we knew that the rule of the country was to take only one egg from a nest; but sometimes we broke that rule when we went bird-nesting in groups of two or three. We boys knew that magpies were both undesirable and despised, so we would go to quite heroic efforts to force our heads and shoulders up through a thorn-bush to stretch a hand into a Magpie's nest. Then we would remove and destroy all twelve to fifteen eggs. They were indeed prolific layers. We would have treated crows the same way, but their nests were not as common or accessible.

Summer meant long, enjoyable days, helping our parents on the farm or in the garden; foraging in fields and orchards; or seeking adventure on the hillsides, cliffs, sand-dunes and bays. Each evening, any remaining daylight would be filled with impromptu games of football or cricket on 'the bank'. Sometimes our mothers would find time to take us to Mewslade Bay for a paddle and a picnic, hoping that the clouds and showers stayed away. On wet days, we could play Cowboys and Indians around the barns and sheds of one of the farms, until the farmer told us it was teatime and sent us home. There were plenty of ways for young boys to entertain themselves.

In the autumn, after getting used to being back at school, our youthful enthusiasm turned to threshing, conkers, fireworks and harvest suppers. Autumn also represented the start of a new football and rugby season. With Christmas to look forward to, as well, there was a distinct air of excitement.

Perhaps because most of the horse-chestnut trees in our Parish seemed to congregate at Pilton Green, it wasn't until we were almost teenagers, that we tested our skill at conkers—usually on the school-bus. Some boys would go to the trouble of using traditional methods to shrivel and harden theirs, just so they could boast when it had defeated a dozen or more opponents—but they all broke, sooner or later.

Soon, fireworks were the main attraction, with families and social groups organising themselves to provide the best show that their budgets would allow. Mischievous boys invested their pocket money primarily in the loudest bangers, such
as Mighty Atoms and Canons. There was much glee in loud, unexpected explo-
sions. Rockets, cart-wheels, squibs, jumping-jacks and cones were favoured for
family entertainment.

One Guy Fawkes night, my father discovered that a rocket stick had been
accidentally snapped in half. He tried to bind the broken pieces together with
string, but it didn't work, so he just stuck it upright in a large Spooner's pop bottle and hoped for the best. By the time it was dark, our nervous little sheepdog
had gone missing—seeming to anticipate that trouble would result from all the
smoke and noise. We had no idea where he was. We waved a few sparklers, lit a
couple of squibs, followed by a jumping-jack. Then, my father lit the touch-
paper on the defective rocket. We all stood back, not knowing what would happen. The rocket started out of the bottle; then suddenly flew horizontally down
along the inside of the garden hedge. There was a loud yelp in the darkness. We
had found our missing dog.

Foggy days, which occurred most frequently in early spring and late autumn,
seemed to create a different world—a feeling of loneliness and isolation. Even if
visibility had been more than only about ten yards, there would be very few people to be seen. The mood was set by the mournful sound of the foghorn from the
lightship guarding The Helwicks sandbank.

The sea-fog could make it so dark that it would fool the wildlife into untimely
action. Hedge-hogs might be found marching about in the damp grass of our
small field, looking for grubs. We would have liked to keep them as pets, but they
were not very sociable. They would roll themselves into a tight ball, which made
it tempting for small boys to try using them as footballs; but they were too heavy
and spiny. Then there were barn-owls that were otherwise rarely seen. Once, a
huge, ghostly, white owl drifted slowly past, within about three yards of where I
stood. I could only gape in amazement at its (at least) four-foot wingspan. I never
saw such a sight, before or after.

On foggy evenings, as with rainy ones, or the occasional bitterly cold ones of
the winter months, people were glad enough to huddle indoors. The oil-lamp
would be lit early. It was at such times that our parents might impress us with
tales of yesteryear. They talked about how the shops had been full of a wonderful
variety of goods (and the prices were cheap) before the war. But they didn't
explain that it was the Great Depression that had pushed the prices down, while

many people were out of work, suffering great deprivations. I daresay the rural areas, poor though they were, didn't experience the hardships of unemployment to the extent that the towns and cities did. My father would tell amusing stories about old-timers I never knew, or about daring "rocket crew" rescues on Paviland cliffs.

Following the excitement of the Christmas season, the dull, leaden-skied days of midwinter were always an anticlimax. These were days when the fields and hedges were brittle and bare, the beaches and shorelines were unwelcoming, and we children looked for other ways to amuse themselves. It was the time of year when young daughters (or even sons) might get some valuable sewing, knitting and darning lessons from their industrious mothers.

I liked to visit friends who had good sets of Dinky toys or interesting card or board games. One local boy, Terry Williams, who was several years older than I, had a slide projector and some fascinating pictures of vehicles and planes. Otherwise, there were the evening radio serials, plays, and comedy shows. Sometimes there was a Saturday shopping expedition to Swansea or a visit to my grandparents in Gorseinon. I was much less resistant to these kinds of outings, in the winter. At this time of year, my father might even find time to take me to see the Swans play; then, we would fill my mother's shopping list, before catching the bus home. Woe befell Joff if he forgot anything on the list.

We kids wished for snow, which would transform our world into an exciting foreign environment. When we did get snow, it was often an overnight surprise, almost as exciting as Christmas. We could only dream of skating on frozen ponds, but we could make snowmen and enjoy fierce snowball fights whenever we got out of the house or the classroom. It was about the only time I wore the wool gloves and balaclava which my mother had knitted. With or without gloves, we would play in the snow until our icy hands brought tears to our eyes.

In 'the cottage', heated only by a single, open coal-fire, I liked to huddle close to the grate, watching my mother perform her household chores, while daydreaming about great adventures or sporting exploits. My short trousers allowed the heat of the fire to make telltale, diamond-shaped patterns appear on my legs.

My mother would often find the time to read, play a board-game or simply make my little sister and me laugh with her ready sense of humour and abundant sayings. In turn, I would poke fun or just act silly until she laughed herself breathless.

But as soon as the weather eased, I was gone, only to return at mealtimes—and not always then.

46

Grammar School

… much learning doth make thee mad.

The Bible: Acts 26:24

IN my father's day, the costs associated with attending grammar school would have been a financial burden to his parents. Weekly lodgings at Gowerton would have been necessary. Also, there were still three siblings junior to him; therefore, my father, Joffre, although gifted with above average intelligence, did not take the opportunity of going to grammar school. In the late 1920s, it was only possible to have a secondary education if you could afford the inevitable expenses of clothing, food and shelter. His older sister, Doris, had previously become the first member of the family to achieve a grammar school education in this way. Daily transportation in Gower was too slow, despite the Vanguard Motors' charabancs.

A significant portion of the family's living must have been gained through producing their own food, including meat, eggs, poultry, dairy products, vegetables and bread. Other necessities, such as rent, farm hardware, coal, salt, oil, candles, clothing and foot-ware, as well as the services of various craftsmen, placed constant demands on any cash available—especially in the years leading up to the Great Depression. Afterwards, everything was cheaper.

With the improvements in roads and transportation, my father's youngest sibling, Leonard, became the first of our family to make the daily journey to Gowerton, in 1933. He would catch the bus to Killay and take the train to Gowerton; but on the homeward journey, he often had to walk the last three miles from Scurlage. He left grammar school after four years and returned to work on the family farm. By then, the opportunity of a secondary education was gradually becoming more of a reality for Gower children.

By 1950, after the Penclawdd Secondary Modern School had opened, there were dedicated school-buses for children from various sections of Gower. Our bus collected children from Rhossili, Horton, Porteynon, Scurlage, Llandewi, Reynoldston and (sometimes) Oxwich and Penmaen.

However, the only way to be accepted at the grammar schools—boys and girls had separate schools—was to pass the dreaded 11+ examination. The examination was held once a year: only two attempts were permitted. It was a full day of tests, covering English Comprehension, English Composition, Mathematics and Mental Arithmetic.

Some claimed that the infamous 11+ exam determined, in the space of a single day, the extent of a child's opportunities for education and a career. This seemed daunting, even unfair; however, the system worked very well for ninety-nine percent of children. For one thing, there was a second chance, if needed—with a whole extra year to prepare. Secondly, it was an undeniably objective system. Thirdly, children did not dwell on the potential lifelong effects of this exam, even if some parents did. Lastly, business people and farmers could afford to send their children to private school, if they felt that a secondary-modern education would be inadequate.

The summer of 1951 was a heady time for me. I had passed my 11+ with flying colours, if not quite as gloriously as my teacher, Miss Thomas, would have liked. She had me earmarked as a potential prime-minister; while her brother, George (better known as Dodi), who played the church organ (and sang) with great vigour, encouraged me to become a Bible scholar, perhaps even a bishop some day.

The Korean War was at its zenith. As we saw from the daily newspaper reports and diagrams describing the ever-changing battle lines, the situation had recovered dramatically since January, when the United Nations forces had been pinned into a small corner of the peninsula. In April, a few of the "Glorious Glosters", who had been surrounded and decimated by Chinese troops, had fought their way back to their own lines. But all of that seemed a long way away—and almost insignificant compared to the global conflict that had ended just six years earlier.

My parents prepared to send me off to an exciting new world, that September, complete with all the required regalia of the Gowerton Boys Grammar School. They were determined that I should make the most of opportunities that they could hardly have dreamt of. There were several trips into town during the warm August weather to ensure that I had everything I would need for that momentous first Monday in September of 1951. My priority was to choose a satchel, which would become my constant school-day companion for the next seven years. Then, I selected a geometry set, a fountain pen, pencils, rulers, and exercise-books for a dozen different subjects.

For clothing, I needed a couple of pairs of short, grey trousers; a navy blazer and a school badge to be stitched onto it; a school cap and tie; three white shirts, two grey v-neck pullovers with maroon trim; four pairs of grey socks with maroon trim; four underpants; and a gym-shirt, shorts and plimsolls. I also acquired a good pair of black leather shoes.

In all, my parents spent the best part of a hundred pounds to outfit me. It was a lot of money to them. It was probably the biggest investment they had made since they had purchased our thatched cottage from the Penrice Estate for about four hundred pounds, some three years earlier.

There was a strange smell of newness to all this paraphernalia. It heralded the imminent experience of being one of about seventy new students, divided between Forms 1A and 1B. There was the feel of new clothing and equipment, as well as the sight of about five hundred strange new faces (including a headmaster and some twenty teaching staff) to get used to.

Hitherto, I had been used to just one female teacher who taught me every-thing I needed to learn. Now, there was a different male teacher for each of almost a dozen compulsory subjects—Art, Woodwork, Music, French, Welsh, History, Geography, English, Algebra, Geometry and Science. There were anti-quated, gloomy classrooms; battered desks; well-worn textbooks; the soft, insipid taste of the drinking water that had not been filtered through limestone rocks; and the day-in, day-out taste of food prepared and served in the school dining hall. It was a very different world.

Our Form Master was Howard John, an athletic, somewhat aloof, disciplinar-ian. Fortunately he was a Gower man himself and took a kindly interest in boys from Rhossili. My parents seemed just as thrilled when he described me as a "real boy" in my first term report, as they were about my placing second in my form.

As with all schools, there was a cacophony of sound at the mid-morning and lunch-hour breaks—some of it was in Welsh (of which we Gower boys under-stood nothing)—as five hundred boys sought out their pals to enjoy boisterous fun and games. Some dashed to the fives-courts; others to the rugby posts, where a couple of rugby balls were available for drop-kicking and catching practice. In the summer months, four or five sets of basic cricket equipment (four stumps, a bat and a ball) would be issued and set up in the school field. However, some of us Gower boys preferred to practice our football skills with any round ball that was available. The school did have a couple of ancient footballs, but they were kept under lock and key.

On top of all this strangeness, we travelled by bus for well over two hours a day, then we had to do homework, after tea. It was just as well that social life was minimal for working-class kids in southwest Gower. Also, I had never worn a tie or cap in my life, but now I was obliged to wear a tie from the time I left home at about 7:30 AM until I returned home about 5:30 PM. For the first few weeks, my complexion was usually some shade of green by the time I reached Middleton. To survive, we all had to adjust to the rigorous routine.

On the way home, the school-bus would stop at Shepherd's shop in Parkmill for ten minutes, or so. Most of us would rush into the shop to spend our daily pocket money on such treats as Walls ice-cream, Spangles, Cadbury's chocolate, pop or weekly comic books like Dandy and Beano. We were amused by the antics of Dennis the Menace, Billy Bunter and Keyhole Kate, but there were also more exciting new publications, which depicted the adventures of a technological marvel dubbed The Iron Fish; or the schemes of a Martian regime headed by their evil leader, known as The Mekon.

The break refreshed us, so that we Rhossili and Porteynon kids could endure another thirty to forty minutes on the bus. When the bus was a double-decker, the boys were segregated from the girls: usually we boys were allocated the use of the lower deck, where the conductor could keep an eye on us. There were regular arguments and pleadings as to whether the bus should go to Porteynon or Rhossili, first—eventually followed by the raucous cheering of the winners.

At school there was competition for all kinds of sports. It seemed as if there was one chance for everything. In the 100-yard dash, several other kids, who were used to such competitions, took off like hares while I was still thinking about it. I knew I had good stamina for longer distances, but there, too, the competition seemed fierce—at least among the older boys—and there seemed to be no opportunity for development, particularly if staying behind after school was not a practical option.

At home, I developed considerable aerobic capability by training at the bays with a ball to chase, or running around the cliffs. My young neighbour, John Densley, used the mileometre on his new bike to help me determine that my cliff-top circuit was close to four miles (home to home). On at least one occasion, I tried a middle-school cross-country race, but the best I could do was sixth place. I was not at all familiar with the route, so I just followed those in front, the best I could. John was there to encourage me as we mud-spattered, panting runners returned to the school field for the final stretch.

The school was fiercely "rugby only", which meant that football (my favourite pastime), was frowned upon. About once a decade, an unofficial football team would emerge to represent the school against one of the neighbouring grammar schools—usually in the Easter holidays. Otherwise, we heard awed whispers about the exploits of Tanner and Davies; or Lewis Jones, who had left school just before I started. Of course, we all admired the mercurial scrum-half Onllwyn Brace: sometimes it seemed as if some of the inter-school matches were arranged so that the whole school could watch him play. In contrast, there was my unpretentious (sometime) classmate, Norman Gale, who was never expected to become such a stalwart for Swansea, Llanelli and Wales.

I liked rugby well enough when I was involved in the action, but the constant kicking into touch, set scrums and line-outs made the game seem tedious, much of the time. I once played on the wing in an inter-house match. Only once was the ball passed out along the line; but the outside centre (who was considered a "natural" rugby player) saw fit to hold on to it when he was tackled, even though I had a clear run to the line. Thus I missed my one opportunity for rugby glory at Gowerton.

In one of our gym-period games, I managed to disgrace myself by using a well-honed football skill. Classmate Michael ("Specky") Taylor, a tall, bony, red-headed policeman's son, was charging through a crowd of players. It looked like he would break clear to score a try. As he rushed past me, it was all too simple for me to gently tap one of his ankles with the toe of my boot, rather than take the trouble to tackle him.

Poor Specky almost tied himself in a knot as he fell. "Who did that?" he demanded, as he scrambled to his feet. Realising that the normally good-natured Specky would be quite a handful when he was angry, I acted as if I didn't know. But veteran coach Bill Bowen whistled for a penalty; then looked at me sternly (yet with a twinkle in his eye). "Cyril, you were close enough to make the tackle!" he said.

Although I was well-versed in road-cricket and beach-cricket skills, I was not enthusiastic about the formal game. Unless you were a bowler or wicket-keeper (prized roles which often seemed to be claimed by the loudest voices), it seemed like a slow, boring afternoon. When I finally got a turn to bat in an inter-form game, I played a solid shot in the general direction of mid-on. It was my call and I started to run, but the batsman at the other end yelled "no!" A second later, he had second thoughts, shouting "come on!" Already back at my crease, I turned and ran gamely for the other wicket, but I was run out. There went my opportunity of cricketing glory.

Generally, I enjoyed all physical activities, including gym classes which subjected us to unaccustomed challenges: somersaulting over the horse, exercising on wall-bars, walking the beam or climbing ropes. However, the one sight that stirred some real excitement in me—a set of boxing gloves and a punchball—seemed to be more of a "prop", as far as our school was concerned. Rugby and music were what really mattered, though there was plenty of focus on athletics and cricket, in the summer. The only time got to play with a football was inside the gym—and then we had to play five-a-side while sliding around on our backsides!

Possessing minimal musical talent, I was unable to participate in the school band, though I did make a game attempt to learn to play the recorder when I was in my second year. My poor parents became all too familiar with my imperfect rendition of *O God, Our Help in Ages Past*. I could only wonder at the talents of those who participated in the choir and orchestra, comforting myself with the thought that such activities were perhaps not really suited to a rugged southwest Gower boy.

In my third year, I was voted vice-captain of Form 3A in an unenthusiastic election. Nevertheless, I took my responsibilities seriously. One of my duties was to help collect the weekly dinner-money (which was about two-and-six a week) while our Form Master, gym-teacher Emlyn Evans, read out the names. On one occasion, Mr. Evans sent for me, afterwards. He asked whether I knew why he was ten shillings short. I immediately stuffed both hands into the pockets of my short trousers and found a crumpled ten shilling note in one of them. I began to mumble an explanation for my absentminded mistake, but Mr. Evans cut me off: "No one thinks you tried to steal it, boy," he said.

There were three, twenty-minute dinner sittings crammed into the lunch-hour. The first and second sittings were quite formal, with regular attendees sitting in tables of eight. Students stood silently behind their chairs until the standard dining-hall prayer was uttered by the teacher on duty: "For what we are about to receive, may the Lord make us truly thankful, for Christ's sake. Amen."

The two most senior boys sat opposite each other, at one end of the table, with the others ranked by seniority. Since all tureens of food (even the gravy boat) started at the head of the table, there was sometimes little or nothing left by the time they reached the two junior boys. It was not uncommon for the teachers on dining-room duty to reprimand some of the seniors and direct how much they could help themselves to.

The third sitting was decidedly informal. It didn't matter who you sat with, as long as a particular table was filled. Often, extra tureens of food would be available, but that wasn't the only advantage. There was no lining up outside the door, so I could play football or fives (i.e. handball) continuously for forty minutes, then fill my stomach before returning to lessons. A late lunch also helped me to survive until I reached home, at about half-past five. At times, the third sitting was so popular, that table-heads and/or prefects from the first and second sittings would come to search for "volunteers" to fill their tables.

Although the dining-room staff was a group of wonderful ladies, who prepared and presented the food extremely well, about the autumn of 1954 some of the more rebellious fifth and sixth-form students started a petition to demand better school meals. This was aimed at an improvement in quality and variety. With a little persuasion, the idea caught on and perhaps eighty percent or more of us signed. Dr. James and his senior teaching staff were apparently outraged at this preposterous act. I suspected they were gallantly drawn to the defence of the good ladies.

Form Masters were sent to speak sternly to their charges. We felt as though we had done something quite unacceptable; some of the nervous students in the junior forms said that they thought the petition meant they would somehow get a fairer share of food on their regular dining-room tables. We were offered a chance to withdraw our names from the petition; the trickle became a flood. Soon there were very few signatures remaining; but I would always feel guilty for withdrawing mine, albeit under pressure.

In our Form 4A English Literature class, we studied Henry V in great detail; therefore, it was no surprise that a trip was arranged for us to travel by train to London to see Richard Burton performing the leading role at the famous Old Vic theatre. It was a memorable occasion, yet it was spoiled by an unfortunate incident.

On the long homeward journey, four of us decided to wander to the dining car. As we sat down, we saw that a small bottle of French wine, no larger than a ketchup bottle, was standing in the centre of the table. We knew it would take some time before the waiter could attend to us, so one of the boys suggested simply picking up the wine and walking out. Two of us indicated our objection to the plan, but soon there was only one objector. I felt I had no alternative but to go along with them. After all, it was just a prank, really. I suppose I was learning something about peer-pressure.

Though I soon separated from my classmates and never knew what happened to the wine, I felt a sense of shame. It was, therefore, a bad surprise for me when, next morning at assembly, our headmaster, Dr. James, announced the "shameful incident". I felt as though he already suspected who the perpetrators were. I felt like a criminal on the lam. I spoke to no one about the incident, not even my fellow miscreants. But I didn't know whether any of them had bragged to other classmates. It was several days before I began to relax. I had learnt another valuable lesson.

Dr. James was a kindly, yet un-charismatic man, who maintained a serious expression and was a disciplinarian—not surprisingly, with five hundred boys to contend with. One Monday morning at assembly, he expressed the utmost horror at having seen two boys, wearing their school uniforms and caps, eating fish-and-chips out of newspaper in the vicinity of the United Welsh bus-garage, in Swansea. On another occasion, he berated those of us middle-school boys who had developed a preference for wearing short duffel-coats known as "donkey jackets", which were particularly favoured by many of the North and South Gower boys. He referred to us as a "donkey-jacketed gang"; but I was sure it was just because he felt the coats detracted from our uniforms.

I sat outside Dr. James's office on at least one occasion, waiting to see what punishment he would mete out; but I was fortunate: my particular infringement of the school rules did not warrant any strokes of the cane. Others were not so lucky since such misdemeanours as smoking took place in "the bogs", with even some of the prefects participating.

On one occasion, I missed school on an important day, but it was not deliberate. A bad cold or neuralgia caused me to miss the unannounced interviews for selection of a school team to represent us in the inter-school Top of the Form competition, which aired seasonally on the wireless. Windsor Bowen, who was almost always top of our class, was selected to represent Forms 3 and 4. However, I was happy that a Rhossili boy, Peter Crozier, was selected to represent Forms 1 and 2.

At the end of seven years, I could count the number of days I had missed school on the fingers of one hand. Attendance was my highest priority. The only time I stayed home without a very good reason was when I reached the second year of the sixth form and I became eligible for selection as a prefect. I didn't have much doubt that I wouldn't be selected—I hadn't participated in anything at school for about three years, except for the "rebel" football series against Bishop Gore. Even so, the tensions of my teenage years meant that I found the possibility of being selected or not being selected, equally appalling. It was a no-win situation.

It became a long seven years. I daydreamt on the long, early-morning journeys on the school-bus. The inevitable complexities and stresses of teenage years ensured that things got worse, rather than better. After managing to do very well in my O-level examinations, I found that school became less rewarding for me. In my two years as a sixth former it meant little more than attending classes and studying for exams. It was largely thanks to some good friends and classmates, Meirion Davies from Pontlliw, Ieuan Evans from Penclawdd and Ken Peebles from Gowerton (as well as the Bishopton/Pennard boys I played football with) that I could find school palatable for such a long time.

Outside school, when I wasn't trying to focus on my homework, I could still wander or jog the length and breadth of the parish, or enjoy the surf at Fall Bay, while I continued to ponder my future. Although sports activities at 'the bank' were becoming less frequent, I enjoyed coaching my young friend, John Morris, and my cousin Colin, who was almost a decade younger than I. The three of us, though comprising such a wide range in ages, were great pals.

For two seasons, I caught the bus on Saturdays to play football for Bishopston in the Swansea and District Under-18 league. It was helpful for my self-confidence to develop friendships (if only on the football field) with my team-mates from Pennard, Merton and Kittle, as well as Bishopston.

Soon, I would be on my way to fresh pastures, though I wasn't sure where.

[Endnote: In retrospect, I have to acknowledge that other Rhossili boys, such as Len Beynon, John Densley, Leo Harding and Colin Jones were far more successful than I, in adapting to the challenges of attending Gowerton.]

47

The Overlander

Once a jolly swagman camped by a billabong ...

Traditional Australian Anthem

THE Thomas family of Rhossili—the eleven siblings who were born around the turn of the century—were a disparate bunch of strong characters. They included Ada, who became the long-serving headmistress of the village school. Her brother George (known to locals as Dodi), having had a successful career with a large London department store, was a gentleman farmer and the church organist. He owned the Worms Head Hotel (until he sold it to Guido Heller, in the mid-1940s) as well as the Broad Park guesthouse. Then there was Sid, a stocky, tough man who had spent some years in Australia, before settling down in Rhossili.

Another brother, Jim, moved to Morriston to work in the steelworks. There was Sophia who migrated to Alberta, Canada and Margaret who migrated to South Africa, where she became quite well-known as a singer. There were three more sisters, named Laura, Molly and Nancy, and two brothers, William and Arthur.

By all accounts, Arthur and Sid, along with their older brother, William and sister, Laura, took off to Australia in the early 1920s, seeking their fortunes in the gold-mines. William, tragically, suffered a broken back from an accident and spent the remainder of his life confined to his bed.

By the mid-1920s, Sid found his way back to Rhossili after some adventurous escapades, working as crew on some lengthy voyages on tramp steamers. Soon, he married a pleasant Llangennith woman, May Tucker. Their only child, Gordon, was born in 1930. With the support of his family, Sid enjoyed success as a farmer, tea-room proprietor and car-park operator.

Arthur, though, spent the best part of his working life in Australia, experiencing both good times and bad. During the depression years, he lived as a hobo (pronounced how-bough in Australia), stealing rides on freight trains, criss-crossing the continent to find work. He enlisted with the Australian Army in both world wars. In the second one, he correctly anticipated that he would be posted to duties in the United Kingdom, so he would be close to his native Gower.

During his varied experiences, many of which had to do with stock farming, he became adept at turning his hand to most of the skills that someone who lived in The Outback would need. Probably he was the most remarkable and resourceful product of Rhossili since Edgar Evans. Arthur was tall and lean; his face was fine-featured, furrowed and kindly. In the early 1950s, he could have been mistaken, in both dress and physical appearance, for the actor Gary Cooper, as he appeared in the western films, *Vera Cruz* and *High Noon*.

About 1952 at Gowerton Boys Grammar School, there occurred the rare event of a film being shown to the whole school. The film was called *The Overlanders* (1946). It was a fascinating docudrama about a group of Australian stockmen moving their herds through wilderness and drought, encountering many hazards and hardships along the way, to escape the threat of a Japanese invasion of northern Australia in the early years of the war. The film must have been considered a valuable educational experience for us schoolboys because of its authentic geographical, historical and cultural content.

The reason that those of my generation came to know Arthur Thomas was that he came back to live in Rhossili in the early 1950s. He was accompanied by his second wife. He settled down for about seven or eight years, mainly farming sheep in a couple of his brother's fields and on the common grazing lands around Rhossili cliffs. He constructed a large, stout shed in one of the fields at the bottom of the Vile, near Sound, so that he could perform such routine tasks as dagging and shearing.

Because the Thomas family were distant cousins of our family, my father felt he could ask Arthur to help in constructing a badly needed shed near the east end of 'the cottage'. The old lean-to had been demolished when 'the cottage' was renovated in 1953. Arthur eventually found time to visit us and find out exactly what my father had in mind. After that, he took over. He estimated and ordered all the material, then went to work.

The shed would be large enough to house a small car, if need be. He concreted the entire floor, first setting solid six-inch square, treated timbers in place. Then he completed the framework with four-inch square, treated timbers. Finally, he finished off with corrugated metal sides and roof, and a pair of large doors, also of timber and zinc construction, facing the road. There was also a back-door for daily use. It would last for more than thirty years, before it needed to be re-built. Arthur did almost the whole job; all my father had to do was unload and move the material.

Although Arthur settled well in Rhossili, there was much that he missed about Australia. Perhaps it was the easygoing, outspoken Aussie culture; perhaps it was the wide-open spaces; perhaps it was his sons from his first marriage who (I had heard) were professional shark-hunters in the waters around Tasmania. Whatever the reason, Arthur suddenly sold off his stock and returned to Australia.

But Arthur could not forget the salty, windswept cliffs of Rhossili. Several years later, he and his wife came back to spend a couple more years in our parish, before returning to Australia yet again. Arthur moved to and fro between Gower and Tasmania, several times. At one time he operated a picnic ground at a place called Wattle Glen, in Tasmania. On at least a couple of occasions, he built and sold a bungalow to help finance his next sojourn in Rhossili.

When Arthur's health was finally failing, he returned once more to Rhossili to spend his last few months. When he died he was cremated; then his wife carried his ashes back to Australia. As was the case with Edgar Evans, Arthur Thomas's remains would not rest in Rhossili.

[Endnote: The Thomas family were cousins of my father and his siblings. Both he and the late Gordon Thomas (one of my generation) were very conscious of this fact. The connection is probably through the maternal side of both families.]

48

A Rainy Saturday in Middleton

Thou waterest her furrows, Thou sendest rain into the little valleys thereof ...

Anglican Prayer Book

THE huge, chilly tears splatter on the sodden fields and pastures. In the farm-yards, dunghills begin to liquefy. The heavy drops tap out a monotonous rhythm on the corrugated zinc roofs of farm buildings. Hayricks and corn-mows are unperturbed under their reliable tarpaulin covers, but the downpour tests the integrity of those few cottages which still have thatched roofs, finding its way through any weak spots to drip into strategically-placed buckets—like the one in the corner of my parents' bedroom.

Rivulets form on the paved road and, picking up minute debris as they go, find their way between the stone chippings, then into the shallow gutters along the roadsides. The roads, now washed almost clean of dust, congealed mud from tractor wheels and the droppings of cows and horses, seem to welcome the opportunity to recapture their freshness. The rivulets become bolder as they band together to rush in ever-increasing volume along the gutters towards the nearest drain—partially blocked by clumps of dead leaves, twigs and dried grass—or down short, muddy slopes, under gateways.

The stream, propelled by run-off from the hill, rushes, alternately roaring and chuckling, downwards from the spring at Sheep Green, crossing under School Lane at Brook Cottage, then, reinforced by more run-off from the fields, becomes a torrent, pouring over the chute at Riverside, where the last of the faithful, hard-working cart horses sometimes slake their thirst. Finally it charges through the double-barrelled steel pipes that cross 'the bank' and, emerging in Broad Hay, heads towards the limestone cliffs of Mewslade Bay as urgently as if it were the White Rabbit. "It's raining, it's pouring; the old man is snoring ..."

Unwilling to stay in the house and read last Christmas's Boys Annual any longer, I watch for the rain to ease as the leaden skies lighten a little. Then, dressed in my old jacket, woollen pullover, short trousers and well-worn studded boots, I race down the road to Middleton. Like my father, I never wear a hat. There's no one about, so I jog out along Rhossili Lane as far as The Green, then walk aimlessly back to 'the bank'.

The rain has eased, but all is quiet. Farmers, workers and their families have found things to do indoors or have gone off to town on the bus, if they don't own a car. Tractors sit idly in their sheds, resting their steel or pneumatic wheel-rims. Poultry and livestock are sheltering in their hen-houses, cow-stalls and stables. Less fortunate creatures take what shelter they can find in the sodden pastures. Even the inquisitive farm-dogs are dozing in the barns, this afternoon. At dusk, the roads will be invaded by fat slugs, snails and a few adventurous toads.

'The bank', so often on weekday evenings busy with energetic boys (of all ages) playing football, while old-timers look on and cackle, is unnaturally quiet today—even for a Saturday. The soaked memorial bench is not inviting, as the elm tree drips even more rainwater onto it. The half-past two bus arrives, but it doesn't need to stop. The spray thrown up by the heavy tyres almost makes more noise than the engine as it roars past.

A solitary veteran farm-worker trudges home from his half-day's work at Great Pitton farm. He plods wearily past with a nod and a smile. It must have been his turn to "do the things" this Saturday. He wears an empty flour-sack across his shoulders, two corners fastened together below his chin with a piece of wire. His cloth cap and trouser-legs look damp, but at least he didn't have to work in the cabbage-field today. Perhaps he had a dinner at the farmhouse before heading home to enjoy what's left of the weekend.

I hang around 'the bank' for about half an hour. Boy, it would be wonderful to play football today, battling both the elements and the opposing team, enjoying sliding tackles, dodging flying boots and scoring spectacular goals. South Gower must surely be playing football at Scurlage or elsewhere, this afternoon. But unless I can cajole the other village boys to become as football-crazy as I, I will have to wait for a few more years for opportunities to play hard in this kind of weather.

I decide it is time to retreat back up the steep slopes of School Lane to 'the cottage'. A fresh shower begins, forcing me to shelter under some tall trees between Jessamine farm and Riverside, until the downpour eases. The leafy cover, already saturated, quickly becomes porous: I have to stand awkwardly on the steeply sloping ground, one arm hooked around a narrow tree-trunk to avoid sliding back onto the road, while dodging the worst of the drips.

Finally, it's easing off. I can see there's a "butt" to the rain-clouds in the distant sky, over Porteynon way, but there'll be more showers before it clears up. Better not delay; I'll head home as fast as I can. A nail from one of the studs on my right boot has pierced through the sole, so I begin to limp as I make my way home, passing Harry Gammon's house, where my boots had been created. There will be no more need for made-to-measure boots, just a few repairs. The house seems forlorn and lifeless, today. Tears of hopelessness drip from the eaves.

Oh well, back to my adventure books and meccano-set, I suppose. I hope my father has remembered to get the accumulator charged up, so we can listen to the football results on our bakelite wireless, at five o'clock. When my mother gets home from town on the half-past six bus, we'll meet her at 'the bank' with an umbrella. She's bound to bring something tasty for our tea, some laver-bread and mushrooms for Sunday breakfast and a joint of lamb or beef to roast in the cast-iron oven alongside the coal-fire, for our Sunday dinner.

Then there's usually a BBC suspense play at eight o'clock on Saturday nights—perhaps about trappers lost in the Canadian wilderness, an adventure in the South Seas, or some desperate men delivering lorry-loads of nitro-glycerine in Central America.

Life doesn't stay boring for long.

49

A Watershed Year

From every house the neighbours met,
The streets were filled with joyful sound ...

Tennyson

ONE year which must stand out in many old-timers' memories is 1953. The major event of that year was, of course, the coronation of Queen Elizabeth on June 2nd. She had already become Queen immediately following the death of her father, King George 6th, in early 1952.

The news of the King's death was considered so important, that classes at Gowerton Grammar School were interrupted by senior boys being sent to inform every teacher, in every classroom. I think it was our French teacher, "Jack" Thomas, who gravely informed our first-year class, Form 1A, of the sad news. He said a few words about how the King had been ailing for some time. The eldest daughter, Elizabeth, would automatically become the new monarch.

The coronation was a joyous event throughout the land. Just a couple of years before, Churchill had been returned to power as Prime Minister, which could only add to the sense of patriotism. Memories of the disastrous East Coast floods in January had begun to fade. The Korean War was coming to a close.

In Middleton, strings of miniature flags of various sorts were stretched between the giant elm tree and adjacent rooftops, including Middleton Hall and the village hall. They had to be high enough to allow the United Welsh double-deckers to pass underneath. There were commemorative mugs, plates and other hardware in everyone's home. Every child seemed to have a small paper Union Jack on a short stick to wave. At the village hall, on the special day, there were real flags and more streamers.

All television sets were black-and-white. Very few people in the village owned one—certainly none of the farm-workers. One or two families bought one in time for the coronation—or perhaps to watch the FA cup-final between Blackpool and Bolton Wanderers, which preceded it by a few weeks.

At the Worms Head Hotel, which catered strictly to residents in those days, a couple of TV sets were reported stolen, just a day or two before the big event. This, in itself, was sensational in a village where crime was virtually unknown. The thieves were not aware that a couple more (rented) TVs were sitting in the village hall, with the doors unlocked.

On Coronation Day, the two hired TV sets were set up in the hall, so that everyone would be able to watch the event. My father, Joff, told us about a previous coronation, in 1937, when two wirelesses had been hired for a similar purpose. Apparently, one of the village elders had argued that "We'll ha' t' be careful t' turn 'um on the same time, by, or one'll be a bit behind t'other!"

After some important preliminaries, which included a couple of short speeches by local councillors, the coronation was carefully observed, at least by most of the adults. After the first hour, the children were just as interested in a second helping of jelly-and-blancmange. There must have been about seventy-five percent of the village population in attendance. Only the VE and VJ bonfires competed with this turnout.

Later, there were organised sports in Will Morris's field, just past the village hall, opposite The Ship farm's rickyard. For us children, there were some hilarious competitions like egg-and-spoon races, sack races and three-legged races. There were also high jump and long jump competitions. The tall, athletic Howard Chalk easily won the 100-yard dash for our age group. I think Ron Beynon came second. Howard also won the high jump, though I managed to do well, finally taking a hard tumble in trying to go higher than anyone else. I ended up sharing the second prize with Peter Crozier. The women and girls competed in their party dresses; we boys competed in our short pants and sandals, while some of the men who competed, did so in their best trousers and shirts.

In the men's 100-yards, 220-yards and one-mile races, Ernie Beynon, Roger Harding, Eric Gibbs, Dudley Thomas and Len Jones were all strong competitors. In the 100 yard race for the over-forties, the diminutive Alec Thomas and long-legged Wilfred Beynon competed fiercely. I felt disappointed that there was no mile race for us boys, because I knew I was used to jogging long distances. Although he said nothing, my father, Joffre, must also have felt some disappointment; at thirty-eight he was too old to take on the young men, yet he didn't qualify for the over-forties, either.

Then it was back to the hall, where Dudley Thomas had us kids join him in a humorous song about various musical instruments. After that, we filled ourselves with more jelly, blancmange, Devonshire splits and a variety of cakes, until we were happy to follow our exhausted parents homeward. Then, Doug Davies took over as the MC for an evening of entertainment and dancing for the unencumbered adults.

There were several other notable events in 1953, which would long be remembered by sports aficionados. The conquest of Everest by a British expedition led by John Hunt was a huge event. Hillary and Tensing were the ones who reached the summit. A Welsh climber and his partner had been very close to it, on the previous afternoon, but had not felt confident that they could reach the summit and return safely. At that time, it was the success of the expedition and the safety of individuals, which mattered. In subsequent years, there seemed to be more and more focus on who was actually first to set his foot on the summit.

Then there was Stanley Matthews's cup-final. The amazing, veteran star—the most famous player in the world—was thirty-eight years old and had never won an FA cup-final medal. He and his team-mates, including Stanley Mortensen, triumphed over footballer of the year, Nat Lofthouse, and Bolton Wanderers. Meanwhile, the much-loved veteran jockey, Gordon Richards, won his first Grand National. Both these exemplary sportsmen were at the end of their best years, though they both continued to participate until they were fifty years old.

Of all the notable events of that year, it was perhaps the advent of the first television sets which would ultimately have the most profound effect on village life, especially the younger generation. As we began to see much more of the outside world, many of us set our sights on experiencing life far beyond the confines of our native Gower.

It was also a watershed year for me, personally. Although I would still wear short trousers for another year, I had now become a teenager. Although Lita Roza's recording of *How much is that doggy in the window?* was a huge favourite at the time, and Frankie Laine's spiritual rendition, *I Believe* was the biggest hit of the year, I was beginning to take an interest in more romantic pop-songs, such as the ones soon to be released by Pat Boone and Doris Day. Inclined to be an idealist, I was beginning to daydream about a seemingly distant future and a life of my own.

It was the last year I would enjoy just being a kid. I was about to find that the hormones, the tensions and the uncertainties of the teenage years would become increasingly difficult to handle.

50

Growing Pains

Man for the field and woman for the hearth:
Man for the sword and for the needle she:

Tennyson

I THINK I first realised I was growing up when I began to give serious thought to living my own life, apart from my parents. For many boys, this phenomenon occurs at a surprisingly early age. This phase accelerated the development of my ability to survive in the world, even though self-confidence was lacking, at least at a social level.

The ideas came first—but that's all they were. Serious thoughts of independence didn't occur until my mid-teens. The ideas had a lot to do with hormones and expectations. They were powerful motivators, promoting a sense of urgency which accelerated my anticipation of an exciting future. Yet time seemed reluctant to move along in those teenage years.

In the hot summer weather of July 1953, I began to take matters into my own hands in a way I hadn't before. We were still billeted at Middleton Hall, waiting impatiently for the completion of renovations to 'the cottage'. One Saturday morning I was hanging around the living room, waiting until it was time to catch the one o'clock bus. We Rhossili boys were going to Horton to take on Horton and Porteynon at cricket. I was alone in the farmhouse.

As I sat in a well-worn armchair, idly reviewing the sports sections of Friday's *Evening Post* and *Daily Express*, it felt warm and stuffy. It was going to be a hot day. My hair had become overgrown: my father had been too busy with work to make an appointment with Vaughan Price, a farm-worker who lived in a "tied" cottage at Great Pitton farm. He and his brother Jim, who lived at Brook Cottage, had been hired at the Brecon Agricultural Fair, in the 1930s.

I borrowed aunty Doreen's hand-mirror. No doubt about it, my hair was badly overgrown; in fact, it looked and felt ridiculous—but the heat was the worst thing. After half an hour, I decided to try to give myself a trim. I soon found a large pair of scissors and began to cut. When my parents came in at dinner-time, they found me with a very uneven haircut, to put it mildly: there were chunks missing everywhere.

Soon, the one o'clock bus flew past on its way out to Rhossili End. But by this time, my mother had convinced me that I couldn't possibly go to play cricket "looking like that". Although I felt devastated at the thought of missing this rare inter-village cricket match, I knew she was right. I knew there was no ready solution to the problem. I felt trapped, albeit because of my own impetuous actions. I realised I would have to pay the obvious penalty.

Just then, Brian (Butch) Beynon knocked on the door, anxiously reminding me that the bus would be arriving any second. Keeping my face straight towards him, so that (I hoped) he wouldn't notice my new hairstyle, I solemnly advised him that I couldn't come to the cricket match. Butch looked as disappointed as I felt, but he could see I was serious. He went off to tell John Bevan and the others.

My self-administered haircut was so bad that my father had to arrange for Vaughan to come to Middleton Hall on the Sunday evening to complete the job I had begun on my own. It seemed a very long Saturday and Sunday that I spent indoors, especially when I could have been playing cricket and going to the bay.

Finally, at about seven o'clock on Sunday evening, Vaughan arrived. He was a tall, lean, soft-spoken man. He couldn't help smiling when he saw my handiwork. He commented that I had chopped my hair a bit high over one ear, but other than that he would be able to restore things to a more-or-less normal "short back and sides". I was not only relieved, but my head felt much cooler for the remainder of the summer.

Having survived a "lost weekend", it felt good to return to my normal routine. Catching the school-bus on Monday morning, I learnt that the Rhossili team had just managed to win a close-fought cricket match.

One dull, chilly afternoon in early January 1954, at the tail end of the Christmas holidays, I was hanging aimlessly around 'the bank' when Howard Chalk came by. There were flurries of sleet from time to time. Howard said his father had told him to check on their sheep, which were grazing on the cliffs above Sound, between Tears Point and the Kitchen Corner. I said I'd go along with him.

Howard was a tall, athletic teenager; he was already into long trousers. I was more than a year younger, still wearing short trousers, so my bony knees were feeling rather cool as we set off down the Vile Lane. We jogged some of the time until we came to the top of Fall Bay, then we took the higher path around to Tears Point. We turned west, keeping in the lee of the rocky ridge.

The leaden skies indicated that daylight wouldn't last much after four o'clock. We plodded along, counting sheep bearing Ingram Chalk's mark. Periodically, we checked over the edge of the cliff. Not too far from Tears point, we found a pregnant ewe trapped in a v-shaped gully about six feet below the cliff edge. We tried for a while to free the sheep, but it was just too tight and awkward to manoeuvre—and there was a sharp drop below. We decided that I should stay and watch the sheep, while Howard reported back to his father.

I knew I was in for about a three-quarter hour wait in the gathering gloom. The sleet intensified at times, becoming almost blinding in the light breeze, though not settling in any great quantity. I crouched in the cleft of the rocks above the trapped ewe. In the solitude, I allowed my mind to wander off into a future which seemed quite utopian to a boy not yet turned fourteen. I would achieve complete personal independence—with the exception of a job, of course: I never doubted that work would always be a priority in my life.

Where, I wondered, *is the girl I will spend the major part of my life with*? Was she a Gower girl, or someone from a city in England, or perhaps from a foreign country, speaking a strange language that I would need to learn? It was as if I were trying to communicate telepathically with my future bride. If only we could become aware of each other, we might get together without delay. How wonderful that would be.

Daydreaming helped the time to pass; then Howard and his father, Ingram Chalk, arrived with a length of sisal rope. Ingram quickly secured the rope around the sheep, using a bowline knot. He tried to lift the sheep as Howard and I pulled steadily from the cliff edge. Soon the ewe was safe; apparently undamaged, she trotted off to join her companions.

With the rescue successfully completed, we set off through Rhossili Vile, towards home. It was just about dark when we reached Hampstead, but I still had some distance to go. There were no lights other than those escaping from kitchen windows, but it was no concern—I rarely used a torch, anyway. At 'the cottage', the welcoming lamplight, the warmth of the fireplace and a plate of stew and mashed potatoes, reminded me of the many good things that life with my parents had to offer. *Perhaps I shouldn't leave home for another year or two*, I thought.

One Saturday in the spring of that year, there was an air-show at Fairwood Common. My father, Joffre, and I caught the half-past two bus, which made a special stop for the show. Howard happened to catch the same bus. None of us had ever had a ride in an aeroplane. I didn't know that my father had a secret ambition to experience flying, though I had often heard him speak with admiration about the Spitfire and Hurricane pilots who had chased the German bombers away from Swansea and Cardiff.

I believe it cost us ten shillings each—a princely sum at that time—but my father, then almost forty years old, enjoyed something that he had always wanted to experience. It would be many years before he would have the opportunity to fly again. The single-engine plane, carrying only four or five passengers, sputtered into life and taxied out to the runway.

We could observe the pilot's actions as well as the instrument panel, as the small plane weaved and banked above the aerodrome and the surrounding countryside for about ten minutes. My father must have been fascinated to get a birds-eye view of the fields at Lunnon and other places where he had worked during and after the war, but I was overawed by the sensation of flying in the noisy machine; I think it was about the same for Howard. A few years later, though, we would both join the Royal Observer Corps.

It was in the autumn of the same year that uncle Len took my friend, Peter Crozier, and me to see a landmark science-fiction film called *The War of the Worlds*, which was showing at the Carlton cinema on Oxford Street. Peter and I were "trekkies" of our generation. We had enjoyed listening to such exciting radio serials as *Journey into Space*, as well as reading a variety of science-fiction stories and comic books. The truth was, of course, that uncle Len, still a young man in his early thirties, was just as desperate as we were to see the film; but in those days, adults didn't admit to such frivolous desires.

Due to the terrifying scenes of aliens invading Earth, we were supposed to be at least sixteen years old, even when accompanied by an adult. I was wearing my very first pair of long trousers. I was not particularly tall for my age; in fact, Peter, who was about a year younger, was slightly taller than I. There were a tense few minutes as uncle Len purchased our tickets. Trying to appear relaxed and unconcerned, Peter and I followed him into the safe anonymity of the darkness, where he gave us a couple of toffees to chew as we waited for the film to start.

We were not disappointed: it was as if all hell was let loose when the aliens attacked our planet. Not even the massed fire-power of the United Nations could stop them. Our planet was only saved when the aliens succumbed to the invisible microbes that frequent Earth's atmosphere.

We were still in a mild state of shock, not talking very much as we had a cup of tea and a sandwich at the Garage Cafe until it was time for the Rhossili bus. It wasn't until we were back in Middleton that I began to feel safe from alien invaders.

It was a warm Sunday in August, 1955. Predictably, I was at Fall Bay. The bay was fairly crowded with "visitors" as we called anyone who was not from Gower. Many of these visitors returned year-after-year to stay at the guesthouses or campsites. The tide was halfway out and there was a strong swell, due to the stormy conditions of the previous week. There were fairly large waves that were good for bodysurfing. There were no locals on the beach, though there were a few regular visitors that I recognised.

I was relaxing on the dry, powdery sand after half an hour of non-stop surfing when there was a disturbance among some of the people. A few were shouting that someone was in trouble in the tide, while one man rushed up the pathway to fetch the lifebelt and line. Jumping to my feet, I saw that a robust-looking, middle-aged man had got caught in the current as the tide began to ebb around the base of Lewis Castle. He was being carried around towards Mewslade and couldn't fight the current.

Soon, a lean fit-looking man about thirty years old was trying to carry the lifebelt out through the surf. The trouble was, there was a whole row of men, women and children hanging on to the line, all wanting to play a part in the rescue. Not wanting to appear uncaring, I joined in and got a hand on the line, too. Then I realised that we were actually holding back the man who was trying to take the lifebelt out through the surf, so I let go, hoping others would do the same.

In retrospect, I was probably more aware than the adults of how the situation should have been handled—but I was only a fifteen-year-old, so how could I give people orders? The young man who had the lifebelt seemed tense and apprehensive: he looked like he needed almost as much help as the man who was in trouble.

By this time, the swimmer had managed to find a way to catch a large wave, which helped bring him back in; whereas all of us would-be rescuers hadn't managed to get the lifebelt beyond the surf. As he found his feet on the sandy bottom, he accepted the proffered lifebelt as a token of our efforts.

For some time afterwards, I was haunted by the thought that events might not have ended so well. I had witnessed a dramatic example of the dangers of indecision in hazardous circumstances.

For many boys, hormones had another predictable effect. They developed aggressive behaviour, which was coupled with the expectation of fulfilling the compulsory National Service requirements (which were not abolished until 1958). The Second World War was soon followed by the Korean War. For more than three years the newspapers carried accounts of the ebb and flow of battles on the Korean Peninsula, culminating in the uneasy truce at Panmunjon. I had every expectation that, sooner or later, I would have to join the armed forces.

By 1955, several of us in my fourth form at Gowerton Grammar School decided we would like to join the Fleet Air-arm. No doubt we had been influenced by reports of American and British Navy pilots doing battle with Russian MiGs over Korea. My parents were adamantly opposed to my plan to enter the forces at sixteen, after my O-level exams. My headmaster, Dr. James, let it be known that he disapproved of my throwing away the opportunity of a university education.

Nevertheless, I replied to a Fleet Air-arm ad in the daily newspaper. I outlined my O-level expectations and requested application forms for entry as a trainee pilot. A few weeks later, a package of forms arrived. When I opened them, I saw that they were for making an application to become a navigator. *But the navigator sits in the <u>back</u> seat of the plane,* I reminded myself. That was not an attractive idea. No one seemed to agree with my ambitions to be a pilot; therefore, I concluded that it must be I who was wrong. In any case, I knew I had astigmatism in my right eye, so I would be unlikely to pass the medical exam as a pilot. I supposed it just wasn't meant to be.

Instead, I turned my attention to working towards a degree in Electrical Engineering. Unfortunately, that didn't help the main problem—the one to do with the hormones. From the earliest teenage years, I had felt the need for a fulfilling relationship. But in our small village, it was embarrassing to be seen out with a local girl. The psychological insecurity initiated by puberty didn't help. The lack of financial independence only added to the problem.

My aggressive inclinations were mainly relieved on the sports field, though sometimes there was a wrestling bout or a fist-fight; but socially, my limitations caused me to become increasingly introverted.

[Endnote: In retrospect, I believe that an early break from the education system, at about sixteen, would have been much better for me. The teenage years can seem unbearable. No doubt practical, vocational programmes, such as apprenticeships, whether in the armed forces or in industry, would benefit the great majority of teenage boys.]

51

The Boys Brigade

... while a foreign troop was landed in my country, I never would lay down my arms ...

William Pitt

EVERY July, for almost a decade, ranging from the late 1940s to the mid-1950s, the Birmingham Boys Brigade would encamp for about two weeks at the lower end of Great Pitton farm's steeply-sloping field, which was separated by a low dry-stone wall from the lane leading to Mewslade Bay. It was an ideal location for these city boys to get down to the bay for a swim, and to the cliffs for fishing and hiking.

There must have been about four score of these sojourners from England, accompanied by about a dozen adults. Yes, they'd need adults to protect them from us tough Gower boys, alright! They were usually housed in about half a dozen large circular tents and a number of smaller, rectangular ones. The youngest boys and the adults were fortunate to enjoy the shelter of the Old Chapel. There was a large, oblong marquee which served as a cook-house and dining area.

Even Tarzan of the Apes would have found this a daunting challenge to his domain, I thought, as we stared from our leafy perches high in a sycamore tree, located in the small wood on the other side of the lane. My companion was Colin Dye, a regular summer visitor from Norfolk. There were just the two of us, but we were quite fearless—at least, as long as we weren't discovered. It didn't cross my mind that, although Colin's mother and grandparents were "old Gower" people, my trusted friend had, himself, been born and raised in England.

The English invaders had no chance of spotting us in our leafy hideout, but we could observe every detail of their camp. We watched as they moved around in twos or threes, carrying towels and toothbrushes, or readying themselves to go

219

to Mewslade Bay for a swim. At noon, responding to the call of a bugle, they rushed eagerly towards the marquee. We were feeling a bit hungry ourselves; perhaps they would invite us for a meal. *No, what am I thinking about? They are the enemy; we are thirteen-year-old veteran spies who mustn't be caught!*

A cacophony of sound resulted from the enthusiastic employment of meal-tins, cutlery and chattering voices inside the marquee. While they were eating, perhaps we could have slid down from our tree, climbed over the low stone wall and slacked off the guy-ropes on some of their tents. But there always seemed to be a few individuals who hadn't rushed off to join the melee. Perhaps they just weren't hungry? Perhaps they were feeling homesick?

We decided instead to resort to a few catcalls and whistles. A couple of the boys stared towards our hiding place. Another one joined them. After a few minutes we catcalled again. They began walking slowly towards the stone wall, one of them pointing towards the wood that concealed us. We kept quiet to see what would happen. We couldn't risk being discovered, because we'd be trapped in the tree, with no way of escape. They might have starved us down from our perch and who knows what may have followed. We began to feel vulnerable. The hunters had become the hunted. Fortunately, we were well hidden. The boys soon gave up trying to spot us and wandered off to find their friends and play some cricket.

By now, it was well after our dinner-time. We decided to return in mid-afternoon, when their camp might be deserted. But it never was. There was always an adult or two looking after the place. We'd just have to put up with the provocation of this invading force and hope they weren't planning to stay too long.

On the middle Sunday of their stay, the Boys Brigade always paraded to the 11:00 AM service at St. Mary's Anglican Church. Even up at 'the cottage' we could hear their drums and bugles as soon as they had formed up and started on their half-mile march.

I would race down to 'the bank' and wait with some of the other kids as the sound of the drums indicated the parade had reached the Lower Shop. Then the bugles would cut in. What a stirring sound! Led by the band, the whole company marched, by threes, through Middleton, with a few kids from Pitton trying to keep up at the rear. It was a magnificent sight.

After the church service, they would march back to their camp, having won much grudging admiration and respect from us local boys. Of course, we hoped (in vain) that the village girls would not be too impressed.

Most summers, cricket and football matches were arranged between the Boys Brigade and us locals. I played in one football match. There was a wide range of ages in both teams. I was about the youngest, at fourteen years old. The others included Colin Dye, Roger Harding, Chris Beynon, Ernie Beynon, Vaughn Price and Len McVitie. In previous years, talented players like Len Beynon and brothers Leyton and Douglas Kent (who worked at Great Pitton farm) had usually ensured victory for the locals.

In this particular game, in 1955, we played on a sloping, uneven grass-field out towards Pitton cliffs, near Alveley. There were some rudimentary goalposts, even cross-bars, but no nets. Our kick and rush game was almost effective, but in the end, the Boys Brigade team was more disciplined and they beat us by a couple of goals. *We aren't very well prepared for playing football in July*, I thought. There was also an annual cricket game, but I never had the opportunity to play in that team. My friend, Colin Dye was about the youngest of the players.

[Endnote: While we youngsters never really had the opportunity to make friends with these annual "invaders", we came to enjoy their visits, especially their Sunday parades. Many of those city boys must have treasured their visit to such a remote and rugged part of the British Isles. For them, the memories would last a lifetime, no doubt.]

52

Football Headlines

Oh, talk not to me of a name great in story;
The days of our youth are the days of our glory ...

Lord Byron

MY fascination with football increased as I grew up. To me, playing football was the ultimate expression of who I was. It was an obsession at times, which was only fuelled further by those dramatic challenge matches between Wolverhampton Wanderers and some prominent Russian clubs such as Moscow Dynamo and Spartak, in the early 1950s. Wolves always seemed to win, but only by a goal or two, even though the matches were always played at Wolves's Molyneux ground. All the games were cliffhangers.

Harry Morris, who lived at Rose Cottage, was one of the first in the village to own a black-and-white TV. It was no coincidence that he was a lifelong football enthusiast. I shared a love of football with both Harry and his oldest son, John, which is how I came to view those historic football matches.

A few years later, it was the Busby Babes (Manchester United) who captured our imagination. Their exploits involved them in tough competitions such as the European Cup. Then came the Munich air disaster, which occurred a couple of months before I turned eighteen. Manchester United fans everywhere felt an unspeakable loss. The unique talent of Duncan Edwards was gone forever, so was the heart of the team. Nevertheless, time heals. The inspirational play of young survivor Bobby Charlton, Harry Gregg, Dennis Viollet and others helped the famous club to recover themselves over the following decade.

I think it was at Easter, 1955, that someone in our school (Gowerton) organised a couple of football matches against Bishop Gore, who were a football-playing

222

school. Our school was strictly rugby; so football was usually ignored. I think it was due to our school's strong rugby culture that both friendly matches were played in the Easter holidays. Anyway, somewhat grudgingly, permission was given to form a football team representing our school—but just for two matches, mind you!

We won both our matches against Bishop Gore by a goal or two. The games were played with perfect sportsmanship. The first was played at a sloping park in the Killay/Dunvant area; the second on a flat pitch next to the Mumbles road. In the second match, I played at halfback. Early in the match, one of the Bishop Gore players was called offside. I took the free kick just outside our penalty area and side-footed it back to the goalkeeper, without looking. Unfortunately, our goalkeeper had decided to stroll away from his goal area. It was a classic own-goal. Fortunately, I managed to score one for our side before the end, so it evened things up.

By the time we played that second match, the *Evening Post* had got wind of what was going on. They took a photograph of our team before the match started. Next day, the photo was in the *Evening Post*, along with the eye-catching headline: "While School's Away, the Boys Will Play—at Soccer!" I was dismayed. It was not the kind of publicity that would likely result in more football matches for us Gowertonians.

More drama was to occur when Swansea Town decided to run a developmental team in the Swansea and District league, in the late 1950s. At eighteen, I was one of the younger players in the South Gower side. Frankly, we were a disparate bunch of kick-and-rush individuals, of varying ages and skills. Gone were the heady days of stars like Ernie and Len Beynon, Don and Brian Shepherd, Eric and Lindon Lee, and Dennis Hughes. There was no team coach, no regular practice, no game plan: we just turned up and played. As long as the ball was kicked up-field, there was a sense of hope. Anyone who dared to pass the ball back towards his own goal would usually earn some disapproving looks from his teammates. Even so, we were able to pull off a few wins, here and there.

We played our away match against the Swans on a perfectly flat, green pitch in the northern outskirts of Swansea. It was a dull day; the turf was soft, but true. The young Swans ran rings around us. They won by about eight goals to nil, without breaking into a sweat. I was overawed by the way their left winger, Barry Jones, could bring a dropping ball under control with the outside of his right foot, without seeming to break his stride as he swept down the wing. I can't remember any other match I played when I just wanted it to end. It wasn't the one-sided score that bothered me; it was how completely inept we were, that day. We couldn't do anything right.

For the return match at Scurlage, on a dull, cool day late in the season, the Swans showed up with a very young team indeed. Most of them were two or three years younger than I. They were unbeaten, while we languished near the bottom of the division, so they had fielded a very young side. We fielded much the same team as for the first match. Our main advantage was that we were used to the uneven surface of the awkwardly sloping pitch, while the Swans were not. Even as they were still trying to get the feel of the strange field, we scored our first goal.

This gave us some heart, while it seemed to make them less confident. We were Gower boys defending our home turf, so whenever they had possession of the ball, we ran straight at them, without paying too much attention to the ball. This tactic prevented them from settling down. Eventually, we scored a second goal. This truly depressed the young Swans. For the rest of the game, they and their coach complained ceaselessly to the referee about our rough tactics, while we enjoyed the game more and more. The headline in the following Monday's *Evening Post* was, "Lowly South Gower Beats Mighty Swans".

On that famous day, both our goals were scored by Gerry Fisher. Gerry came from somewhere in Gower. He drove a mobile ice-cream van. In fact, he usually drove it to home matches, arriving at the last minute, having been selling ice-cream all morning. Gerry was not the most graceful of football players. Often his shots lacked direction and consistency, but he had powerful legs, so when he hit the ball cleanly, it was impressive. Gerry hit the ball cleanly, just twice that day. They were two beautiful "daisy cutters" reminiscent of the Swans's Mel Charles.

Gerry was the undisputed man of the match. He brought football fame to South Gower. But we made sure he shared the honours with his rag-tag bunch of team-mates, who included goalkeeper Cliff Howell; veteran defenders, Les Clement, Emmett Hughes and Manty Griffiths; as well as Laurie Jones, Islwyn Bennett and our sixteen-year-old star, Wyndham Parry.

53

Car-Park Tedium

I go to encounter for the millionth time the reality of experience ...

James Joyce

IN the summer of 1956, I found myself working as a general farmhand for Gordon Thomas and his aging father, Sid, when they found they needed someone to fill in as car-park attendant. I knew that the chief coastguard's younger daughter, Anne Dorling, usually did this seasonal job; but she had decided to make herself busy elsewhere. No one could blame her. The car-park attendant's job could be rather tedious; it was very quiet in the weekdays—in contrast to summer weekends, when at least one extra attendant was needed.

In some ways, it was a nice change from farm-work, whether picking potatoes, stacking hay-bales in the old Vanguard bus-garage, dipping sheep, or just going from field to field, mending fences with Aubrey John, an ex-merchant seaman. Fencing along the top of the hedges had proved to be an awkward, difficult job. I had been filling in for Gordon's friend, the flame-haired giant, Derek Dorling (Anne's brother), who was away doing his National Service.

By contrast with farm-work, the car-park provided the opportunity to meet a few interesting people and exchange pleasantries with any locals passing by. I think I should also have taken the opportunity to do some reading, but I had lost interest in that healthy mental exercise. *Besides, school's closed for the summer, so it's time to relax my brain*, I thought. Gordon's cheerful, energetic mother, May, now became my boss, keeping me supplied with change and books of tickets.

Often I would get the opportunity of a brief chat with Stan or Molly Walters when they came home to The Cottage for lunch or tea. I also got to know their shy, be-spectacled five-year-old son, Robert, whom I like to address as "Bob" because it seemed to puzzle him. Sometimes, Eddie Tucker's little daughters would drop by and play around the attendant's hut. The older girl, Julie, was dark-haired with fine features; the younger one, Anne, was blonde with a round face. Even so, weekday afternoons were mostly quiet. When the time came to pack up for the day (at about five o'clock during the week, but earlier, if the weather was bad), I was truly glad to be un-tethered from my post.

Weekends were very different. There were streams of cars and a number of coaches. On Sundays, an extra field had to be opened up to accommodate the traffic. There would be at least two of us selling tickets. There was also a steady stream of locals (just when I didn't have time to stop and talk) taking a stroll "out the end" to buy an ice-cream.

I managed the car-park as conscientiously as I could. Dealing with so many customers, I had the opportunity to compare the best and the worst sides of human nature. It also seemed to bring out both the best and the worst in me. On one occasion, a car cruised deliberately past the hut while I was selling a ticket to another motorist.

I knew the driver had seen me, so as he drove past, I took a couple of quick strides and banged on the roof of his car with the heel of my hand. The driver, a tall solidly-built chap in his thirties, was so infuriated that he stopped the car, rushed over to me and began demanding to know what right I had to bang on his car. I told him he was required to stop at the entrance. He went on haranguing me for a couple of minutes, but finally he ran out of steam and charged off—after he paid his shilling.

On the other hand, a good deed I had done would have been long forgotten, if it were not for chance. Several years after I had worked at the car-park, my cousin Frances was recuperating in Morriston hospital from a very serious operation. An elderly woman in the next bed told her that, although she was an invalid, she loved to visit Rhossili.

She said that on one particular occasion, her companions explained to the young man at the gate that she couldn't get out of the car, but wanted to enjoy the beautiful view of the bay and the hill. She recounted how the boy had quickly run down along the rows of cars and located a space at the front, with an excellent view: she had enjoyed that day tremendously.

Frances assured her that she knew that young man very well.

54

Close Calls

Grant to us such strength and protection, as may support us in all dangers ...

Anglican Prayer Book

FOR a number of years I enjoyed a strong friendship with John Bevan, the youngest son of Jack Bevan, a businessman and senior lay-preacher at the Methodist Chapel. This friendship was strengthened by my regular attendance at the Methodist Chapel Sunday-school for a few years, where I was a diligent student.

Although John did not share my fanaticism for football and rugby, nor for spending time at the bays, we nevertheless enjoyed playing cricket (or sometimes French cricket) with a soft ball at 'the bank', which resulted in us spending a lot of time together. John had great reactions for slip catches; in fact, a few of us became very competitive in this area, but John's long arms gave him an extra edge. He was also a great imitator of the bowling styles of contemporary "greats" like Bedser, Lock, Laker, Loader and Bailey.

John and his father often went to support Glamorgan—and Parkmill man, Don Shepherd—at the St. Helens cricket ground. On a couple of occasions, I was invited to join them for the afternoon. John and I would catch the ten o'clock bus into town, then we would meet his father at the family's electrical and plumbing supply shop in The Uplands; from there, we could walk down to the cricket ground. They were memorable experiences, even though being an onlooker on the opening day of a three-day cricket match was not my favourite entertainment. I much preferred being involved in the action, rather than just being a spectator.

John's great passion in life was always farming, though. I was sometimes frustrated with him when I was trying to organise Rhossili boys for inter-village football matches. John always found it hard to give up his precious Saturdays helping his uncle Jack Richards at Jessamine farm. *How can milking cows be more interesting than chasing a football?* I wondered.

It was not surprising that John's Christmas presents included some magnificent farm-sets, complete with realistic animals, fences, vehicles, tractors, trailers, buildings, even trees. Father Christmas certainly knew what John wanted—and John certainly deserved those fine presents. I spent several pleasant afternoons at Sunny Mead in the Christmas holidays or on rainy days, playing at farming. Sometimes I would be invited to stay for tea with John's parents and his older siblings, Jane, David, Elizabeth and Pauline.

Strangely though, I would later associate John with a couple of near-disasters, which we were fortunate to come through unscathed. Perhaps it was something to do with our time spent at the Chapel Sunday-school, diligently learning our Bible lessons, which subsequently protected us from severe injury.

John could throw a ball powerfully. On one occasion, I saw John and one of the younger sports enthusiasts, John Morris, playing around with a cricket-bat and "soft" ball in Wilfred Beynon's field opposite the Post Office. As I clambered over the wall at The Ship farm's loading stage to join them, John saw me. He turned and hurled the ball high in the air from the other end of the field. It was a perfect throw; the ball was dropping straight towards me. As I took a couple steps into the field, I watched it descending, accelerating at a steep angle.

Suddenly my love of football took over: I had an urge to "head" the ball back as high as I could, to see how far it would go. But for some reason (which I have never quite understood) I changed my mind and caught the ball perfectly, with both hands cupped close to my chest. The ball was not "soft"—it was a cork cricket-ball! Shocked though I was, I said nothing to the other two boys.

In the other incident that left a lasting impression with me, our roles were reversed. We were in our mid teens, and a gang of us ("the boys") were setting out on a summer evening to go dragnet fishing at Rhossili Bay. A local farmer's son was driving the tractor. The open-sided trailer was loaded with a dragnet, our changes of clothes and at least half a dozen enthusiastic teenage passengers, standing upright.

The two or three boys at the front of the trailer could hold on, but the rest of us could not. As we passed Broad Park guesthouse, the boy driving the tractor in top gear, decided to cause some excitement by swerving from side to side across the road. We all laughed, but it was scary. Suddenly I realised I had lost my balance and was going to topple backwards off the side of the trailer, probably striking the road, head first.

In an instant, I reached out with my hand and pushed against the boy standing next to me, in order to regain my balance. Thankfully, it worked. But the boy I had pushed lost his balance. He went tumbling head over heels off the rear of the trailer. To my immense relief, he quickly scrambled back to his feet, shaken but with no obvious injuries. As the tractor screeched to a halt, he ran after us and climbed back onto the trailer, apparently unscathed.

That boy, who had unwittingly saved me from unknown injury, was John Bevan.

[Endnote: Those were by no means the only "close calls" of my younger years, but they were a couple of experiences with potentially deadly consequences—sharp lessons on the importance of applying common sense and safety even in our leisure activities.]

55

Travelling and Adventuring

An adventurous child, thanks to the gods.

R. L. Stevenson

MIKE Roberts and I became friends the time we first met. That was on the 1951 school trip to Bristol Zoo, which was jointly organised by Knelston and Rhossili Schools. It was a rare and memorable occasion, involving about a dozen of the senior students from each school. A coach was hired to collect us from our various hamlets; then we caught the train at High Street Station. We were all dressed in our best sports-clothes, as if we were going on a Sunday-school trip. We were accompanied by our headmistress, Ada Thomas and her counter-part from Knelston School. Our infants' teacher, Lily Button, was left in charge at Rhossili School.

For most of us, it was our very first ride on a train. At High Street Station, tickets had to be purchased, but that was all looked after by our teachers; if they had distributed them to us, some would have been lost, I'm sure. Marching up the platform towards a carriage near the front of the train, we had time for a look at the engine. The clanks and hisses, the smell of coke and steam, reminded me of the steam engine which drove the threshing-machine in the autumn, and the steam-rollers that paved the roads. But the train engine was much larger and more powerful, as it stood hissing and snarling impatiently.

Then, it was "All aboard!" Doors slammed, the guard blew his whistle, and the engine struggled to gather speed as the steam pressure built up. We settled down to a couple of hours of wonderment, staring out of the carriage windows as the scenery constantly changed—from fields with crops or livestock, to rows of terraced houses, to bustling town centres, to quiet villages. Once in a while, the train whistle screamed loudly—again reminding me of the threshing-machine and steam-roller engines. Sometimes the train galloped along, making the characteristic clickety-clack sounds; at other times, it slowed right down as it approached railway stations or junctions.

Eventually, we reached the famous Severn tunnel. We held our breath as we began the long slow journey underneath the broad river. We were instructed to make sure all the windows were closed to keep out the billows of steam and grit from the engine. The minutes ticked by. *We must be right under the middle of the river by now.* That was a fearful thought. It was almost pitch black outside and the carriage lighting was dim. At last, we felt the train climbing towards the exit. We'd had enough of tunnels for now; soon we would emerge in England.

Finally, we reached Bristol railway station. From there, it was all sunshine and fun. Everyone had a great time at the zoo. There was so much to look at—many fascinating animals and birds we had only seen in picture books. We stared incredulously at the camels and the giraffes. Elephants and monkeys we had seen before, on rare visits to the circus.

Whenever the word went round that one of the big cats was moving about, or was being fed by its keeper, we all rushed to stare. There was a bit of fuss when one of the girls from Knelston School annoyed a caged animal by poking at it with a peacock feather, through the wire mesh of the cage. One of the boys unintentionally threw his friend's cap into the Gorilla's cage. The Gorilla, probably overdue for his lunch, proceeded to make meal of it. Otherwise the visit went smoothly.

The return train journey passed without great excitement, though not without the usual delays. Our coach was waiting patiently, near Atkinson Sports shop in the High Street. Then, on the way home, our teachers prompted Mike and me to collect a tribute of appreciation for the coach-driver, on behalf of both schools. It had indeed been a day of wonderment and new experiences.

Mike and I started grammar school at the same time, though we were allocated to different forms. We had different pals and sporting interests, but always remained good friends. We had more involvement when four or five of us teenage boys from Rhossili began to catch the six o'clock bus to Horton, once a week to participate in the thriving Wolf Cub troupe. I was assigned to a different group from Mike; but although inter-group competitions were quite fierce at times, we always remained on good terms.

Mike was a fanatic for diving and swimming in the tidal gullies at Horton beach, while I loved bodysurfing at Fall Bay. It was inevitable that we would trade visits to show off our favourite haunts and skills. One Saturday morning, Mike caught the bus to Middleton, from which point we made our way down the Vile Lane to Fall. The tide was well on the way out and it was fairly calm. Just my luck—there would be no showing off at bodysurfing, that day.

We had a rather quick dip in the sea because the water was cool and murky. Then, as the tide continued to ebb, we decided to explore some of the caves and cliffs between Fall and Mewslade. It was late spring and seagulls were nesting all over the cliffs. There were chicks in many of the nests. I suggested climbing up to the lowest nests to see if there were any un-hatched eggs. I was the local boy, so I lead the way, with Mike close behind.

We were only about twenty feet above the sand when an adult gull swooped close to us, screaming plaintively. We ignored it, but it swooped again, even closer, this time. I began to feel nervous, but I wasn't going to suggest a retreat. We climbed another couple of feet. Suddenly, the gull dived. Hanging on to the cliff with my left hand, I threw up my right arm to protect myself—to no avail. With precision that would have impressed Bomber Command, the gull unloaded the distinctly fishy contents of its bowels underneath my arm, over my chest and also over Mike. I was grateful that my face had been spared.

Well, that was that. The gull had shown us who ruled the roost on those cliffs. With hardly a word we backed down the cliff-face as fast as we could. When we reached the sand, we headed for the water. We were going to need another dip in the sea, like it or not. After we had dried off, we felt better. We sat on some rocks (well away from gulls) and ate our cheese and marmite sandwiches, and a slice of homemade cake, washed down with lemonade.

A couple of years later, at Easter 1955, a ten-day trip to southern France was arranged by Dr. James, the Headmaster of the Gowerton Boys Grammar School. Surprisingly, only about eight students took advantage of what, at the time, was quite a rare opportunity. We were accompanied by a distinctly greater number of adults, including Dr. James and his wife.

It was not a cheap holiday, yet it did offer great value. Mike Roberts and I were two of the fortunate ones whose parents thought it worth the sacrifice to pay for their sons to make the trip. I believe the cost was about fifty-five pounds—a lot of money, then. It was about six weeks' wages for my father. Then there were some clothes I needed, plus spending money. Fortunately my mother had several part-time jobs.

We travelled primarily by train all the way from Swansea to Lyon in the south of France. We stayed at a small (but well-known) town called Aix-Les-Bain. It had a dramatic history stemming from the German occupation, since it was located in the heart of the area that had been dominated by the collaborative Vichy French. Old hatreds still ran deep. However, our focus was on sightseeing trips to the Swiss Alps and Geneva. We also visited the wine-growing district of Grenoble.

On the daytrip to the Swiss Alps, there was a tense moment during the cable car ride up to a high plateau. There was a power failure which caused the cable car to stop abruptly and sway to and fro, in midair. We observed that two or three of the women in our party, who had been constantly chattering loudly, seemed to suddenly run out of things to say. Fortunately, power was restored in about ten minutes, and we went on our way to hike across a glacier and visit an ice-cave.

Although our school French was of limited use, the experience of travelling so far, and the exposure to a completely different culture and climate, was an invaluable experience. The only negative thing I can recall was that our hotel constantly supplied us with hard-boiled eggs, both for breakfast and for packed lunches on our daytrips. When I got home, I asked my mother not to give me any boiled eggs for breakfast for at least the rest of the year.

In 1957, Mike suggested we take a two-week hiking trip to the Benelux countries and perhaps as far as Germany. In late July, after saving some money from a few weeks of potato-picking, we set out from Swansea, carrying rucksacks containing a change of clothes, some cooking utensils, a few cans of food, basic toiletries, sleeping-bags, a ground sheet and a small tent.

We got a ride as far as Newport and it was already past teatime as we ambled out along the main route to London. After an hour of thumbing there was no luck. This hitch-hiking business was already starting to lose some of its appeal. Then, a large van pulled up. The driver said he was returning to his base in south London.

We were lucky. We threw our rucksacks into the back of the van and climbed up with the driver, who proved to be a very decent chap. He drove us all the way to his home on the outskirts of London, by which time it was just getting dark. He said we were quite near to an Underground station, but if we liked, we could sleep in the back of the van. It was a chilly night and the wooden floor of the van felt hard. At six in the morning we were already awake. It was gloomy and cool, so we were glad to get on our way to find the Underground station. We crossed to the southeast side of London, where we caught a bus which was headed towards Dover. We had to change buses at Canterbury; but at last, we reached the cross-channel ferry terminal.

We sailed to Ostend where, by late afternoon, we managed to find our way out of town on the main highway towards Holland. By now, it had been a long day, so we decided to camp in the middle of a huge road junction. While Mike lit our small cooker, I opened a couple of small cans of tomato soup. I was surprised to find that the colour of the soup in the two identical cans was quite different. One of them must have gone bad, I reasoned; therefore, we should throw one of them away. After some thought and discussion, we decided that the paler of the two looked the more suspicious, so we shared the other one.

In the morning, feeling refreshed, though still unwashed, we set off in a positive frame of mind. We stopped to stare at some huge, flat barges being towed along the canals by bored-looking horses. Each barge-master seemed to be accompanied by family members. We wondered what it would be like to live on a barge. A few days would be long enough for us, we agreed. Then, we managed to thumb some rides which took us through Rotterdam and eventually to Amsterdam. We stayed a couple of nights at youth hostels, which we much preferred to camping. We could shower, get something to eat, then head out to sample some of the Pilsner lager beer which was virtually unknown in Britain, at that time.

We found Amsterdam a fascinating city. We took a tour-boat on the canals, where our guide pointed out many places of interest, including the haunts of some famous Dutch artists, as well as the red-light district. To us, Amsterdam seemed to be one big red-light district. We also spent an overnight stop at a rather basic hostel in the Dutch countryside with windmills all around us. There was no doubt that it was indeed a very flat country. We stared dubiously at some of the dykes that kept the Zeider Zee out.

We travelled back past Rotterdam and arrived at the historic German city of Aachen. It was a lovely city with many large church buildings; but our objective was to find the youth hostel before it got filled up. We found it in good time and were settled in before "lights out" at about 10:00 PM. A couple of English boys kept on talking, aloud. One of them, who had a rather shrill voice, was especially verbose. Suddenly, a young but harsh voice with a strong German accent growled, "Shut up, English pigs!" We were glad we weren't English. There was no more talking: we were soon all asleep.

On our way towards Brussels, we were surprised to see a little Volkswagen "beetle" stop for us. The driver had his wife and child with him. Even so, he managed to squeeze the two of us, plus our rucksacks into the vehicle. He was a professional of some sort, perhaps an accountant or a lawyer. We soon realised that he was one who was still appreciative of the wartime sacrifices of the British people. The union jacks on our rucksacks had paid off.

On the journey, our benefactor conversed with us enthusiastically. He was quite fluent in English. He advised us that two essential ingredients of a good education were travelling and reading. (Mike and I must have taken his advice to heart. Subsequently, Mike would spend many years living and exploring in various countries in the Middle East and Asia, while my career would take me westward to North America, and eventually to Australasia.)

Our ride took us as far as Bruge. There, the kind man showed us where he lived, before dropping us off at the Youth Hostel. After we had settled in, Mike followed up on an invitation to visit the home of the man and his family, but I was feeling a bit under the weather. Later, we took a walk around the town, sampling a couple of lagers and some local bakery products.

Moving on to Brussels, we found the World Fair in full swing. The "cold war" was at its most intense and there was strong rivalry between the Russian and American pavilions. The Russians focused strongly on their traditional culture, classical music and technical achievements in space—after all, they were ahead of the Americans in the space race, even though Yuri Gargarin's historic flight was still more than three years away. Yet it was the Americans, with their unerring sense of organisation and showmanship, who managed to draw the largest crowds. They had a steel-band playing Caribbean music, which (when I thought about it) had little to do with American culture.

Finally, tired of walking around the huge park, we rested. I sat on a low wall with a bunch of leaflets in my hand, perhaps looking a little exhausted. Suddenly, an old lady stood in front of me speaking rapidly in her own tongue (probably one of the Flemish dialects). After some minutes, I gathered she wanted to buy some of my leaflets. I tried to explain that I wasn't selling them. That didn't seem to work. Then I tried to give them to her, but she insisted on knowing how much she should pay me. After a few minutes, a passer-by was able to explain the situation to her. With an embarrassed smile, she went on her way.

When we had disembarked at Dover, Mike implemented a pre-planned tactic to notify his sister that we were back in the country. He made a person-to-person call, giving his name to the operator. When the operator informed Mike's sister that he (Mike) wanted to talk to her, she simply said that the (named) person was not at home. The operator advised Mike to "try again later" and refunded his money. So Mike's sister knew that we were back in Dover. Unfortunately, she had no ready means of informing my parents.

Our adventures were not quite over, though. We overstretched ourselves in our eagerness to reach home. At dusk, we were stranded on the English side of the Forest of Dean. We were thinking about sleeping in a field, when we saw a car's headlights approaching. We told the driver we were heading towards Newport. He was hesitant, but sounded very congenial. He told us to get in as he was headed in that general direction. There were two other men in their late twenties, in the car. We piled in alongside the one in the back seat. But we soon realised that the driver was the only one who was even close to being sober.

As we drove along, we realised that we were not following the main road, at all, although they were heading in a westerly direction. At some point they took a sharp right turn, so we asked them to drop us off. They obliged and went on their merry way, probably feeling satisfied at their "good deed for the day". We were left in the darkness, trying to find our bearings.

By this time, it was past midnight. We were on a secondary road, somewhere in the Forest of Dean. (I wasn't aware, at the time, that it was the area where my maternal grandfather had been raised.) It was a chilly night. Setting up tents in the darkness, in an unknown field, did not appeal to us. There was some faint moonlight penetrating the clouds, but we had only a vague idea of direction. As we stumbled along a by-road, we reached a crossroad with a sign which we managed to read with the aid of a weak torch: it said, "Chepstow 12 miles". What a relief!

Now, all we had to do was walk for twelve miles, through the forest. We were grateful that our rucksacks were no longer laden with canned food or even any fluids. We'd had nothing to eat or drink about six hours. With little left to snack on—perhaps a chocolate bar or a packet of crisps—we tramped on in the darkness.

About four hours later, we saw the glimmer of streetlights in the distance. We had found the town of Chepstow. By 5:00 AM, we had reached Chepstow railway station. The only problem was that the first train to Swansea didn't leave for more than two hours. We waited patiently for an hour, before we could buy a cold sandwich and a cup of tea. But we didn't care.

We were as good as home!

56

Spud-bashing Woes

... if any would not work, neither should he eat.

The Bible: 2 Thessalonians 3:10

GOWERTON Boys Grammar School was closed for the summer. All GCE exams had been completed. Suddenly all those months of mental concentration were over. As a teenager with football, bodysurfing and girls on my mind, it had been difficult to focus on my studies. Now, all I could do was to wait for the GCE results to appear in the *Evening Post*, though I was pretty sure I'd only failed Latin and Woodwork.

It was time to earn some money—some to help my parents; some to spend on beer whenever I could get over to The Ship at Porteynon; some to save. Conveniently, I heard that Great Pitton farm needed as many potato pickers as they could get, to start at 8:00 AM on Monday. They'd pay one-and-six a hundredweight. The fields were somewhat dry and stony, so the early crop of potatoes would not be large. It would take time and effort to fill each bucket and hundredweight sack.

My mother called me at 7:00 AM. She had a timbre to her voice which seemed to penetrate to my very core when she acted as my alarm clock. I reluctantly woke up, dragged myself out of bed and put on the oldest shirt, trousers, socks and shoes that I could find. A hearty breakfast of bacon and eggs was spattering in the frying pan, along with a couple of pieces of fried bread and a sliced tomato—a working man's breakfast! I allowed time for the walk down across Alf Bevan's and uncle Len's fields to the Chapel, then over the stone stile, across Donald Button's triangular field and up to Great Pitton farm.

When I arrived at the potato field, I had to wait while the youthful farmer, Chris Beynon, still a teenager himself, sorted out some problems with his Oliver potato lifter. The Oliver was popular with farmers who employed pieceworkers because it laid the potatoes on the ground in a swathe less than three feet wide. (Small farmers made do with the "spinner", which could fling potatoes and helms in a swathe about four or five feet wide, but was much more economical and trouble-free.)

Finally, rows of potatoes were being opened up and the tawny treasure was laid on the ground. I set out sacks at the intervals I estimated it would take to fill a bucket. It would require four twenty-eight pound buckets to fill each hundred-weight sack. By this time, a gang of female pickers arrived from Penclawdd. A raucous bunch of experienced pickers, they quickly made themselves at home, selecting bags and buckets. The loudest of the bunch was a buxom, vivacious red-head about twice my age, but with many times more experience of life. While working, she and her mates carried on intermittent conversations, mostly about the men in their lives—or perhaps about pop-stars they wished were in their lives.

No stranger to potato picking, I got started as quickly as I could. After a couple of hours of steadfastly focusing on the differences between spuds, stones and lumps of dried dirt, the small of my back began to protest. It became a welcome relief to stand up to empty the bucket; unfortunately, it seemed to take quite a while to fill one. My mind, protesting at the simple repetitive processes now required of it, insisted on reflecting on exam questions about Geography, Physics and Calculus.

Lunch was brief, perhaps half an hour for a thermos of tea and a few sand-wiches. About half-past four, a halt was called. We finished off our rows and helped veteran farm-workers George Beynon and Vaughan Price to load our sacks onto a trailer. My total was twenty-eight-and-a-half hundredweight bags—not a great pay day, but the money would be appreciated. I was shocked to see that the redhead had filled thirty-one sacks, while most of her mates had done just as well or better than I. *Perhaps I've been too fussy in sorting the spuds from the stones and the dirt.* I thought.

As I trudged homeward with an aching back and legs, dented pride and a frus-trated intellect, I knew that things would get worse, before they got better. The second and third days would bring increasing pain and slower performance. I knew from past years that the pain would ease after that. I hadn't yet figured out how to neutralise my overactive brain, though.

I found ready employment at Great Pitton farm for a couple of summers. By con-trast, a couple of years earlier, I had one solitary opportunity to pick potatoes for farmer Bevan Tucker in Higher Pitton. Even on the first day, I had the feeling I was on trial. Bevan was a no-nonsense kind of man.

There were three or four of us local boys, trying to earn some pocket money in the school holidays. They included Nelson Proctor and his mischievous younger brother, Stewart (better known as Twgi). They lived in a "tied" house—the old farmhouse at Corner House farm—as their father, Bert, was employed by Bevan Tucker.

We had been going at it for a couple of hours in the large, steep field on the southeast side of Pitton Cross hill, when something landed with a plop about five yards from me. I ignored it; but a minute later, something whizzed past me again, a bit closer. Was someone playing "silly beggars"? I looked around, but everyone else had their heads down, working hard. Bevan Tucker was on the tractor, busy opening the next row for us with his Oliver potato harvester. He probably wondered what I was up to.

I decided to be more wary. Bent over, I caught a quick movement some distance behind me, followed by another small potato whizzing past. It was young Twgi, no doubt about it. He pretended to be working, not knowing that I'd finally spotted him. I decided to let him know I was onto him. I picked up a potato and flung it just past him, thinking that would be the end of the tomfoolery. I was looking at him with a grin on my face, as he looked up: he laughed. Now, perhaps we could get on with the job.

Unfortunately, Bevan Tucker had seen my actions. He said nothing; just glared. I got back to work and worked hard for the rest of the day, though the crop was sparse and uninspiring. Even so, when I was paid my modest earnings, I wasn't invited to return the next day.

Potato-picking was an opportunity to make good money for a hard day's work. Although my father worked for five-and-a-half days a week on the farm for regular wages, there was often the opportunity to do piecework on the weekend. Sometimes he would use his holiday entitlement to spend a week making some extra money.

Some Sundays, we worked on mature crops of large Aran Banner potatoes at Kings Hall farm, which was owned by Alf Bevan. They were large and easy to pick, as the rich but powdery earth didn't cling to them. For several years in the mid-1950s, the going rate for main-crop potatoes was a shilling a hundredweight; therefore, a good picker could make at least three pounds in a day. Of course, that meant filling your bucket and emptying it into a sack, two hundred and forty times.

At lunch times, finding some shade under a hedge, we would enjoy the sandwiches my mother had prepared for us, along with a slice of fruitcake or apple pie for dessert. Alf's kind-hearted wife, Myfi, would bring a can of hot tea and some cups for the pickers. After that, Joff might offer me a hand-rolled cigarette to puff on.

But not many of the farm-workers or their sons, sought out such fatiguing work, especially in the hot weather. Farmers were often hard-pressed to find sufficient pickers.

57

The Cleveland

What is a ship but a prison?

Robert Burton

IT was a dull, almost misty afternoon in late June, 1957. The breeze was light though restless: definitely not a stormy day. Russell Jones from East Pilton farm, John Bevan and I were hanging about on 'the bank' wondering what we might do to alleviate our boredom—perhaps play some French cricket, since there weren't enough of us to get a football game going.

It was getting late in the afternoon when one of the Beynon boys from The Ship farm, either Ron or Brian, brought word that a ship had run aground in Rhossili Bay. At first, we were incredulous, but he assured us his father had just come home from the fields at Parsonage and said that a big ship of some kind had drifted right onto the beach. We quickly decided to check it out. Somewhat sceptically, the four of us hurried out to The Green, but no ship was visible from there; though we could see that the tide was well in.

We began to doubt that the story was true. We walked down the narrow lane behind the church, to the bus terminus. There, we could get a good look at the far end of the bay. Yes, there was a ship alright, quite a big one, but it was almost at Hillend. This meant it was more than a mile away, down the steep path past the Worms Head Hotel, along the edge of "the warren" towards the Old Rectory, then down onto the beach. Then there was a long jog along the damp, packed sand, as the tide was already starting to go out.

The ship had drifted to within fifty yards of the high-tide mark and it was now sitting in less than two feet of water, as the tide ebbed. It was perfectly upright, broadside to the beach, with its bow pointing in the direction of Burry Holms. Wavelets lapped around it. There was a small crowd of thirty or more people

241

standing in groups, well clear of the ship, discussing the spectacle in hushed awe. It might as well have been a ghost ship in the fading light of the dull afternoon. We wondered what to do next: it wasn't in the nature of Rhossili boys to just stand and look.

Slowly the tide continued to ebb; we waited impatiently for about half an hour, as the water receded. We decided to remove our socks and shoes and paddle out to where a thick tow-line dangled almost vertically from the ship's bow. The hawser must have been about three inches thick. The bow was close to twenty-five feet above the sand.

On impulse, I grasped the hawser with both hands and started to climb. I had been used to climbing the guy wires of electricity poles, where feet could not be used to any advantage; but this thick hawser was a challenge to my small hands. Nevertheless I steadily climbed towards the top, gripping with my knees to support my weight.

Scrambling over the overhang of the bow proved to be the biggest challenge. After some manoeuvring, this was achieved. As I caught my breath and looked around, I saw that Russell had followed me up the tow-rope. He was about three years younger than I, but he was fascinated by ships. I tried to help him past the difficult overhang, but was unable to do so. Worried in case we got into a dangerous situation, I urged him to slide back down the rope, though I sensed that he was bitterly disappointed.

Once aboard, I set about exploring. Disappearing from the view of my companions, I padded cautiously past the forecastle in my bare feet, then round towards the after-deck. There was one open-ended room where strange looking electrical and mechanical controls and equipment abounded, but as one might expect, all bulkheads were firmly sealed; therefore, my exploration was limited. Added to this, much of the detachable equipment on the superstructure such as guns and radar components, had been removed.

The ship struck me as being surprisingly compact, with hardly room to enjoy any form of outdoor exercise, other than walking. I didn't think I would enjoy being a sailor on this ship. Nevertheless, it felt exciting to be aboard a real warship for the first time in my life.

After only five minutes or so of exploration, I retraced my steps towards the bow. On the way, I met a young man I didn't recognise. He was about three years older than I: he passed me with barely a glance. I reached the bow and began the tricky task of manoeuvring myself past the overhang and getting a firm grip on the hawser: then, I was sliding down, hand over hand to safety.

I had to confess to the others that I had not been able to get into anything very exciting; I hadn't been able to see the inside of the ship at all. After half an hour or so, we could see that nothing would be done about the ship that evening. It would be stuck in the sand for several days, at least. We plodded back along the sands, towards Rhossili. It would be well past teatime when we reached our respective homes.

Over the next few days, we learnt from the newspapers, as well as by word of mouth, that the ship was a decommissioned Royal Navy destroyer, which was being towed to Burry Port to be broken up for scrap. For some reason, the hawser had snapped as it was being towed across Rhossili Bay in calm conditions.

The Cleveland remained beached at Hillend for many months, defying all efforts to re-float her before it was finally decided to break her up for salvage. But I never went near her again—the novelty had worn off.

58

The Royal Observer Corps

You see, but you do not observe.

Arthur Conan Doyle

THE Royal Observer Corps (ROC) was stood down at the end of the war, but not for long. The tensions of the cold war caused the Ministry of Defence to re-commission it in 1947. Farm-worker Phil Richards of Pitton Cottage was the Chief Observer in Rhossili. In the mid 1950s, Charles Brown took over as the Chief Observer. He worked for farmer Bevan Tucker and occupied the "tied" farmhouse known as Corner House, at the bottom of Pitton Cross hill, after the Proctor family had moved to Scurlage.

Charlie's first recruit was Alan Button, the teenage son of his neighbour and workmate, Will Button, who was himself a former wartime ROC member. Howard Chalk and I were soon recruited; then a year or so later, sixteen-year-old Nelson Proctor, from Scurlage.

Charlie held meetings about once a week in his sitting room. We were drilled with aerial photos and silhouette cards, as well as a slide-projector to recognise enemy (i.e. Russian) aircraft such as Ilyushin Bear and Beagle bombers, and MiG 13 and 15 fighters (though we never actually saw any of them). It was equally important to be able to recognise friendly aircraft, such as the RAF's Canberra, Victor, Vulcan and Valiant bombers, and Javelin and Meteor fighters; or the US Airforce's Saber, Starfire and Stratofortress.

In accordance with the risks of nuclear age, the ROC was also developing a capability for detecting, measuring and reporting radioactive fallout, so we learnt how to measure Roentgens, and how many indicated a dangerous level of radio-activity.

In 1957, after about a year of preparation, Alan, Howard and I were sent off to a one-week ROC summer camp at RAF Tangmere, in Sussex. This was an enlightening introduction to life in the forces. We were accommodated in large marquees, each housing more than a dozen volunteers. There were (mostly young) men from as far away as Scotland. We experienced a few wet days when a rivulet ran right down the middle of our marquee. It was difficult to be ready for mid-morning inspections under those conditions.

We had to make our own beds, shine our boots and turn out for inspection or any events which were posted on the notice board. The canteen food was quite varied and plentiful, if plain. We did not get tired of it in our short stay. We found that draft beer and "scrumpy" cider were cheap and available in our recreation time at the NAAFI bar; cigarettes too, if we had been interested. Life in the forces didn't seem at all bad.

We could enjoy saluting any officers we passed, just to make them salute back. Once, I saluted a group of three senior officers as we passed them, and wondered why only one of them returned my salute. I was quite puzzled until Alan pointed out that I wasn't wearing my beret. Indeed, I was fortunate not to be reprimanded.

We were encouraged to join in organised recreational activities, such as inter-squadron cricket matches. My performance at a cricket match was mediocre, to say the least, yet there was a supportive attitude among my team-mates. This was the kind of psychology that could bring out the best in military personnel.

In some ways it was a long two weeks, but a very worthwhile experience for us. We returned to Rhossili, finding it a bit quiet and boring, at least until the school holidays were over. But soon, we were putting our training into practice, if only under simulated conditions.

In Sid Thomas's field behind Howard Chalk's parents' house, Hampstead, a new concrete observation post had been built to replace the wooden wartime one. Sitting in the upper level, about fifteen feet off the ground, we had a clear view of land and sea for about three quarters of the compass, but to the northwest, Rhossili Down created a blind spot.

A couple of times a year, ROC exercises would be arranged to coincide with RAF exercises. These exercises were held on Sundays or weekday evenings (in the summer months). Our unit would be required to man the post for between four and six hours. Dressed in our light-blue uniforms and equipped with binoculars and a radio headset, we each took twenty-minute turns reporting all aircraft sightings—with our comrades in supporting roles, or resting. Other posts in the area were Penmaen, Penclawdd, Sketty and Pontarddulais. Whenever we sighted aircraft, we reported them in a predetermined sequence, such as: aircraft identity, quantity, direction spotted, estimated elevation, direction headed.

We were very well drilled in spotting and reporting to our Group Control in Carmarthen. However, in the age of jet aircraft, it soon became apparent that by the time we had made our report, the aircraft was already being spotted and reported by the next ROC post, in Penclawdd or Penmaen. Sometimes we only heard (but could not see) the low-flying jets, if the hill blocked our view.

Although our reporting was always as accurate as possible, "That was ... a jet!" soon became a standing joke with us.

[Endnote: In 1968 the Rhossili post was closed. After that, only the Penclawdd post remained operational in Gower.]

59

A Tribute to Archie

To strive, to seek, to find, and not to yield.

Tennyson

EDGAR Beynon (better known as Archie) was the fourth son of Wilfred and Sally Beynon of The Ship farm. Born in 1934, he was six years older than I. He was below average height, very thin, short-sighted and anaemic in appearance. Archie, though, was someone special. He did more to warm the hearts of people in the village than anyone I can think of.

In a parish where many worked hard all their lives; where others made fine academic, sporting and career achievements; where there were faithful churchgoers and chapel-goers of admirable character; and where men prided themselves on their toughness and durability, Archie somehow outshone them all, in my memory. In his short life, he became well-known and well-liked throughout southwest Gower.

Archie was already in the senior class at Rhossili School when I started there, in 1945. I have a clear recollection of another boy bullying him, jumping on his back, pummelling his ears and knocking his glasses off. I was about eight and I didn't like what I saw. However, I don't think the perpetrator made a habit of annoying him. Archie enjoyed playground sports, especially the traditional game of shinty (similar to field hockey, but with few rules).

Well before he left school at fourteen, Archie was a more than useful hockey player, joining in any matches arranged on the firm sands of Rhossili Bay, but he was, above all, a lifelong football fanatic. As his strength allowed, he would often join in the rough and tumble football games on 'the bank' until he became too exhausted to continue; then, hiding his disappointment, he would go off to do some chores on the farm. He was often teased, but it didn't dampen his enthusiasm. He wouldn't hesitate to let us know when we committed a foul or displayed bad sportsmanship. Sometimes, it felt as though he were my second conscience.

Despite his enthusiasm, we knew Archie had no chance of securing a regular place in the South Gower football team. He was too frail; he would be too easily hurt. Neither was he considered robust enough for fulltime farm-work. Fortunately, Archie was able to get part-time work, helping Will Williams at the Post Office as a grocery clerk. In the 1950s, very few villagers owned a car, so the Post Office and the Lower Shop were the main source of groceries for the households of farm-workers and small farmers. Archie's main functions were stocktaking and filling orders for groceries and general household commodities.

Archie fitted into his job perfectly. When villagers turned up at the Post Office for a couple of grocery items or the *Evening Post*, only to find they'd missed most of the customers they liked to talk to—no problem. With twinkling eyes blinking behind his wire-rimmed spectacles, Archie would get them caught up with the latest news in the most humorous and diplomatic manner. He always had time for everyone.

All who lived in the village in those days must have their own reminiscences of Archie: he belonged to us all. In some sense, his era fitted in with the last of "the old Rhossili"—the days of old-timers matching wits at draughts; of quoits being played on fine evenings in the meadow at Middleton Hall farm; of yarns spun (partly in the Gower dialect) on 'the bank' until it got dark; of hobnailed boots and leather gaiters; of waistcoats, pocket watches and collar-less, flannelette shirts; of a rudimentary hockey game called shinty being played in the schoolyard; and of a stick game called cat-and-dog.

But Archie wasn't finished, yet. After his eighteenth birthday, he was called up for two years of National Service. He had to report to the Army at Aldershot. No worries, we all thought, he can't possibly pass the medical requirements; he'll be sent home soon enough. Instead, Archie was put through basic training and became a driver in his regiment. He did a tour of duty in Germany during the cold war. Whenever he came home on leave, we lined up to talk to him to hear what he had to say and to ask questions. He was a local celebrity.

In his time in the army, Archie developed a taste for a strange American beverage called Coca-Cola. Soon he had us trying this new drink instead of our customary Dandelion and Burdock. But Archie had also developed a passion for driving. Not too long after being discharged, he purchased a new economical, two-seater Austin A35 van. Two other locals, Horace Rosser and Howard Chalk, owned similar vehicles. There was some opposition from his parents, but Archie had also learnt independence in the army.

Having returned to his old job at the Post Office with increased confidence and professionalism, Archie made the most of his new-found mobility. He could drive to town to see his beloved Swans play (gladly taking along anyone who wanted to join him). He could run family or neighbours to appointments or fetch anything they needed. Although Archie was a teetotaller, preferring Polomints or Coca-cola to alcohol, his younger brothers, Ron and Brian, would often persuade him to transport a bunch of village boys to the Kings Head in Llangennith for a few pints. He'd drop them off and return for them later. There were often five or six of them crammed into Archie's van.

Archie was a great supporter of the South Gower football club, as well as Swansea Town. He could be heard yelling advice from the touch-line during our home matches, while we struggled and fumbled on the field. He would readily help out with anything for the club, whether it was marking lines or fetching players who didn't have transportation. On Monday evenings in the Post Office (especially if the Swans had lost, that weekend) Archie would sometimes get into heated discussions with any customers who dared make derogatory remarks about his beloved Swans.

About 1951, there was a locally-produced concert at the village hall, following the annual harvest supper. One comedy skit had skinny, seventeen-year-old Archie and two husky young men of the village, dressed in leopard skins, taking turns to lift a bar with huge round black dumbbells on the ends. The first two men struggled hard, before (apparently) collapsing with exhaustion: finally, skinny Archie stepped forward; he picked up the bar with one hand and walked off the stage. The village hall erupted in cheers. The dumbbells had been black balloons.

Archie didn't shoot game-birds, didn't do any fishing, ferreting or snaring rabbits—but he loved mushrooms. On those mild spring and summer mornings when there had been some rain the day before, Archie seemed to have scoured the cow pastures from Middleton to Kings Hall before most people were awake. I sometimes dragged myself out of bed at eight o'clock and searched for mushrooms in vain, only to learn that Archie had been there at the crack of dawn. Darn that Archie!

[Endnote1: Cat-and-dog was a traditional stick game for youngsters, comprising two pieces of wood about the thickness of a shovel-handle. One piece was about six inches long, whittled to a point at both ends (the cat). The other piece was about two feet long, pointed at one end (the dog). Either end of the cat was tapped sharply with the pointed end of the dog, so that the cat flew into the air, where it was struck sharply. The game was often played along a roadway. Each player would try to reach a circle, about eighteen inches in diameter, with the least number of turns.]

[Endnote2: The last chance I had to meet Archie was when Swansea Town played Preston North End in the FA cup semi-final at Villa Park, in 1964. By then, I was working and living in Birmingham. I was supposed to meet Archie and two other villagers (including my father's cousin, Horace Rosser) near Villa Park, but arrangements were vague. We used the Royal Mail for communication in those days.

It wasn't a lucky day for the Swans, either—they lost 2-1. Their diminutive centre-forward lost his nerve with a couple of excellent opportunities, early on. A Preston defender sealed the game midway through the second half with a speculative but well-directed shot, from the halfway line.

About two-and-a-half years later, I received the news that Archie had died. He could not have been more than thirty-two years old, but that had been long enough for him to do a lot of good in the village, while seeing and enjoying more of life than most villagers had, up to that time.]

[Endnote3: Just a few years after Archie's passing, the village school closed forever. It was converted into an Outdoor Pursuits centre. This, in itself, signified a major change for Rhossili as a community. All that was left were souvenirs for those who could grab them—a gigantic papier-mâché wolf's head, left over from a pre-war performance of *Little Red Riding Hood*; the school hand-bell; the painted wooden shield. In my mind, though, someone who was no longer with us had already taken ownership of the school's motto—"Strive to Win!"]

60

A College Education

To spend too much time in studies is sloth.

Francis Bacon

AT the end of the summer of 1958, I commenced studies in Electrical Engineering at Swansea University College, in Singleton Park. Having experienced increasing difficulty in focusing on my Applied Math, Pure Math and Physics subjects at Gowerton, I did not have much choice in the matter of which university I could attend. The alternative was to repeat my final year, so as to improve my A-level results. I could not easily have faced that prospect. I had completely lost my appetite for school.

I really did not know what I wanted to do next. Going on to university had become more a matter of meeting everyone's expectations (including my own) than pursuing a field of study for which I had any real enthusiasm. On the other hand, studying electrical engineering offered a new environment with the promise of expertise (if somewhat theoretical), which would propel me towards a worthwhile career.

I therefore took note of the Chancellor's remarks at the formal welcoming dinner for new students. He emphasised that, although learning the self-discipline of studying was an important goal, life at university was very much about participation in recreational and socially-interactive programmes. I took that to mean I could focus on the gymnasium and the sports teams: in that sense, I was happy to take the Chancellor's advice.

I was still football crazy and I had trained hard on Fall and Mewslade bays to develop some exceptional skills and stamina, but physical and psychological limitations held me back. Problems with my left ankle and knee brought me to a point where I could hardly walk as I tried out for the university football team,

251

though somehow, I could still chase a football. But I could not cope with being "under the microscope" of the selectors when they finally decided to give me a ten-minute tryout with the first eleven. The net result was that I missed selection and, in any case, I had to take a break from football to rest my painful joints.

It was because of my enforced rest from football, that I took note of the boxing team, training hard in the college gymnasium. As I watched their elimination and sparring bouts, I felt an overwhelming urge to get in the ring and take them on. I felt I could tackle any of them. Thanks mainly to our Middleton neighbour, Ron Densley, I felt completely at home with a pair of boxing gloves. Good hand speed was a natural gift. In no time, I was on the boxing team; it so happened that there was a dearth of welterweights, so I had no real rivals.

All I had to do was take a perfunctory medical exam; then, a couple of weeks later I was ready for the visiting Aberystwyth team. My injured leg would be no problem in the ring. I watched a few bouts as I waited for my turn. A lean, muscular redhead stood confidently in the opposite corner. I stared back innocently. I felt nervous, but certainly not fearful. Our team manager offered me the encouraging advice that my opponent was a very good boxer and also that he was a southpaw, which would make him particularly difficult to deal with. A few words of caution from the referee, a quick touch of the gloves and we were ready to go.

The bell rang; there were a few seconds of sparring; then, I took a sharp right-hand lead on my left cheekbone. I kept my hands up, focusing my gaze on the heart of the other man, as Ron had taught me. Bang, bang: I parried his right lead, but a long left found its way between my gloves, leaving a welt on my forehead. One more right-hander stung my ear when I tried to circle to my right, as one should against an orthodox boxer. This wasn't working, but I had already seen the chink in the other man's armour.

The fight was still only thirty seconds old as I stepped straight forward with a left lead. My chin was on my chest, my eyes focused on my opponent's heart. He responded with another sharp southpaw lead. The difference was that my left lead was a feint. I moved towards my left, allowing his lead to miss past my right ear. Even as he was still following through, I countered with a hard right hook. I didn't need to see his chin to know where it was. My opponent was not only stopped in his tracks, he fell like log.

Unfortunately, the ring was set up on the gym floor: a canvas sheet was all the padding there was, so the poor chap took an additional bang on the back of his head from the floor. He was counted out: the fight was over in only forty seconds. From then on, my reputation seemed to have more effect than my fists, as opponents from the university colleges of Cardiff and Bangor seemed to have accepted defeat before the bouts began.

In the meantime, I had settled down to playing centre-forward for the second team. My team-mates were a likeable and easygoing bunch. There were Paul and Chris, a couple of chirpy Londoners; Alan, a stocky outspoken lad from Portsmouth; tall Dai John, who anchored the defence; and skinny, unpredictable Paul Crotty. I felt quite relaxed and confident in my sports activities. By Easter I had scored thirty goals and my record in the boxing ring was 5-0.

During the Christmas and Easter breaks, I sometimes spent a few days at my grandmother's house in Gorseinon. From there, I took a few training sessions with my younger cousin Phillip Davies at the Pengelly boxing club, located at a nearby farm. The farmer's son, Mansel, was well on the way to becoming a pro. Fortunately, he was in an even lighter weight class than I, though I did spar with him, on occasion.

On one occasion, we travelled in a couple of cars to attend an amateur boxing competition at a venue near Merthyr Tydfil. At that time, I'd only had two previous bouts, but all I was expected to do was fight another welterweight novice who was our "stable-mate" at the Pengelly club.

Unfortunately, the other lad discovered he had no stomach for the fight. He asked me not to hit hard, even before the fight started. I felt embarrassed and confused. We started off the first round sparring cautiously, then moving in for a few flurries. I was pulling my punches, but the knowledgeable crowd were not fooled. My opponent was probably even more obvious than I. The small crowd began to boo. I started to use my hard, straight left to stir my opponent into action. Each time it landed on his face, his head was jolted back, but still he would not retaliate; he just tried to hold on in the clinches.

Those three two-minute rounds seemed like a long time. When the referee raised my hand at the end, I just wanted to get out of the ring; however, there was a presentation of a small trophy, which I accepted reluctantly. It was the only boxing trophy I would receive—and it was for a non-fight!

An experienced boxing official, riding in the same car as I, asked about my experience and training. When I told him he had just witnessed my third fight and that I was training myself, he was quite amazed: he asked if I would consider turning professional. Not feeling very proud of my latest performance, I told him I would be tied up at the university for a while.

The following season, I formally won the University of Wales welterweight title at a tournament in the Swansea U.C. gymnasium. My semi-final opponent from

Cardiff, a stocky, awkward boxer, surprised me by insulting me in the clinches. This perplexed me because I'd never seen him before. Was this the way to treat strangers? I became angry at what I considered to be very unsporting conduct. Fortunately, he wasn't able to take advantage of my loss of focus, but I couldn't get a clean shot at him either, and I had to settle for a unanimous points decision.

Ironically, a photograph from this semi-final fight appeared in the *Evening Post*. It looked like an impressive knock-down, but in fact, my opponent had slipped and fallen as I, annoyed by his insults, pursued him relentlessly, flailing like a windmill. I didn't realise it at the time, but a Scurlage man, Dick Daney, who had been working on some renovations at the gymnasium, was among those cheering me on. Dick couldn't have been too impressed with my performance, yet he returned the same evening to see me win the final, against an Aberystwyth boxer.

A few weeks later, I was on my way to the Universities and Hospitals Boxing Championships in Dublin. There were three of us from Swansea and one each from Cardiff, Aberystwyth and Bangor. This was an expenses-paid trip, but it involved a great deal of travelling—by train from Swansea to Holyhead, then by boat from Holyhead to Dublin. There was a night's rest in a dormitory, a fried breakfast, an official weigh-in and a preliminary bout in a college gymnasium at about 1:00 PM. It was Saturday, March 5th 1960.

The weigh-in provided a surprise: I was considerably lighter than I had expected; in fact, if I hadn't eaten breakfast, I would have made it at the light-welterweight limit. The officials asked if I wanted to take an hour to try to reduce my weight by a pound and a half. I responded that I had come to fight as a welterweight and that's what I wanted to do. However, the rest of the day, I found myself fighting a couple of opponents who were light-middleweights. Once more, I had observed an unfavourable aspect of boxing.

In my preliminary bout, I met a very strong opponent, representing Dublin University. He was very well built and certainly looked stronger and heavier than I. My assessment proved correct: Within seconds of the start of the bout, I was dumped unceremoniously on my backside. This was a new experience. They say you don't see a good punch: I certainly never saw that one. Even so, I realised to my surprise, that I wasn't hurt. As the referee started counting, I got back on my feet; he got as far as six.

Thinking I was in trouble, my opponent moved in confidently. I covered up, expecting a charge and a welter of punches; instead, the other man paused in front of me, seeking an opening in my defence so he could pick his punches. His hands were lowered, his chin was exposed. Big mistake! My favoured right hook couldn't miss from a distance of eighteen inches. My opponent fell back across the ring. I waited patiently as he slowly got to his feet. I didn't know whether he was any more hurt than I had been.

Without hesitation, I walked straight up to him and delivered another hard right from close range. I was surprised that he did not seem able to cover up. He fell like a log. Again he scrambled back to his feet. Once more I walked in and delivered a right hook. This time, my opponent wasn't getting up; his corner threw in the towel; and the referee stopped the fight. The first (two-minute) round still wasn't over.

The rest of the afternoon and early evening, the six of us who had come to represent the University of Wales, marched around Dublin, carrying our kit bags over our shoulders, without much thought as to what we could do with our time. We didn't go into any pubs to sample the Guinness, as four of us would have to box again, later. We crossed the Liffy several times, on one occasion bumping shoulders with three rough looking Irishmen in their mid-twenties. They stopped and glared at us, as we stared back at them. They seemed ready to take on the six of us. After a brief exchange of comments, we wisely continued on our way.

In the evening, I had a semi-final bout against a tough, stocky opponent representing Durham University. It was in Ireland's National Stadium. There was quite a crowd in attendance and there were real dressing rooms under the stands, even massage tables for boxers to rest on, just like in the films I'd seen. Watching other boxers making nervous preparations, I had no clue what I should be doing to make the best use of my time. I had been on my feet almost all the time, since eating breakfast at 7:30 AM. It was starting to feel like a long day. Finally, at about nine o'clock, I was called to the ring.

My opponent was heavier but shorter than I, so he proved difficult to handle. I always found taller opponents easier. This one was a solid puncher, too. Perhaps I should have used my footwork to stay away from him and my accurate left hand to score points, but we mixed it up for three hard rounds. Early in the fight, the bridge of my nose was bruised and my nose began to bleed, though I hardly noticed it. Finally, the three two-minute rounds were over.

My opponent was justly awarded a majority decision. I shrugged my shoulders and headed for the showers; however, to my surprise, the knowledgeable Irish crowd gave me a great ovation and several shook my bandaged hands enthusiastically as I made my way back to the dressing rooms. None of our team made it past the semi-final. We caught the midnight ferry for Holyhead, but not before someone had given me a copy of the Dublin Evening Mail with a photo of my afternoon KO success dominating the sports page. That was sufficient reward for me.

While I liked the self-reliance aspect of boxing, I had experienced some examples of the less pleasant sides of the sport, which were troubling to me. In spite of the notoriety I achieved with the boxing team, my heart was in football. I enjoyed playing with the university second team, where there was not too much tension and politics, so one could simply get on with the game. I could sometimes fit in a game or two with South Gower, especially in the Christmas and Easter breaks.

My mother claimed she "put her foot down" on my boxing career when I arrived home from Dublin with a bruised nose and a pair of black eyes. In the end, though, it was I who decided I got more pleasure from scoring goals than punching opponents' faces.

During my first two years at the university, I had spent almost all my recreation time (and quite a lot of my study time) in the gym or enjoying the football and boxing excursions to venues in other parts of Wales. Then there were the fantastic jazz-bands, featuring artists like Acker Bilk and Chris Barber, which played at our college dances.

As my third and final year loomed, I realised that I would need to buckle down if I was going to attain even a pass degree. (I had lost the privilege of competing for an honours degree at the end of my first year.) Although I was promised a serious shot at the university first team, I knew I would still be dogged by the same problems that had resulted in disappointment two years earlier. I decided not to be distracted by sports until I had completed my degree.

From Easter until my final exams at the end of June, I was at home with my parents at 'the cottage', working to a rigid schedule of preparation for all the subjects I would be tested in. This involved reserving one-third of each day for recreation, while following a flexible schedule of study in the remaining two-thirds. This system meant that, in late spring, I was able to spend many sunny afternoons swimming and running with our part-Jack Russell terrier, Pip, at Fall or Mewslade. Often, we had the bays to ourselves, at that time of year.

My self-discipline worked well. Tough as it was to crack some of the erudite mathematics of electrical theory, by the time the examinations started, I was completely relaxed and confident—the finals were a "breeze". I had no doubt that I had done well in every subject, though I felt some regret that no matter how well I did, I would still receive only a pass degree.

But I had indeed followed the Chancellor's advice—other aspects of university life had been at least as important as my studies.

61

Pip

I HAD just turned fifteen when my father, Joff, asked me to ride my bike over to Porteynon and fetch a five-month-old terrier pup. Somehow, he had agreed with George Eynon to take the part-Jack Russell bitch. I rode my bike there on a dry Saturday morning in June and located George's house about halfway down Porteynon hill, just above the church.

The dog was handed over without much ceremony—I don't think George was home at the time. I didn't even get a chance to talk to his pretty teenage daughter, Rosemary. She was about three years younger than I, and had only recently started catching the double-decker school-bus that transported us to the secondary schools at Gowerton and Penclawdd.

I'm not certain whether the pup was already named Pip, or whether Joff chose the name, but Pip became part of the family for well over twenty years. She had mostly Jack Russell features, including the characteristic brown and white patches, which extended to her sharp, intelligent face.

I had taken a collar and about six feet of old clothes-line with me, so I rode back to Rhossili, taking the shortcut through Margam lane, with the brown and white pup trotting willingly alongside my maroon and white bike. Soon I had passed Pyle Well and was free-wheeling down across Pilton Green when a large farm-dog charged, barking loudly, from Bert Fisher's house. Pip dashed between the wheels of my bike, jerking the line in my hand. In the confusion, I lost my balance and fell off. Otherwise, it was an uneventful journey.

257

We'd had dogs before, but Pip really was different. She became well-known throughout Middleton. For the next five years, Pip and I were almost inseparable on weekends and school holidays. Pip would often accompany me to the bays or on my runs around the cliffs above Mewslade, Fall and Rhossili—which was about a four mile circuit from 'the cottage'. If I decided she couldn't go along with me, she'd sneakily follow down Sheep Green hill, trying to keep out of sight; I'd have to yell at her to send her back home, her tail between her legs.

Pip loved to spend an afternoon at Fall Bay. When the tide was in, I'd throw her into the sea to practice her swimming; however, I usually gave her a drink of fresh water as a reward. When the tide was out, she was good company for running laps on the beach or exploring in the direction of Mewslade.

In the summer of 1957, I worked part of the holidays for Rhossili farmer, Gordon Thomas. One afternoon, after I'd walked home for my dinner, I allowed Pip to come back to work with me. We were dipping sheep in the yard adjacent to the old Vanguard bus-garage. About five o'clock, as I was trudging homeward along Rhossili Lane, I suddenly realised that Pip should have been with me. I assumed she must have wandered off and made her own way home, though she had never done that before.

At first, I didn't care—dumb dog! But as I reached the Post Office, I began to feel concerned. Wearily, I turned and retraced my steps to Gordon's yard. No sign of Pip. I looked into the dip, still full of water and disinfectant; there she was, gallantly dog-paddling around in the dip, unable to find a way of escape. Perhaps the hot weather had made her walk down the steep slope at the exit to cool off, or maybe she had become very thirsty by the end of the day. Of course, I was relieved to find her unharmed and I felt thankful as I marched homeward, once more.

Pip must have been one of the best bargains of all time. My father certainly would not have paid much, if anything, for a mongrel bitch. As far as I know, Pip never saw a vet in all her life. She gave birth to at least a dozen sets of mongrel pups, many of which were drowned in a bucket of water immediately following birth, in keeping with traditional practice for disposing of unwanted litters of pups or kittens.

But Pip's real value came through in her Jack Russell heritage: she was an excellent watch-dog. She was never coddled—invariably spending the nights locked in our corrugated-zinc shed, with a worn-out blanket for a bed. Neither stray animals nor prowlers could come close to 'the cottage' without being detected.

At the beginning of September, 1961, I left Rhossili to follow my chosen career. I spent one last beautiful, late summer afternoon enjoying the fresh sea air of the cliffs and the hill. Of course, I was accompanied every step of the way by my faithful friend, Pip. And for one last time, my parents were anxiously searching for me at dusk.

The next morning, armed with a basic engineering degree from Swansea U.C., a slide-rule, a suitcase and a sense of adventure, I set off for Birmingham and my first permanent job—with the General Electric Company at their huge Witton engineering plant. Alone, I caught the bus to town, then the train from High Street Station. I don't know what my parents were feeling; I just knew they were happy for me. That day, it felt as though the world was at my feet.

In my heart I knew I would probably never return to live in Rhossili, but I preferred not to dwell on that thought.

[Endnote: From time to time, I returned to enjoy a great welcome from my parents and the people I'd grown up with. It's true, there's no place like home; and it was always Pip who gave me the most enthusiastic welcome of all. She lived for a good twenty-three years. I had been gone from Middleton for many years when she died, but my parents missed her badly.]

62

Joff's Legacy

Example is the school of mankind ...

Edmund Burke

MY father, Thomas Joffre Jones (known simply as Joff), was born in May, 1915. He was the tenth child in a family of thirteen. He was named after the French General, Joffre, who was a popular hero in the early phases of the First World War. Perhaps this helped set him apart from his siblings. In fact, he became more independent and isolated, as the years went by. He named me Cyril, which is quite an unusual name in Wales (even in Gower), which perhaps influenced my own perception of being "different".

Joff was a gifted man, as we all are, in various ways, if we stop and think about it. He had exceptional physical gifts of strength and stamina. He was six feet tall, athletic, big-boned, with iron-hard hands—his wrists were twice as thick as mine would ever be. But he was also gifted with above-average intelligence. He was able to master reading comprehension and the concepts of mathematics with equal ease. He never went beyond primary school—leaving when he was fourteen—but he was awarded a special prize, as the best male student. He passed the County written examination for grammar school, but probably did not make the long journey to Gowerton to attend the oral examination, which was required at that time.

He passed up at least one other opportunity of further education. While he was still in his teenage years, a well-off cousin of the family offered to send him to a boarding school with his own son; but the opportunity was not taken. Joff may have felt he needed to stay with his ailing father on the farm. Perhaps there were not enough resources to support the inevitable extra costs. Perhaps, he just couldn't face a strange environment.

A few years later, he went to stay with his married sister, Doris, who lived on the outskirts of London—a world very different from rural Gower, especially at that time. But after several months of commuting to work night-shifts at a dairy, he returned to Rhossili, unable to make the adjustment from a seaside village to the hustle and bustle (not to mention smog) of the London area. He was glad to return to Rhossili and the hard work at Middleton Hall farm.

Soon, the war years provided Joff with all the work he could handle. Exempted from call-up because of the desperate need for farm labour, he served first in the Home Guard; then he transferred to the Auxiliary Coastguards. For several years, he was employed by the Wartime Agricultural Committee, providing mechanised farming services to farmers all across Gower and beyond. He became about as well-known across Gower as any workingman could be.

And when the smoke cleared (so to speak) he was a married man with two children to support. He had learnt to work day after day with no recreation other than his newspaper, a cigarette and the wireless (when it worked). He had become an old-fashioned workaholic. He didn't even know when he was close to exhaustion—he always had the stamina to go for an extra hour or two or three. If there was daylight and there was work to be done, Joff would be there.

I learnt not to expect much of Joff's time or attention: it was normal for farm-workers to be at work ten or more hours a day. For Joff, during the war, it could be as much as thirty-six hours at a stretch, in the summer months. Harvesting often required working until about 9:00 PM; then, if it was his night on watch, he would have to be at Thurba Head from midnight to 6:00 AM. It was a tough walk, in both directions, especially in the winter months. Then he would be needed back on the farm as soon as he could eat his breakfast. Sometimes he worked extra nightshifts when others were unwell.

Joff deserved a career that would have been more intellectually challenging—or, at least, a farm of his own. He occasionally recounted how his widowed mother had urged him to accompany her to the family lawyer's office at Gowerton, in the early 1940s, so that the tenancy rights of the farm could be signed over to him. However, fearing the reaction of his many siblings, he declined to take this course of action. By default, as it were, the tenancy of the farm fell to the youngest sibling, as all except one of his elders married and moved out to find their own homes. Unfortunately, he was not able to make a "going concern" of it, so the farm was sold in the mid-1950s.

In the early 1950s, Joff became interested in a farm manager's job in Surrey, though he may not have got as far as actually applying for it. Then about 1954, he and my mother spoke of migrating to Australia. Ironically, it was I (the wanderer) who dug my heels in and refused to go—I suppose that's what fourteen-year-olds do. Without me, my mother wouldn't go, so that was that.

His preoccupation with his own thoughts caused Joff to be absentminded, at times. One winter evening, after eating his tea, he announced that he would take the bucket of food-scraps down to Middleton Hall farm to feed the pig he was fattening up for us. My mother always put the food-scraps in a particular bucket. However, she often soaked clothes in buckets before she washed them to ensure that the end result would be spotless.

Joff didn't check too carefully; he just grabbed a bucket from the back-kitchen and headed for Middleton. It was only when he got back home that my mother realised that the bucket of scraps was still there. He had carried a bucket of my mothers' best linen (not old stuff) down to Middleton Hall farm and fed it to the pig. He raced all the way back to the pigsty, but pigs are renowned for eating just about anything—and this one had not turned its nose up at my mother's linen.

On another occasion, he reached into the china cupboard and grabbed a tea-pot (instead of a milk-jug) which he carried halfway to Middleton, intending to fetch fresh milk from Jessamine farm. He must have felt very foolish walking back up Sheep Green hill, carrying that empty teapot. Of course, we reminded him about these hilarious events, from time to time.

Repetition of such stories gave us many a good laugh over the years, yet they certainly did not detract from my sense of respect for both my parents, not only for their personal qualities, but also for their many years of self-sacrifice so that my sister and I could enjoy a much better life than they ever had.

As the years went by, the effects of Joff's unfulfilled potential began to show. He became more introverted and less satisfied with his life, without really under-standing why. Although apparently physically healthy and robust, he began to realise that his back and his joints would eventually pay the price for the years of wear and tear. And he had become too set in his ways, trapped in his narrow existence.

He did not have time to participate in village activities, except perhaps for a once-a-year bus-trip to Porthcawl, Tenby, the circus or a Christmas pantomime. He did not attend church, though he never liked to miss the Sunday hymn-singing on the wireless; nor did he have any recreational activities, once he had given up the occasional game of football. He had turned thirty by the time the war was over.

By the end of the 1950s, Joff was becoming increasingly disillusioned with life in the parish he had always called home. He was also less tolerant of other people's weaknesses. One of his favourite humorous quotations was: "We must gladly learn to suffer fools." Yet he could not practice it.

[Endnote: After I completed my studies at Swansea U.C. in 1961, I spent little time with my parents. Yet Joff's influence in my life has been constant: the memories of his devotion to honest, hard, physical endeavour have never deserted me. I was well into middle age before I could believe that any kind of office job was real work.]

63

Vignettes of the 1940s

Memories are hunting horns, whose sound dies on the wind.

Guillaume Appollinaire

It is a warm day in the early summer of 1945. In one of the fields above the Chapel, my mother is on her hands and knees, thinning and weeding rows of carrots. I'm helping some of the time, learning how to do a proper job (in between throwing lumps of earth at the white cabbage butterflies). It is fortunate that it is mostly cloudy; otherwise we would be parched by now.

For lunch, we have brought some tea (including milk and sugar) in a tin can. We use the lid for a cup. There are some sandwiches, too—uneven slices of white bread with cheese, cucumber and marmite. My mother stops work about four o'clock and we walk up across Alf Bevan's fields to 'the cottage'. She has to light the coal-fire and start preparing the evening meal.

◆   ◆   ◆

It is the month of May 1946. It is a quiet day at 'the cottage'. My parents are out working. I feel more than a little bored. I reflect on what the Weston boy who lives across at Windy Walls has been saying about the newts which frequent the abandoned well on the hillside. I decide it's time to try my hand at newt-catching. But what makes a good newt-trap, I wonder? Perhaps a shrimp-net; but I don't have one.

After half an hour of brainstorming, my thoughts alight on my mother's chip-basket. Perfect. It has holes to allow the water to escape, but not the newts. Twenty minutes later, I'm dipping the basket into the scummy water at the old well. It doesn't take long to come up with a couple of newts. I pop them into a jam-jar that I've brought along. Soon I have three newts; but I don't find them as fascinating as I expected.

When I arrive home, I realise that I can't just replace the chip-basket, knowing what it's been used for. I decide to get rid of it, by hiding it in the rubbish. I'll have to worry about it, next time my mother decides to "make a few chips". In the meantime, I've got a jam-jar with some newts in.

◆   ◆   ◆

It is late February, 1947. The blizzard has been so intense, the wind so severe, that giant snowdrifts have formed over some of the houses. 'The cottage' is almost buried. On the side facing the hill, especially, it is completely hidden by the drifts. Not yet seven years old, I can't be much help to my father as he digs his way through a solid wall of snow to get out of our only exterior door (on the sheltered side of the house) so that he can go to work.

The roads are plugged. German POWs are employed to help clear them. Food supplies at the village shops are running low. It is almost a week before fresh bread from Davies's bakery at Reynoldston can get through by tractor and trailer. Chains are necessary for the tires of any vehicles attempting to negotiate Pitton Cross hill. Tractors with metal wheels tipped with spugs are better able to function on the snow-packed roads, but they are not easy to start in freezing weather. People who are caught low on their coal supplies are desperate to borrow from neighbours. The snowfalls and bitter cold will persist for more than a month. This is one winter when the snow and ice will eventually lose their appeal—even for us kids.

◆   ◆   ◆

It is shortly after Christmas, 1947. This year has been an unusually hard one, in several respects, but there is still time for one more unwelcome event in the village. A fourteen-year-old girl, Jean Marks, has died of "consumption". She is the only child of Fred and Evelyn, who live in one of the old coastguard houses at Rhossili End. The other two houses are occupied by the families of bus-driver, Harold Jones, who shares Fred's passion for hunting and fishing; and farmer, Sid Thomas.

My mother explains that young Jean began to notice a drop in energy during the spring—feeling exhausted when walking up the steep slopes of the cliff-lands, like those around Fall Bay. Signs of consumption were all too evident. She was taken away to Craig-y-Nos for diagnosis and treatment.

As Jean's condition worsened with the contagious disease, several of her friends and neighbours visited her at the hospital. After she was sent home, in late summer, Jean's sick-bed was placed near the sitting-room window, so she could still talk through the open window with some of her teenage friends.

The funeral is a poignant occasion, attended mostly by the men and teenage boys. Women, especially those of Welsh tradition do not usually attend funerals; they involve themselves in the preparations and catering.

[Endnote: Within just a few years, tuberculosis became a curable disease.]

◆   ◆   ◆

It is a Saturday afternoon in the early spring of 1948. My father still follows the seasonal tradition of harvesting gulls' eggs. The eggs must be collected within a day or two of being laid. It is a bit early in the season—not many eggs have been produced; yet he searches between Lewis Castle and the Devil's Chair. Finally, he decides to climb down the side of the cliff, below 'the chair'.

He soon becomes lost from my sight, below the edge of the steep, grassy slope. After about ten minutes, I begin to panic: my father is the most important person in my life. It is an agonising wait, but soon his blond head appears. He has found three fresh, speckled eggs for tomorrow's breakfast.

◆   ◆   ◆

It is a grey, mild Saturday in the early summer of 1948. Ron Beynon and I find ourselves exploring the lane and fields between Hoarstone and Fernhill farm. We take a good look at the ruins of the old cottage, once known as Whorestone. Then we decide to check out some fields on the opposite side of the lane, which belong to Middleton Hall farm. Perhaps we'll see some rabbits, even a fox. What we do find, in fact, is a couple of stray horses that we know don't belong there. A single strand of barbed wire hanging across the shut-way has not kept them out. They are munching on the fresh grass in the hayfield known as Western Park.

Conscientious farm boys always try to do what their fathers would do. I climb onto the hedge at one side of the shut-way and support the strand of barbed wire on the shoulder of my old, torn jacket. Ron trots off to round up the horses and is soon "hallooing" them towards the exit. The first horse passes just underneath the barbed wire, but the second one is a few inches taller. The top of its head jolts the barbed wire on my shoulder and I feel it dig into my left ear. It doesn't hurt much; but when I get down off the hedge, Ron takes a look at it. He doesn't say anything, though I notice that he looks concerned. I cup my hand to my ear and we decide to set out for home.

Perhaps we'll get some help from an adult. Fernhill farm seems deserted. I take my hand away from my ear and see that it holds a pool of blood. I begin to panic; this is a real nuisance. When we reach Fernhill Top, I find "aunty Ol" at home. She takes a look at my ear, wipes off some of the congealing blood and tells me it's not a terribly bad cut.

I feel relieved as we hurry down the road to 'the cottage' where my mother assures me that I'll live; then she cleans up the cut with some cotton-wool soaked in something which stings. In a few days, it will be forgotten, though the scar will last a lifetime.

◆　　　◆　　　◆

It is mid-summer, 1948. My uncle Len is mowing hay in the field directly opposite the Chapel. He prefers his little Fergie tractor to a horse, any day. He uses a scythe to cut a swathe of hay near the gateway, before bringing the hay-mower into the field. It is already four o'clock, just time for a couple of laps around the field, before tea.

Len wheels the tractor sharply around, into position; then gets off to set up the mower blade. He has to sharpen a couple of the triangular teeth with a hand-file. A couple of the other teeth are broken. The oil-can is put to good use. After some adjustments, we're off. The clack-clack of the mower blade accelerates as the tractor speeds up. After a couple of turns around the field, the blade hits a large stone, hidden in the grass. A couple more of the triangular teeth are broken and the driving rod jams. There will be no more hay-cutting for a couple of days.

◆　　　◆　　　◆

It is a dull afternoon in 1949 in "uncle Tom" Williams's potato-field at Kinmoor. The potatoes are sparse and small: the stubborn dirt sticking to them is damp and peaty. Tom opens a couple of rows with the popular "spinner". Tom, his wife Olwyn, and I work hard to fill the hundredweight sacks. Their daughters, Sylvia and Cynthia, do their best to help.

It is slow going, but we manage to fill about a dozen hundredweight sacks. That will be sufficient for what he needs, Tom tells us. He is pleased with my help. Before I go home, he gives me three shillings and sixpence. It is the first pay-day of my life. Without hesitation, I give my hard-earned wages straight to my parents. They are grateful for some help to pay what they owe Will Williams (the Post Office) for groceries they have needed to buy "on tick".

◆   ◆   ◆

It is a Friday in late June of 1949. Miss Thomas is taking her class (about twenty of us) on a once-a-year picnic, this time to Cefn Bryn, where we can walk to Arthur's Stone. It is a treat not to be missed. Most children have brought their packed lunches. Because I live close by, my mother has told me to come home at lunchtime, so she can have my good shirt ready, as well as some sandwiches. When I get home, I find my mother has nothing ready for me—and she is "in a state".

Gradually, I understand that it has something to do with my little sister, who is due to start school in the coming September. Apparently, she was playing in the garden about mid-morning when she suddenly disappeared, even though she was known never to wander off from the house. My mother began to search for her—on the hill behind 'the cottage'; in the neighbouring fields; then eventually as far as Fernhill, Hoarstone and Pitton. Returning home exhausted and panic-stricken, my mother decided to check the bedroom, where she found my sister had fallen asleep.

Unfortunately, my mother decides she cannot let me go on the school picnic without a clean, pressed shirt and a packed lunch. Now it's my turn to be devastated. My father, Joff, who has come home for his dinner (which won't be much, today), suggests I should go back to work with him, for the afternoon. I agree. I don't have much choice.

Joff has to be back at George Thomas's farm by about one o'clock. I follow him down to Middleton, where Miss Thomas (who happens to be George's sister) and all her class are waiting for the one o'clock bus. She is surprised to see that I'm heading towards Rhossili End with my father. No explanation is provided by Joff; I mumble something about having to help my father, this afternoon. Miss Thomas seems to realise something unfortunate must have occurred.

◆   ◆   ◆

It is the autumn of 1949. Uncle Len decides his breeding sow is ready for servic-
ing. From one of his neighbours, he borrows a trailer with sides and a tailboard.
He backs the trailer up to the upper corner of the yard, close to the pigsty. The
sow is coaxed, none too gently, into the trailer.

After the tailboard is secured, a strong net is thrown over the trailer and tied
down at the corners. We set off to drive more than two miles, through Margam
Lane to Moor Corner farm, where Ivor Parry and his son, Will, are expecting our
arrival, thanks to the wonders of the telephone.

The boar has to be coaxed out of his comfortable sty to be introduced to our
sow. I've never seen such a huge pig in my life; it must weigh about forty score. I
know from experience—having previously accompanied uncle Oliver in taking a
sow by horse and cart to the boar at Weobley Castle—that this may be just an
introductory meeting. There'll be no romance today. Will Parry and Len agree to
leave the sow there for a few days; we'll come back to fetch her, next week.

64

Vignettes of the 1950s

Fond memory brings the light
Of other days around me.

Thomas Moore

It is the early autumn of 1950. Ron Beynon and I are aware that Middleton farmers are waiting for the threshing-machine, which is completing its commitment at Great Pitton farm. We decide we can't wait for the exciting sounds and sights of threshing to reach Middleton, so we head off for Lower Pitton.

When we arrive, at about eleven o'clock, we find the threshing operation in full swing. The farm-workers of Great Pitton farm, assisted by neighbours from Pitton Cross, Pitton and Middleton, are working hard. They have almost demolished one corn-mow, located in the shelter of a large barn. But as they get to the bottom layers of sheaves, rats begin to flee in all directions. The farm-dogs react quickly. There is general mayhem as dogs, rats and men brandishing lethal pitchforks, dash in all directions. The rats lose the battle, but many escape to continue breeding.

Soon it is lunchtime and the men amble into the old farmhouse kitchen, where Mrs. Eileen Beynon has ensured a plentiful supply of sandwiches, cakes and hot tea. Not forgetting our manners, Ron and I hover around the doorway until someone invites us in to have a piece of cake.

◆   ◆   ◆

It is July, 1951. For the past couple of summers, I have been learning to dog-paddle in Fall Bay. This afternoon though, three or four of us boys are spending an

270

afternoon exploring the attributes of Rhossili Bay. The tide is about two-thirds of the way out. We romp in the shallow waters of the bay, leaping over the power-less wavelets for a while; then we decide to explore the features of the small coves along the foot of the towering cliffs.

About halfway along the cliffs, we find a deep pool caused by the rusted iron remnants of the wreck of the *City Of Bristol*. The sandy sides are steep, but it gets deeper near the cliff. Howard, who has learnt the American crawl at his boarding school, decides to swim across the pool to a rocky ledge at the base of the cliffs. I reckon I should be able to dog-paddle for that distance—no problem; the pool is only about six yards across.

But about halfway, I feel an urge to test the bottom of the pool. I try to touch the bottom with my feet; however, I quickly discover that I'm already out of my depth. Worse still, I find I can't restart my dog paddle from my vertical posi-tion—unless I can kick off from the sand. I sink down and the water closes over the top of my head, but still my feet do not find the bottom.

I struggle upwards, clawing the water with my hands. I manage to break the surface and gulp a breath of air, then I sink again. I repeat this process a couple of times, then begin to panic. I choke and splutter on a mouthful of salt water. How can I extricate myself from this predicament? It seems impossible.

I use all my strength to jack-knife my body into a semi-horizontal position, still below the surface of the water and begin dog-paddling as hard as I can. To my relief, my head breaks the surface and I'm making slow progress towards my destination, once more. Howard encourages me, not realising the crisis I have experienced.

This time, I don't stop until I reach the rocky platform. From here, after a brief rest, I can dive and my momentum will carry me back to the shallow end of the pool. I reached my objective with no problem, at all. I have learnt a valuable lesson in survival. Furthermore, I reckon I still have about seven (or perhaps six) lives left.

◆   ◆   ◆

It is a dry, pleasant day in the two-week Easter holidays in 1953. I'm helping my father dig a fresh grave at Rhossili churchyard, near the wall, opposite the church doorway. This is an old part of the graveyard. I take my turn with the pick-axe and spade. The clay is heavy, but at least it's not rock. About three feet down, my father finds some very old bones—the fresh grave has overlapped with a long-for-gotten one. My father decides to place the bones out of sight behind the fresh pile of earth. After the funeral—he tells me—he will replace the old bones, as he fills in the grave. We continue digging down to five feet.

Suddenly, I see some people strolling through the gate, ambling along the path. I see that one is a boy from Bishopston, a couple of years older than I, who also attends Gowerton Grammar School. I excuse myself and wander off to look for a drink of water until the people have passed. My father thinks I don't want to be seen digging graves, but the problem is deeper than that—it is my lack of confidence in social situations.

◆   ◆   ◆

It is a mild autumn morning in 1953 as we Rhossili kids stand along the roadside in Scurlage, opposite Berry Lane. After catching the 7:45 AM United Welsh bus from Rhossili, we are all waiting patiently for our double-decker school-bus, which is collecting the children from Horton and Porteynon.

We hear a car coming. It belongs to Science teacher, Howard John, en route from his home in Overton to Gowerton Boys Grammar School. My pal, Peter Crozier, perhaps feeling more high-spirited than usual, waves his arms wildly and yells "How-dee!" as the car passes by. (We know that Mr. John has been nick-named "Howdy" by the boys at Gowerton.)

Unfortunately, Howard John, in a relaxed mood as he enjoys the fresh Gower air—knowing that he will reach the school long before the school-bus arrives, barely in time for the 9:00 AM assembly—has the windows of his car partly rolled down. Instinctively, I feel that Mr. John's feeling of well-being may have been disturbed.

Later that day, Mr. John questions Peter about his conduct. He is pretty sure who it was that yelled and waved at him, but he also noticed me. The next morning, Mr. John interviews me. Specifically, he asks whether I had observed Peter's actions, on the previous morning. I feel awkward, torn between a teacher that I had learnt to respect (as a Science teacher, as well as my first Form Master) and my friend, Peter.

I spend most of my time observing my shoes in minute detail, as I repeatedly deny that I saw or heard anything. Later, I realise I must have looked as ridiculous as I felt.

◆   ◆   ◆

It is a Saturday afternoon in the late spring of 1954. There is excitement at 'the cottage'. My ten-year-old sister is expecting a brand new bicycle to be delivered. She can't wait to learn to ride it: she knows our mother will soon teach her. She and my mother have been looking down the road all afternoon, but there's still no sign of the delivery van. By teatime, they have given up hope of seeing it, that day.

I arrive home, eat my tea and wander outside. Suddenly, the delivery van is flying up the road, past the school. In no time, I'm left holding on to a shiny black and chrome girl's bicycle. The driver says he'll need to have my mother sign for the delivery, so he heads towards the back door of 'the cottage'.

I look at the sparkling bicycle and a mischievous thought comes to my mind. Never one to miss an opportunity to tease my poor sister, I decide to have the first ride on her new bicycle. I jump on and freewheel down past the school, then turn around at the top of Sheep Green hill and pedal vigorously back to 'the cottage'. I wouldn't want anyone to see me riding a girl's bike.

By now, my sister has realised why she can't find her new bicycle. She is disappointed, upset and angry at me. My mother is exasperated, too: "That bloody boy!" she exclaims to my father.

◆   ◆   ◆

It is August, 1954. There has been a spell of beautiful weather to ripen the wheat. One of the new Combine Harvesters is working at Alf Bevan's Kings Hall farm. Miraculously, bales of straw and sacks of grain are produced right there, in the field. It takes two men to lift each sack of grain onto an open trailer and stand them up, in rows. I work with my father; we grab each sack by its top and bottom "ears".

The tractor pulls the trailer close to the garden gate of the abandoned farmhouse. The sacks must be carried through the gateway of the overgrown garden, then through the front door and up the wooden staircase to the main bedroom, which will be used as a granary. My father demonstrates how to take a full sack directly off the trailer, across the top of his shoulders and carry it steadily to the improvised granary. I'm surprised to find that I can manage it, too. Those sacks weigh at least a hundredweight and a half.

◆   ◆   ◆

It is the spring of 1955. The local football season is over, so I take the opportunity to watch a late season Swansea Town football match at the Vetch Field. They won't get promotion from the Second Division, but that brilliant young forward line of Len Allchurch, Harry Griffith, Terry Medwin, Ivor Allchurch and Cliff Jones, is still sparkling. The Swans win another one at home.

Afterwards I head from the Vetch towards the magnificent Albert Hall cinema, at the junction of Mansel Street and Craddock Street to see a terrific new western film, *The Man From Laramee*, starring James Stewart. But in between, I have a little spare time in which to dream up some mischief.

I wander into Black's Joke Shop, which was about halfway between The Market and the United Welsh bus-garage. You can find all sorts of useless but humorous stuff, there. My eyes alight on a two-inch nail which has been cut into two pieces, connected by a thin metal loop which fits over the side of a person's hand. To complete the illusion, there is a pool of plastic blood around the severed part of the nail. In a flash, I see the possibility of a marvellous practical joke. I make my purchase.

When I arrive home, it is dark. My father is about to go outside to chop some wood with the aid of the light from the kitchen window. Perfect. After a while, I go out and have a brief discussion with him. Shortly afterwards, he comes rushing into the house, clutching his hand. All we can see is a nail sticking out both sides of his palm, with a pool of red blood around it. My sister screams, my mother faints (almost) and the dog runs out of the room.

My father is taken aback by the sheer effectiveness of this practical joke. So am I. It takes us a while to calm my mother down. It will be a week before she can laugh about it.

◆   ◆   ◆

It is a bright, warm Saturday in the summer of 1955. I'm alone at 'the cottage'. My mother and sister have gone to town; my father is working somewhere. There is no farm-work today. Having got up late—almost ten o'clock—I wander down to 'the bank'. All is very quiet there, so I fetch the *Daily Express* from the Post Office and retrace my steps. I notice that the sun seems very bright, today; in fact, it is irritating. I plan to go down to Fall Bay about half-past one.

As I prowl restlessly around the living room, occasionally stopping to read some sports news in the *Daily Express*, a strange phenomenon occurs. It seems as though there is a blank spot in my vision, on the left side. At first, I think it's my imagination. I blink a few times and rub my eyes, but I become more convinced that there really is a blind spot. It seems to be about the size of a half-crown; furthermore, there are now some jagged lines of lights surrounding it. Within a few minutes, most of the vision on my left side has gone: *This is getting worse, I'm going blind!*

Soon, I begin to feel frightened. There is no pain—just the loss of vision; though my head seems to buzz slightly. I keep my eyes open, but that doesn't help. Soon, I feel really scared. I don't know what's going on and I don't have any idea what to do about it. I decide to try what I had been taught at Sunday-school, several years previously—pray. I ask God to restore my eyesight to normal; I promise Him I'll be a reformed boy; then I sit down with my eyes closed, unable to tolerate the mocking, dancing lights any more.

A few more minutes pass. What else can I do? I open my eyes and I'm more than relieved to find my blindness has lessened, almost gone in fact. The whole episode has lasted about a quarter of an hour. In just two or three more minutes, everything is back to normal. I whisper my thanks to God; then search for my towel and swimming trunks.

[Endnote: Although I have often been revisited by migraine symptoms over the years, they have always lasted for less than an hour—and they have always been painless.]

◆   ◆   ◆

The air is still warm but breathless on a late August evening in 1956. There are still a few vehicles in the car-park, though most have departed with the heat of the day. A few people meander, in twos or threes, along the cliff-tops. The sun sits majestically on the horizon across the calm, full tide of Rhossili Bay, ready to bid adieu to its privileged audience.

A perfect, golden pathway lies across the water, seeming to beckon anyone who would, to follow the sun on its journey to the other side of the world. The last of the day-trippers and visitors have left the beach, except for one or two young couples and a family with small children.

The world is stilled, waiting for its next breath, as though awed by its own beauty. There is nothing to do but appreciate the moment, which will fade as the sun makes its graceful departure. There is no time to go knocking on doors, so that others may enjoy the phenomenon.

Up at 'the cottage' my parents are probably tidying up outside, before settling down for the evening. On an evening like this, they will hear the bleating of the maturing lambs from as far away as Pilton.

65

Epilogue

✦

(A Pipe Dream)

For all sad words of tongue or pen,
The saddest are these: It might have been!

John Greenleaf Whittier

WELL intentioned organisations like the Gower Society and the National Trust have achieved considerable success in preserving much of the natural beauty (i.e. farmlands, moor-lands and cliff-tops) of Gower from the evils of development; yet they have been powerless to do anything to preserve the rural community. How could they preserve it? Even if it were within their mandate to do so, it would not be possible to stand in the way of the mechanisation of farming or the agricultural policies of the EU. On the other hand, the EU policy with respect to heritage sites fully supports the commendable efforts of the two organisations. They are not struggling against the tide, as was once perceived by many local people.

A question that has often been posed is whether it is even conceivable that Rhossili could have avoided such drastic societal changes. The answer is that it is conceivable, but at the same time so unlikely, that it would be only a pipe dream. Well, let's take license to dream a little.

The village elders who so strongly and successfully opposed the public licensing of the Worms Head Hotel for many years, were viewed as killjoys by many of us, particularly the younger generation (as we were then). These elders represented a strict moral code which was perhaps the legacy of some combination of the Wesleyan movement, the Victorian era and the religious revival in Wales.

Nowadays, many of us can see that innovation in technological development and entertainment has been far too rapid for the good of mankind. People today constantly seek more conveniences, entertainment and leisure activities. Few would seek a hardworking, austere existence, even if their social security was guaranteed (or perhaps, because it is).

However, there are a few self-contained societies which have set themselves apart and denied most of the technological advances of the modern world. They have continued farming, using all the traditional skills associated with a rural way of life. The prime examples of these people are the Amish societies of North America, who populate tracts of rural land in south-western Ontario and parts of Pennsylvania and Ohio.

Amish society is egalitarian and benevolent in nature. In many respects—except in its rejection of technical progress—it is what the ideals of communism aspire to, but can never achieve. The essential "secret ingredient" is their religious conviction—their firm commitment to their moral values and to the peaceful resolution of all matters through consensus and meditation over the Scriptures.

Did the wise elders of Rhossili, of whom none are still living, even dream of such a society? If any of them did, they must have given up in despair. The social fabric in Rhossili was flawed in two very important respects. First, there were a number of long-running inter- and intra-family disputes, for which there was no forum for resolution. Secondly, there was too much awareness of social "class". Many people considered themselves to be "above" some, yet "below" others.

This class consciousness was largely a reflection of the notorious system for which England is famous—after all, Gower was historically part of the "little England beyond Wales". There were four distinct groups in the village: farm-workers, small farmers, professional and business people and the larger (i.e. well-off) farmers. The first two groups would readily socialise with each other, as would the last two, for the most part.

Of course, the farm-workers and their families were at the low end of the social spectrum. Although children generally ignored such boundaries, and all adults generally treated village children even-handedly, class consciousness was all too evident among adults. As we grew older, it seemed that when farm-workers' children achieved success, there was often barely-concealed resentment in some sections of the community, fuelled by class-consciousness or perceived historical grievances among families.

Today, the farm-workers and their families are gone. The larger farmers manage their tracts of land with an air of powerlessness and frustration. The EU is introducing a system of payments for stewardship—in other words for keeping fields, hedges and farm buildings in good order. There are fewer intrinsic or extrinsic rewards from farming; the farmers' influence in the community has reduced.

The lack of any shops or services within the village (and the soaring prices of houses) has encouraged the dissipation of "local" families. Either they have left to pursue modern, professional careers, or they have retired to enjoy the conveniences of suburban life.

The Amish way of life is an anomaly in our western society. It is essentially based on a very long and rigid tradition of theocratic principles. A few of the Rhossili village elders (or rather, their likeminded offspring) have continued their traditional leadership roles in the church, chapel and parish committees. However, the younger generation and the majority of professionals and business people who constitute the commuter-class, ensure that secular values will dominate.

Life is designed (i.e. predestined) to be temporary. Our parents and grandparents lived their lives; we must live ours. They lived austere, mostly unhealthy, existences. On clear, dry days, they must have enjoyed the beautiful scenery, breathing the salty air and indulging in some recreational activities. There would have been many moments of hilarious homemade fun, if only at the expense of others. Yes, there were sunny days in Rhossili, but more often, it was wet and chilly, overcast, foggy or "wild". For many, any day free of pain must have felt good, especially as they got older. As my father's cousin, Horace Rosser put it: "The only thing that was good about 'the good old days' was that I was young!"

Today, we are much better off. Why, then, do we feel so much sentiment about those fast-fading days, of more than half-a-century ago? The answer lies in a phenomenon sometimes referred to as the J-curve, which can be applied to many aspects of human progress. For example, world population increased from about 2 billion to 6 billion in the last 40 years of the 20th century.

Technological progress has also accelerated dramatically in the same timeframe. Before 1940, there was motorised transportation, even a few tractors. Farm machinery included the horse-drawn reaper-and-binder, the hay-mower, a simple potato-digger, a variety of small two-stroke engines which were used for daily chores such as shredding mangels for feed, and the wonderful threshing-machine. Carthorses remained in common use until the late 1940s, but then such innovations as combine harvesters, milking machines and the electric sheep-shears appeared. By the mid-1950s, farming methods had been revolutionized.

In the 1940s, we boys wore essentially the same garb (trousers, braces, jersey, jacket, shirt, tie, hat and boots) as our fathers had. We had the same teachers, vicar and shoemaker. We learnt the same lessons with nibs, ink-wells and blotting paper. We played the same games—football (sometimes with a bare pig's bladder), rounders and shinty. We were also obliged to do similar chores at home.

We ate the same diet of fried, roasted and boiled food, augmented by seagulls' eggs, laver-bread, crabs, mackerel and rabbits. Horses were used to draw carts, to plough and to provide the energy to operate the reaper-and-binder, just as in my grandfather's youth. Much had not changed in more than a quarter of a century. However, tractors were becoming increasingly reliable and affordable.

Now, there are few left who were brought up with the traditional methods of farm-work and who therefore experienced the full range of manual tasks in the open fields. The point is that our forebears, who had little choice but to live the hard way of life they inherited, are gone. It was their way of life: we were but youngsters who tried to help. We shared in the deprivations of those days, but mostly we were merely observers of our parents' hardships.

Technological progress also brought the radio, electrical power, appliances, television and the telephone. These curtailed the misery of hard work and austere living conditions. The resulting economic progress provided us with unprecedented choices of education, vocation and lifestyle. Who could resist?

Change accelerated so rapidly in the past half-century that we feel disjointed from the very roots of our youth—which is why we reflect on them with so much nostalgia. Ploughing with horses; milking or sowing grain by hand; mastery of the scythe, the hoe and many other implements which had been a way of life for centuries, suddenly became obsolete.

To change or not to change is one of the truly important questions in life. But the past can only be the past. So let it be with "the old Rhossili".

[Endnote: Thirty or so features of Rhossili around 1950, which have since disappeared: home-cured pork; feathering poultry; milking by hand; homemade butter-making; Vanguard garage; rocket practice; ship's "mast"; the "rocket house"; the well; leather gaiters; village shops; village school; nibs, inkwells and blotting-paper; scrubbing board; village cobbler; hobnailed boots; roast rabbit; harvesting seagulls' eggs; the stream; Middleton Lodge farm; stone hitching-post; working horses; the water-chute; the elm tree; "the log"; thatched cottages; field skills (hoeing, scything, sowing); reaper-and-binder; hay-mower; door-to-door shopping; cat-and-dog; quoits; informal team sports; horizontal ash tree.]

An Old-timer's Prayer

"LORD, Thou knowest (better than I know myself) that I am growing older and will someday be old ... Keep me from the fatal habit of thinking I must say something on every subject and on every occasion ... Release me from the craving to try to straighten out everybody's affairs ... Make me thoughtful but not moody; helpful, but not bossy ... With my vast store of wisdom, it seems a pity not to use it all ... but Thou knowest, Lord, that I want a few friends left at the end.

Keep my mouth free from the recital of endless details ... Give my lips wings to get to the point; seal them on my aches and pains, which are increasing (and love of recounting them is getting sweeter as the years go by) ... I dare not ask for grace enough to enjoy the tales of others, but help me to endure them with patience ...

I dare not ask for an improved memory ... but, perhaps, a growing sense of humility and a lessening cocksureness when my memory seems to clash with the memories of others? Teach me the glorious lesson that occasionally I may be mistaken ...

Keep me reasonably sweet. I do not want to be a saint—some of them are so hard to live with ... but a sour old person is one of the crowning works of the devil. Give me the ability to see good things in unexpected places and talents in unexpected people. Give me the grace to tell them so ... AMEN"

Author Unknown

Glossary

batkin	a metal draw-bar used with horses (see Endnote of Ch. 16)
black pudding	congealed pig's blood, with seasoning added; a popular component of a fried breakfast (sometimes eaten in a sandwich)
brawn	otherwise known as "head-cheese" (made from pigs' brains; eaten cold)
butter-fist	a circular board for beating fresh butter, with a short, perpendicular handle on the underside. The board had a raised centre to help the runoff of fluids
by	the author's dialect form for "boy" (sounds like "buy")
caffle	dialect word meaning "tangle"
cat-and-dog	a stick game (see Endnote 1 of Ch. 59)
catkin	pen-sized male and female seed clusters found on willow trees
City of Bristol	an iron-hulled steam-packet, which foundered under the cliffs of Rhossili Bay in 1840, with great loss of life
cockles	small shell-fish, dug out of the sands of the Burry Estuary; then boiled in the shell and eaten whole with salt, pepper and vinegar (or else fried)
corn	grains of wheat, barley or oats
death duties	an inheritance tax on handed-down wealth (see Ch. 44)
dinnertime	12:00 Noon (traditionally, the main meal of the day)
"do the things"	the essential morning chores to do with farm animals, including feeding, watering, milking and mucking-out

faggots	chopped, seasoned pig organs, wrapped in the apron (see Ch. 15)
farrier	a specialist in the care and well-being of horses (including blacksmith's skills)
fives	a handball game, played against a tall, wide wall, sometimes with sloping side-walls.
flitch	the section of pig-meat between the ham and the shoulder (streaky bacon)
football	the more commonly used name for soccer
half-crown	a silver-coloured coin about 1-1/2 inches in diameter (now obsolete); worth one-eighth of a pound
hayrick	a large stack of hay (dried grass) with a thatched or tarpaulin cover
Helvetia	the prominent wreck of a wooden ship in Rhossili Bay
hitching-stone	a stone pillar with an embedded iron ring, for tethering horses while they waited for service at the forge (see Endnote 2 of Ch. 16)
hundredweight	one hundred and twelve pounds (weight)
laver-bread	a traditional seaweed dish of the Gower coast (see Endnote of Ch. 8)
lurcher	usually, a cross between a sheepdog and a whippet, so as to combine intelligence with speed (see Ch. 33)
mow	an orderly stack of corn sheaves (either round or rectangular)
quoits	a game where cast-iron, tapered rings are lobbed at a short stake (similar to the game known as horse-shoes)
rickyard	a central area of a farm which contains mows, hayricks and straw-ricks
Roche Castle	the "rocket crew's" most famous action; all except one of the ship's crew were saved at Paviland cliffs, in 1937

rocket crew	the volunteers who trained to perform land-sea rescues (see Ch. 39)
rounders	an elementary base-ball game with simple rules, played with a soft ball
shinty	an elementary road-hockey game, with few rules
Shipway	the passageway between Worms Head and Kitchen Corner, which sailing ships could pass through in preference to beating around Worms Head
shut-way	(pronounced should-way or shurd-way) a large gap in a hedge, closed off, perhaps seasonally, with a removable barrier, such as bushes, branches, or temporary fencing
sloe	a small, bitter relative of the plum family, which never becomes sweet; the fruit of the blackthorn bush
Sound	the boulder-strewn rocky cove between Kitchen Corner and Tears Point
spug	stubby metal appendages, bolted onto the rear wheel disks of early tractors (see Ch. 10)
stook	a group of six or eight corn-sheaves, leant against each other with ears up, so as to permit maximum drying by wind and sun
straw-rick	an oblong stack of straw (an outcome of threshing operations)
teatime	about 6:00 PM (a lighter meal than dinner, involving tasty treats or salads)
'the bank'	Middleton Bank
'the cottage'	Middleton Hall Cottage
"the dangers"	an area of treacherous water off Tears Point where unexpected breakers betray the presence of rock-shoals
the pictures	films, movies

the Vile   a generally fertile plateau where the fields were divided (i.e. shared) between the tenant farmers of the Penrice Estate

try   in a rugby game, similar to a touchdown in American/ Canadian football

Worms Head   the famous landmark at the tip of the Gower Peninsula

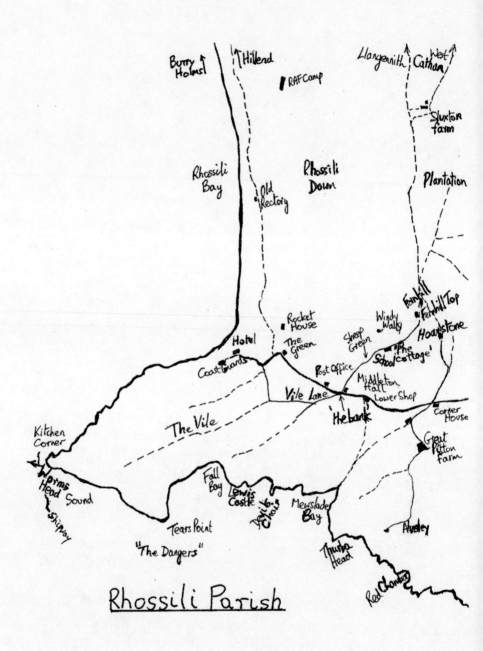

Rhossili Parish

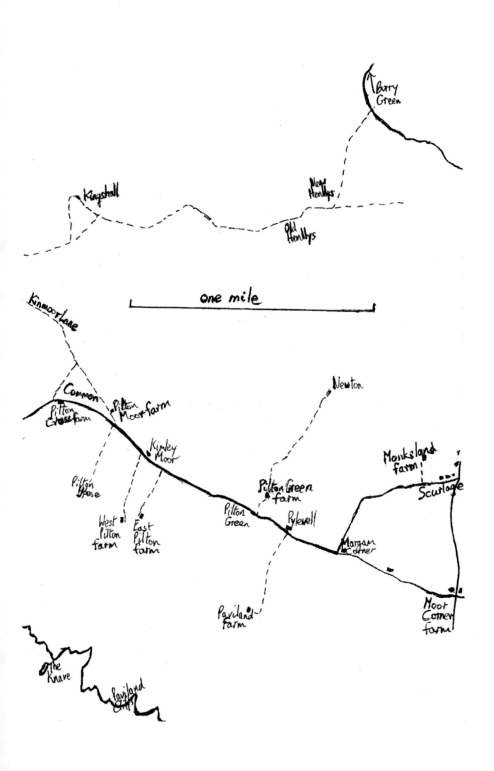

Burry
Green

Kingshall

Near
Henllys

Old
Henllys

one mile

Kinmoor Lane

Common

Pilton Moor farm

Pilton
Grass farm

Newton

Kinley
Moor

Monksland
farm

Pilton
House

Pilton Green
farm

Scurlage

West
Pilton
farm

East
Pilton
farm

Pilton
Green

Bylevell

Margan
Corner

Moor
Corner
farm

Paviland
farm

The
Knave

Paviland
Cliff

978-0-595-70515-3
0-595-70515-4

CPSIA information can be obtained at www.ICGtesting.com
Printed in the USA
LVOW131917190712

290784LV00006B/8/A